Starting with Me

Knowing Myself *Before* Finding a Partner

*Based on the Bahá'í Faith's Teachings
About Relationships and Marriage*

Revised 3rd Edition

Susanne M. Alexander, Johanna Merritt Wu, PhD, and
Jeremy Lambshead

Starting with Me
ISBN: 978-1-940062-33-4 (Trade Paperback)
ISBN: 978-1-940062-34-1 (eBook)

Publisher: Marriage Transformation LLC
Printer: Ingram Spark; United States of America
https://marriagetransformation.com/
susanne@marriagetransformation.com
+1-423-599-0153

©2018 and 2024 Marriage Transformation LLC; all international rights reserved. No part of this book may be electronically shared, scanned, uploaded, or reproduced by any means, without the publisher's written permission. Violations are considered as theft of the authors' and publisher's intellectual property. *Thank you for respecting this legal copyright. Your integrity with this law spreads a spirit of loving respect throughout the world and makes us very happy.* If you wish to share the book, please direct people to our website or an online bookstore where they can purchase a copy. Quoting small portions in study groups, newsletters, and media is permitted. The publisher welcomes inquiries about use.

This publication provides helpful and educational information about relationships and marriage. If expert assistance is required, the services of a competent professional should be sought. The examples and stories included are fictional or anonymous sharing from individuals.

Cover Design: Steiner Graphics and Neda Rahimi

Layout: Marriage Transformation, LLC

Note: Marriage Transformation® is a registered trademark in the United States. The logo of two wings of a bird symbolizing two partners in a relationship or marriage, both in color and in black and white, is copyrighted by Marriage Transformation.

Editorial Note: One of the authors and the publisher was raised in Canada and was taught both British and American spelling and punctuation rules. In addition, many quotations in this book were originally in British English and edited to be American. Until such time as there are global standards for these things, we trust that you will tolerate such variances as you might find different than expected. Thank you!

Dedication

Susanne M. Alexander: *I honor my loving husband, Phil Donihe, who went through preparing for marriage with me, supported me throughout the writing and editing process of Starting with Me, happily gave his input when requested, and daily creates an excellent friendship and marriage with me. He always seems to know when I need a hug!*

Johanna Merritt Wu: *This is humbly dedicated to my parents Oscar and Winnie Merritt, whose example of a beautiful marriage has been an inspiration to so many, and to my precious husband, Steve Wu, who walks with me so sweetly and lovingly through this world.*

Jeremy Lambshead: *With grateful heart, I honor my family members and friends for all they have taught me—and no doubt will continue to teach me—about relationships and marriage. I dedicate my humble contribution to this endeavor to these loved ones, and with special affection, to my future wife and children—should I be so fortunate.*

Starting with Me—Knowing Myself *Before* Finding a Partner

Table of Contents

Welcome to This Exciting Journey! 1
Helping You Navigate the Content 5

Chapters

1. Living an Integrated, Joyful Life: Foundation for a Happy Marriage 9
2. Learning from Family and Relationships 19
3. Observing and Knowing My Character 32
4. Strengthening My Character 50
5. Aligning My Expectations with Reality 70
6. Avoiding Possible Pitfalls on My Journey 82
7. Describing Myself and a Potential Partner 98
8. Creating My Future 123
9. Completing This Stage of My Journey 142

PrepSheets

2   Understanding Influences from the Past 22
3   Assessing and Understanding My Virtues 40
4   My Virtue Development Plan 58
5A My Expectations of Marriage 76
5B My Expectations of a Marriage Partner 78
7A Assessing My Level of Maturity 100
7B Describing Myself 106
7C What to Seek—and Avoid—in a Potential Marriage Partner 119
8A Creating a Vision of My Marriage 130
8B Learning About Marriage by Interviewing Married Couples 133
9   Widening My Circle of Friends and Experiences 150

Appendices

A: Tracking My Action Commitments 158
B: Forming a Book Study Group 160
C: Using Consultation in Marriage Preparation 162
D: Many Sources About Character 168
E: Courses of the Ruhi Institute 170

About the Authors and Publisher 171
Acknowledgments 173
References and End Notes 175
Feedback and Resources 180

Welcome to This Exciting Journey!

Knowing and preparing yourself *before* finding a partner might fill you with curiosity and excitement. If you're also a little nervous, don't worry—it's quite natural, as marriage is a big step. That's why we've created a lot of tools to help you before you're in a serious relationship.

Starting with Me shares new ways to approach relationships and marriage, drawing on the transformative teachings of the Bahá'í Faith (commonly pronounced Bah-HI) as well as related scientific research. We wrote this book:

1. To help people prepare for, begin, and sustain healthy marriages.

2. Or alternatively, to reduce divorces by helping people learn if they aren't ready to marry or need to look further for a complementary partner.

We enthusiastically invite you to join us in increasing your own knowledge and experience and helping build a healthier, more harmonious society.

Introducing a Dynamic Marriage-Preparation Process

People often tell us that they yearn to be in a happy marriage, but their life histories and fears get in the way. They are uncertain what to look for in a partner, and they don't know how to create a unified marriage. We've heard from relationship veterans who have tried many approaches, to no avail, and from youth and young adults who aren't sure how to begin the process. Whatever your life circumstance, take a deep breath and smile, because help and hope are at hand.

Our nine chapters will empower you to prepare yourself for marriage by guiding you to:

1. Live a well-balanced, happy life that includes service to others.
2. Understand and heal from past relationships.
3. Know your character strengths and opportunities for growth.
4. Further develop your character.
5. Understand and refine your expectations of a partner and marriage.
6. Successfully avoid pitfalls along the way.
7. Know what is important to you in a chosen partner and in a marriage.
8. Create your vision of a future marriage.
9. Build friendships, practices, and a support system that prepare you for a happy, unified marriage.

We provide you with meaningful content that will assist you to consider and clarify your values, character qualities, expectations, and goals—and then step into action and learning. Sometimes you will carry out your efforts alone, and sometimes you will invite others to join you.

If something in the book isn't a fit for you, that's fine—we encourage you to take what makes sense and incorporate it into your life, in whatever ways are most helpful to you. Make this book your own.

Note: Sometimes, we use the terms "relationship partner" or "marriage partner". However, we often shorten them to "partner", including in the book subtitle.

Balancing Mind, Heart, and Soul

The Bahá'í Faith proposes a unique approach to marriage, one that includes knowing each other very well, as shown in the quotation below.

> Bahá'í marriage is the commitment of the two parties one to the other, and their mutual attachment of mind and heart. Each must, however, exercise the utmost care to become thoroughly acquainted with the character of the other, that the binding covenant between them may be a tie that will endure forever. Their purpose must be this: to become loving companions and comrades and at one with each other for time and eternity ....[1] 'Abdu'l-Bahá

Bahá'u'lláh taught that marriage should be like "a fortress for well-being"[2]. To extend this metaphor, the foundation materials for building this fortress are such elements as a spiritual and physical connection, a deep friendship, mature behavior, meaningful and unifying communications, well-developed character strengths, couples consciously choosing each other, and a capacity for true commitment. All these factors start with self-reflection and a readiness to create a happy relationship and marriage.

A wise marriage decision doesn't rely on romance, chemistry, idyllic visions of a future life, parental pressure, or practical conveniences. Instead, a marriage will be strongest when the partners share higher purposes—such as raising children, family unity, serving humanity, and contributing to personal and societal transformation.

Romance and passion are often the guiding motivators for relationships. While chemistry and attraction are natural, we invite you to balance these with the beauty and power of mental, emotional, and spiritual magnetism toward a potential partner. Reflection, prayer, consultation with others, and engaging your mind are powerful balancing factors to the attraction you feel. Each of these elements lends itself to a systematic process, guiding you toward healthy, happy choices.

Benefiting from Systematic Processes

This book's approach echoes a process of learning that many Bahá'ís and others are utilizing in their lives and communities:

- **Understanding Reality**: Skillfully assessing our current life and community conditions, capacities, and potential

- **Empowerment**: Taking charge of our own learning and development and recognizing that the responsibility to influence our destiny is in our own hands

- **Consultation and Unified Service**: Each person discovering their roles in life through consulting with others and service

- **Reflection and Learning**: Reviewing what has happened to help us form wise future action steps

- **Transformation**: Individuals systematically improving their character, and communities discovering new ways to function harmoniously

Successive plans for the Bahá'í community's global development emphasize clear-headed, logical, and systematic approaches to its efforts. Following this model, we offer you an empowering process for personal growth and development as part of self-preparation for marriage.

Oddly, many of us dedicate ourselves to our education and employment, applying ourselves diligently to getting a driver's license, a degree, or a work promotion. However, when it comes to relationships, many of us expect it to be effortless. And yet, the inescapable reality is that without *conscious, intentional investment of time, love, and getting to know each other very well*, relationships tend to end in breakup or divorce. A systematic approach to building a future marriage and family requires discipline and attention—just like any serious effort, such as building one's career.

A systematic process does not imply we avoid our feelings—quite the opposite. Creating a special connection and spiritual bond of love and friendship between two people who are getting to know each other—and who are exploring the possibility of getting married—is an important, delicate, and complex process. Couples experience feelings of warmth, love, trust, ease, contentment, and happiness with true friendship. Any happily married person will testify that success in finding a suitable partner—and building interdependence and deep connections with them—requires more than romance.

Applying the Concepts to Your Life

In each chapter, we share concepts from the Bahá'í teachings about relationships and marriage. Questions, quotations, PrepSheets, and activities will help you explore the themes and concepts from different angles. The process of understanding something in theory and then putting it into practice leads to long-term effects. Your personal reflections, emotions, creativity, prayer, meditation, and actions can further expand your learning and powerfully prepare you to be—and to find—an excellent marriage partner.

A reader shared their experience:

"The unique ideas in each chapter--and the profound quotations from the Bahá'í writings--opened my eyes to new and helpful ways of viewing marriage. Then, when I started answering the reflection questions and doing the activities, I began to think in a much more logical way about how these ideas apply to my life, my specific relationships, my own character qualities, and my fears and hopes. I then started to realize I had inconsistencies between my thoughts and my beliefs, which helped me see very clearly what I need to do next to grow. I felt energy and enthusiasm I didn't know was possible--and a new-found hope that my stumbling blocks can be overcome! In short, the benefit I got from Starting with Me really skyrocketed when I began to complete the exercises that help us tailor the concepts to our lives, to maximize their impact.

"I found there is something very powerful about actually deciding on and writing down my answers to these questions, prompts, and exercises. It seems similar to when we are journaling, or talking to a friend, and we give voice to the thoughts and feelings we have about something. Through that self-expression and exploration of our own thoughts and feelings, sometimes a light bulb goes on, and we have unexpected epiphanies and revelations that open up new doors of perception and action for us. All in all, it seems like there's something amazing about taking the time to really decide what I think about each question and to write down and express my answers."

Sharing Personal Experiences

Throughout the book, *in italics*, we share insights from individuals reflecting on their own marriage preparation process. For example, here's what one person shared about the importance of a process-oriented approach when striving for a worthy goal:

"I think that the spiritual goals we are given in the Bahá'í Faith need to be understood in terms of process, rather than as a finished product. The ideal marriage is a goal to be worked toward; it gives direction to our striving. When we look at the ideal marriage as something that we 'should' have, we are likely to feel discouraged, guilty, a sense of futility, and so on. When we understand it to be the goal of a

process, which we can move toward regardless of our current situation, and we start working toward it, we can feel hope and encouragement—and that we're making progress. I believe the Faith teaches us that spirituality is a dynamic process, not a static condition. This systematic process applies to marriage preparation and marriage as well."

We, the authors, also bring our own varied relationship and marriage experiences and insights to this book, even as we each continue to strive to live joyful, service-filled lives.

A true marriage *partner* to live, love, and serve with is a wonderful blessing. When partners are true, intimate friends and spiritual and physical companions, the Bahá'í teachings promise—and scientific studies confirm—that relationships and marriages will be filled with joy, companionship, and well-being.

We invite you to reflect:

"What's exciting to me about taking time to prepare myself for marriage?"

We warmly welcome you to this experience.

Susanne, Johanna, and Jeremy

Helping You Navigate the Content

Accessibility

We hope our writing style is accessible and clear to most readers, but we know it will not be a perfect fit for everyone. Most importantly, we try to be inclusive and aware that our perspective is one of many. To that end, you'll find that our pronoun usage shifts a lot. On some occasions, we'll say "you" to make clear that we'd like you, our dear reader, to think about something or take a specific action or next step. On many occasions, we'll write "we" or "our" to demonstrate we're conveying something with universal qualities.

This pronoun shifting also helps ensure that you do not feel any sense of judgment from us or that we are trying to tell you what to do or how to live. Of course, this is not the spirit in which our suggestions are made. To accommodate the fact that readers may be looking for a male or female partner, and to avoid cumbersome language, at times we will use "them" to signify "him or her"—or "they" instead of "he or she".

Family Terminology

As you participate in this adventure of preparing yourself for marriage, the people who raised you will likely figure centrally in how you think about that journey. We often use the term "parents" to identify the people who raised you and who were vital influences in your early life. If others raised you, or a combination of a parent and others, please know that when we use "parents", we intend you to think of those who were most immediate and formative in your upbringing. It may be a grandparent, a stepparent, a single parent, a foster parent, an older sibling, or others.

In some exercises, we'll ask you to reflect on how your parents influenced your perspectives. We may use the term "parents", but we mean it more widely to mean "primary caregivers". Additionally, who you consider a "family member" may differ from the conventional use of the term, so please read the term "family" to fit your own conception and circumstances throughout the book.

Religious Terminology

Susanne, Johanna, and Jeremy are all members of the Bahá'í Faith. Sometimes it can be a challenge when people are very familiar with a topic and try to share it with others. We have done our best to avoid jargon. You will notice, however, that we love quotations and didn't avoid using them!

These teachings have transformed our lives, and they provide a foundation for all our life choices, so we're excited to share them with you. As in the early introduction of anything new, some names and terminology can seem a bit strange to people hearing them for the first time. Throughout *Starting with Me*, we quote from sources written from the mid-1800s up to the present. Many are translated from Persian or Arabic, so there is wide variation in language usage. For example, when various words are translated as "man" in English, the original terms almost always imply "humanity", or "man" and "woman", interchangeably. Additionally, you may see words capitalized that you are used to seeing in lowercase letters; this is often to demonstrate that something is significant or sacred.

We anticipate this book will be used by people who are from diverse backgrounds and belief systems. We also recognize that some people find certain religious terms or concepts unappealing, perhaps due to negative associations or experiences they've had. For example, some may have negative associations with the term "God". When *we* speak of God, we mean the ultimate and infinite divine goodness that guides and loves all of humanity. If a term we use is uncomfortable, please use whatever fits for you instead.

Likewise, many individuals and groups turn to prayer, meditation, and reading sacred verses as a central and daily means of seeking guidance. So, at times, we suggest including these in your marriage self-preparation process. If personal practices like these are not part of your life or beliefs, feel free to try them out, either alone or with someone accompanying you, or draw on your own practices. For example, when we suggest you pray or meditate, you can focus on a peaceful thought, breathe deeply to create calmness, or orient yourself toward thoughts and actions you believe will bring good to the world.

The Bahá'í Faith and Its Teachings

The Bahá'í Faith is widespread across the globe, with around 6 million members in established communities in almost every country. Bahá'í communities worldwide work to break down barriers of prejudice and collaborate with other groups and individuals to promote the model of a peaceful global society, beginning at the family and neighborhood level. At the heart of Bahá'í belief is the conviction that humanity is a single people with a common destiny. In the words of Bahá'u'lláh, "The earth is but one country, and mankind its citizens."[3]

Bahá'u'lláh taught that there is one God Who progressively reveals vital messages to humanity through Messengers of God. Some you may be familiar with are Moses, Jesus, Muhammad, Krishna, and Buddha. Each has contributed to the spiritual development of civilization, bringing the human race to spiritual and moral maturity. Bahá'u'lláh, the most recent Messenger, has brought teachings that address the challenges of the modern world. Humanity is now coming of age—making possible the unification of the human family and the building of a peaceful, global society.

Among the teachings of the Bahá'í Faith are the importance of prayer and meditation, that each person has an eternal soul, and that each individual is responsible for searching for truth for themselves. The Faith is fundamentally committed to the elimination of all forms of prejudice, the equality of women and men, universal education, the importance of achieving personal moral and spiritual excellence, and the harmony of science and religion. Its teachings promote the importance of marriage and family as building blocks for a healthy, unified society. Bahá'ís believe that lasting social change starts at the local level and is carried out by individuals, couples, and families. In neighborhoods across the country, Bahá'ís and their friends are engaged in a systematic community-building process that cultivates love and translates it into action.

This brief introduction merely scratches the surface of this richly diverse, unique, and fascinating global Faith. We invite you to learn more about the Bahá'í teachings and plans for action by visiting any of these websites: bahai.org; news.bahai.org; bahai.us.

Sources in the Bahá'í Writings

You may already be familiar with the history of the Bahá'í Faith and the various people and entities that have contributed to the body of its teachings or offer guidance. However, in case this is new to you, we've included below a brief orientation and pronunciation guide. Throughout the book, you will see source names and notes connected to each quotation, and you can refer to the list below if you want to understand the reference better.

1. **The Báb** (pronounced BAHb), translates as "The Gate." He was the Prophet-Founder of the Bábí Faith in 1844 in what is now Iran, and He is also referred to as a "Manifestation" of God. He prepared people for the coming of Bahá'u'lláh and the Bahá'í Faith.

2. **Bahá'u'lláh** (pronounced Bah-HAH-oo-LAH), translates as the "Glory of God". He was the Prophet-Founder of the Bahá'í Faith in what is now Iran and Iraq in 1863, and He is also referred to as a "Manifestation" of God. He taught that every human being has a unique purpose to help build a unified world, that justice enables each of us to fulfill this potential, and that the inequalities between

everyone—including women and men, all races, rich and poor—must dissolve. His teachings span the equivalent of 100 volumes and are still being translated.

3. **'Abdu'l-Bahá** (pronounced Ab-dool-bah-HAH), was Bahá'u'lláh's eldest son. Upholding unity as the fundamental principle of His teachings, Bahá'u'lláh established the necessary safeguard to ensure that His religion would never suffer the same fate as others that split into sects after the deaths of their Founders. In His writings, He instructed all to turn to His eldest Son, 'Abdu'l-Bahá, not only as the authorized interpreter of the Bahá'í writings but also as the "perfect Exemplar" of the Faith's spirit and teachings. 'Abdu'l-Bahá wrote extensively and gave talks internationally.

4. **Bahíyyih Khánum** (pronounced Bah-HEE-ah Kahn-oom; Khánum means "lady") was the daughter of Bahá'u'lláh and 'Abdu'l-Bahá's sister. Her character is very highly respected.

5. **Shoghi Effendi** (pronounced SHOW-ghee, e-FEN-dee; Effendi means "sir") was appointed by 'Abdu'l-Bahá to be the Guardian of the Bahá'í Faith after 'Abdu'l-Bahá's death in 1921. He was also authorized as the sole interpreter of the Bahá'í Writings, and he wrote many letters and books, developed the global administration of the Bahá'í Faith ordained by Bahá'u'lláh and 'Abdu'l-Bahá, and explained many facets of the Faith and its role in advancing civilization. After his passing in 1957, there could be no further individual leaders of the Bahá'í Faith.

6. **The Universal House of Justice** is the international governing council, first established in 1963 and elected every 5 years by members of the National Spiritual Assemblies around the world. Its offices are in Haifa, Israel. Bahá'u'lláh conferred divine authority upon the Universal House of Justice. It uses a consultative approach to guide the worldwide Bahá'í community about steps toward the advancement of the welfare of humankind, education, peace, and global prosperity. It is charged with applying the Bahá'í teachings to the requirements of an ever-evolving society, and it is therefore empowered to legislate on matters not explicitly covered in the Faith's sacred texts.

7. **National and Local Spiritual Assemblies** are 9-member bodies elected annually in their corresponding geographic locations. All Bahá'í elections are free of nominations and campaigning. Local Assemblies are charged with promoting the spiritual education of children and young people, strengthening the spiritual and social fabric of Bahá'í community life, assessing and utilizing the community's resources, and encouraging community members to devote their energies and talents to advance collective goals. They help inspire and coordinate efforts to contribute to the well-being of the areas where they serve. National Assemblies serve in a similar manner at the national level, coordinating efforts across a country.

8. **The Continental Boards of Counsellors and Auxiliary Board members** are appointed to assist the Bahá'í community to maintain unity and growth, providing moral leadership without the administrative authority vested in the elected institutions. They often consult with individuals about personal and relationship issues. They also have assigned geographic areas for their service. These appointees serve a set term and are not invested with individual authority.

Managing Your Progress

Throughout the book, we invite you to strengthen your character qualities and virtues. The book's structure includes questions and activities that invite you to systematically reflect on your life and future choices. Your ability to practice reflection, self-discipline, patience, purposefulness, and perseverance will likely strengthen as you complete the book and its suggestions. Additionally, trustworthiness and responsibility are reinforced when we identify and complete goals. A few people can easily keep track of their goals and the tasks they promise to complete. Most people, however, benefit from tools and systematic skill development in this area. To assist you in tracking and completing all the reflections and growth steps in this book, we have provided suggestions and tools in "Appendix A: Tracking My Action Commitments".

Forming a Book Study Group

While you are starting with yourself in this initial stage of a marriage preparation process, this certainly doesn't mean you have to do the process entirely alone. The focus is on developing your knowledge and understanding of *yourself* in ways that help you seek a fitting partner and successfully move forward toward marriage. You may find it useful to complete some of the activities and study some of the content with others. "Appendix B: Forming a Book Study Group" offers suggestions for this. Parents may wish to study the content to accompany their children and youth with friendships and relationships. Youth group leaders may also want to study some of the book in groups. Another way to engage others in this process is to consult with trusted people—as this sometimes helps us see ourselves more clearly.

Note: The Marriage Transformation book, *Relationship Talk: Exploring Meaningful Questions Inspired by the Bahá'í Faith* (Alexander and Wu), is also a good group discussion resource.

Disclaimer Note: Other than the content that is directly from the Bahá'í writings or from another book, the views and perspectives in *Starting with Me* are those of the authors.

Chapter 1
Living an Integrated, Joyful Life: Foundation for a Happy Marriage

A happy life. A purposeful life. An integrated life. One with a joyful marriage that provides eternal companionship and helps contribute order and stability in society. Helping you take foundational steps toward all of these is the goal of this book.

Each of us has the capacity to build a happier, more fulfilling life now. As we're then ready to consider a relationship and marriage, the foundation-building is already underway.

This first chapter asks you to take a broader view of your life. If you are concentrating more on how you will meet someone and know if they're the *right* person, please set these questions aside for now. We will address them later. For now, please think about your life context, such as:

- How you spend time
- What brings you joy and laughter
- How much you are oriented toward helping and serving others
- How much you balance reflection and action
- What brings you peace and contentment
- How you are approaching the progress of your professional life along with the possibility of creating a marriage and family

When you envision yourself in a relationship or marriage, it's natural to imagine you and your partner as very happy. Many of us have been led to believe this state of happiness should begin the instant we meet our beloved, that we are quickly soul-connected, and that this happiness will endure uninterrupted for all time. When difficulties do occur, then it's natural to think something is wrong. While a lifetime of being happy with a partner most of the time is possible, it's merely a delightful fantasy that it's as easy as many hope or as many movies and books imply!

Key Learning Points

- Integrating "being" and "doing" (who I am and what I do)
- Constructing a full, coherent life—Integrating career and marriage
- Creating laughter, happiness, and joy

Integrating Being and Doing (Who I Am and What I Do)

Please read and reflect on the quotations below that frame the benefits of building a purposeful, integrated life.

1. "It is incumbent upon every man of insight and understanding to strive to translate that which hath been written into reality and action. ... That one indeed is a man who, today, dedicateth himself to the service of the entire human race. ... Blessed and happy is he that ariseth to promote the best interests of the peoples and kindreds of the earth."[4] Bahá'u'lláh

2. "The betterment of the world can be accomplished through pure and goodly deeds, through commendable and seemly conduct."[5] Bahá'u'lláh

3. "We cannot segregate the human heart from the environment outside us and say that once one of these is reformed everything will be improved. Man is organic with the world. His inner life molds the

environment and is itself also deeply affected by it…. Through them [the Bahá'í teachings] will the human heart be changed, and also our social environment provides the atmosphere in which we can grow spiritually and reflect in full the light of God…."[6] On behalf of Shoghi Effendi

4. "To follow a path of service, whatever form one's activity assumes, requires faith and tenacity. In this connection, the benefit of walking that path in the company of others is immense. Loving fellowship, mutual encouragement, and willingness to learn together are natural properties of any group of youth sincerely striving for the same ends, and should also characterize those essential relationships that bind together the components of society. … You … are aware of your part in a mighty, transforming process that will yield, in time, a global civilization reflecting the oneness of humankind. You know well that the habits of mind and spirit that you are nurturing in yourselves and others will endure, influencing decisions of consequence that relate to marriage, family, study, work, even where to live. Consciousness of this broad context helps to shatter the distorting looking glass in which everyday tests, difficulties, setbacks, and misunderstandings can seem insurmountable. And in the struggles that are common to each individual's spiritual growth, the will required to make progress is more easily summoned when one's energies are being channeled towards a higher goal—the more so when one belongs to a community that is united in that goal."[7] Universal House of Justice

5. "Experience suggests that a discussion about contributing to the betterment of society fails to tap the deepest springs of motivation if it excludes exploration of spiritual themes. The importance of 'doing', of arising to serve and to accompany fellow souls, must be harmonized with the notion of 'being', of increasing one's understanding of the divine teachings and mirroring forth spiritual qualities in one's life."[8] Universal House of Justice

6. "… [E]very aspect of a person's life is an element of his or her service to Bahá'u'lláh: the love and respect one has for one's parents; the pursuit of one's education; the nurturing of good health; the acquiring of a trade or profession; one's behavior towards others and the upholding of a high moral standard; one's marriage and the bringing up of one's children; one's activities in teaching the Faith and the building up of the strength of the Bahá'í community … and, not least, to take time each day to read the Writings and say the Obligatory Prayer, which are the source of growing spiritual strength, understanding, and attachment to God."[9] Universal House of Justice

"What have you been up to lately?" "What do you do for a living?" These common ways of talking to each other center on actions, accomplishments, and external achievements. As the quotations above support, while we are "doing" essential action, education, work, and service, we also can answer questions about our "being". These could be: "Who am I?", "What is my purpose?", or "What brings me joy?". You may also be reflecting on why you want to be in a relationship or marriage. The answers are complex, because each of us has physical, mental, emotional, and spiritual attributes that are part of the body, mind, heart, and soul. Each of these influences our "being" and our "doing". When you contemplate "Who am I?", you might think of examples such as:

- Your personality: "I'm lively; I'm quiet and shy"
- Your virtues and character: "I'm thrifty; I'm courageous"
- Your spiritual state: "I love to pray; I find it difficult to meditate consistently"

Balancing our "doing" with these and other aspects of "being" helps us live an integrated, coherent life.
We can enhance our "being" by reflecting on and centering our lives around our beliefs and internal purposes, as well as by strengthening our spiritual qualities. Integrating our "doing" and "being" enables us to make choices that align our behaviors with moral and spiritual principles. The Bahá'í teachings

promote service to others for the betterment of the world as an integral and necessary part of leading a fulfilling, purposeful life. One way to serve humanity is to marry and raise a family that contributes to the order, stability, and progress of society. Integrating who you are alongside what you do is a lifelong process; practicing it now will help prepare you for being in a relationship and marriage.

Note: The Ruhi books that are used in the institute process, such as Book 1: "Reflections on the Life of the Spirit", and Book 12, "Family and the Community: Unit 1, The Institution of Marriage", may assist you with your personal reflections and consultations with others. More on the Ruhi courses is in Appendix E.

Reflection

1. What do I include in my life that helps me "be", feeling spiritually centered as a happy, healthy individual?

2. When do I most benefit from time spent "being" and not "doing"?

3. How do I feel when I am not "doing"?

4. What "doing" activities are most important for me to include in my life?

5. What do I generally think of as "service"? How has this section helped me think of service more broadly?

Constructing a Full, Coherent Life—Integrating Career, Service, and Marriage

Choices about our education and profession are part of integrating "being" and "doing". Effectively managing choices in work life and community service includes harmonizing these with our personal life—especially with marriage and family. We invite you to reflect on the quotations below.

1. "It is enjoined upon every one of you to engage in some form of occupation…. Waste not your time in idleness and sloth. Occupy yourselves with that which profiteth yourselves and others. … When anyone occupieth himself in a craft or trade, such occupation itself is regarded in the estimation of God as an act of worship; and this is naught but a token of His infinite and all-pervasive bounty."[10] Bahá'u'lláh

2. "… [A]ll effort and exertion put forth by man from the fullness of his heart is worship, if it is prompted by the highest motives and the will to do service to humanity. This is worship: to serve mankind and to minister to the needs of the people. Service is prayer."[11] 'Abdu'l-Bahá

3. "The more we search for ourselves, the less likely we are to find ourselves; and the more we search for God, and to serve our fellow-men, the more profoundly will we become acquainted with ourselves, and the more inwardly assured. This is one of the great spiritual laws of life."[12] On behalf of Shoghi Effendi

4. "The Bahá'í youth … should be advised, nay even encouraged, to contract marriage while still young and in full possession of their physical vigor. Economic factors, no doubt, are often a serious hindrance to early marriage, but in most cases are only an excuse, and as such should not be overstressed."[13] On behalf of Shoghi Effendi

5. "… Bahá'í youth can accept—and should be encouraged to accept—a responsibility of their own for moral leadership in the transformation of society."[14] Universal House of Justice

6. "… [Y]oung women and men become acutely conscious of the exhortations of the Supreme Pen to 'enter into wedlock' that they may 'bring forth one who will make mention of Me amid My servants'…. This generation of youth will form families that secure the foundations of flourishing communities…. Through their growing love for Bahá'u'lláh and their personal commitment to the standard to which He summons them will their children imbibe the love of God, 'commingled with their mother's milk', and always seek the shelter of His divine law. Clearly, then, the responsibility of a Bahá'í community towards young people does not end when they first start serving. The significant decisions they make about the direction of their adult lives will determine whether service to the Cause of God was only a brief and memorable chapter of their younger years, or a fixed center of their earthly existence, a lens through which all actions come into focus."[15] Universal House of Justice

7. "There are advantages and disadvantages in whatever one does, and there is always some unpredictability about the future. An individual should decide on such matters in the light of his circumstances, possibilities and responsibilities. It may be best for you to consult with the members of your family and close friends who are familiar with your situation and whose wisdom and farsightedness you respect. You may also wish to consult professionals in the fields which are of interest to you and seek their expert advice."[16] On behalf of the Universal House of Justice

Sometimes, under the guise of other interests, people postpone marriage in pursuit of prolonging adolescence or self-focused activities. While reflecting on a career and professional identity is important, trying to figure this out may become an unnecessary distraction from moving a relationship toward marriage. It's common in many cultures for people to say they must complete their education and establish themselves professionally or financially before they can seek a relationship or marriage partner.

Take a moment to consider what timeframe in your life would be ideal for you to marry. What do you think has to happen before you marry? Do your family or any others have perspectives? How does your current thinking relate to some of the quotations above?

In some parts of the world, marrying relatively young and growing together with your partner is counter-cultural, and its benefits are often overlooked. Younger couples have more robust physical well-being, consult about big life decisions and carry them out in unity, and have the stamina to raise young children. Of course, practical matters would still need to be addressed. Marriage at a younger age may require resource support from family, especially when both partners are still in school. It can be challenging for independent-minded adults to accept this help from family—and not all families can offer support. However, this doesn't mean that a marriage at a young age can't succeed.

Marrying at a later age presents its own challenges. Living independently for a long time and developing one's household and financial habits may make adjusting and living harmoniously with another person more challenging. Couples who marry later may have previous marriages and children, which adds complexity. Later marriages can also benefit from family and community encouragement—even if financial support is less likely to be needed than with younger couples.

Although each phase of life brings potential challenges to getting married, excellent marriages can be created at any age. Even if you are beyond the time in your life when you want to raise children, companionship and a partner to offer service with are parts of marriage that can bring great joy at any point in life.

And yet, in a world where divorce has become common, some question whether to marry at all. We understand this. We also ask you to reconsider, as research and the Bahá'í teachings demonstrate many spiritual, emotional, and physical benefits. An individual who was studying the topic of marriage shared their perspective about some of the positive spiritual aspects of marrying:

"It seems to me that primary reasons to marry include having a spiritual relationship and to deeply embrace the development of virtues necessary for marriage and family life. Marriage is a spiritual companionship that continues to evolve, reinforced by each partner abiding by the will of God. Our souls' progress throughout eternity is contingent on our acquisition of virtues, expressed through 'pure and goodly deeds.' Marriage is a fortress where prayer, encouragement, love of each other, and the love of God, help us acquire and cultivate virtues necessary for the development of our eternal soul and for the betterment of this world."

To avoid the false dichotomy of thinking *either* I marry *or* I pursue my career, and to remain open to marriage while building one's education and profession, consider the passage below about viewing life as a "coherent whole".

It is essential then that ever-growing numbers of those in the prime of their lives 'steel themselves for a life of service'[17] to society. Naturally, many matters occupy their time and energy: education, work, leisure, spiritual life, physical health. But they learn to avoid a fragmented approach to life that fails to see the connections among life's various aspects. Such a disjointed view of life often makes individuals fall victim to the false choices suggested in questions such as whether one should study or serve, advance materially or contribute to the betterment of others, pursue work or become dedicated to service. Failure to approach one's life as a coherent whole often breeds anxiety and confusion. Through service, young people can learn to foster a life in which its various aspects complement each other.[18] (Universal House of Justice; Bahá'í Youth Conferences Participants' Handout)

A healthy marriage can provide a partnership that fosters consultation and conversation about life choices, especially when we're young. It offers a structure for mutual support to help each partner navigate many potential life paths, including questions about our education and professions.

It will be helpful to consider what a partnership can bring you and whether you want to adjust anything in your life before starting a serious relationship. For example, you may be well-established in your profession. Assess whether the amount of time you spend working will allow you to sustain a relationship. Alternatively, will moderating your time choices be helpful?

Reflection

1. Did any of the concepts in the quotations in this section surprise me? In what way?
   _____
   _____
   _____

2. Do any of them invite me to consider a new approach or behaviors when it comes to marriage preparation? If so, how?
   _____
   _____
   _____

3. What am I already doing that aligns with the quotations? What would be helpful to strengthen? How could I do this?
   _____
   _____
   _____

4. What is important for me to accomplish before a relationship or marriage? Why? Does this align with the quotations? To what extent are finances a factor in my thinking? What are possible solutions?
   _____
   _____
   _____

5. What might be some benefits of being in a relationship or married while I am attending university or in my early working years? What are some challenges, and how could they be overcome?
   _____
   _____
   _____

6. Who might be able to help me approach school or work—as well as a relationship or marriage—in a more coherent manner, so I don't fall into the trap of thinking of them as a dichotomy, an either-or choice?
   _____
   _____
   _____

7. What are some benefits of marriage even if I am no longer considered a "young person"?
   _____
   _____
   _____

Creating Laughter, Happiness, and Joy

Consider the quotations below on the merits of building joy and happiness in your life.

1. "Soar upon the wings of joy in the atmosphere of the love of God."[19] Bahá'u'lláh

2. "Let not the happenings of the world sadden you. I swear by God! The sea of joy yearneth to attain your presence, for every good thing hath been created for you, and will, according to the needs of the times, be revealed unto you."[20] Bahá'u'lláh

3. "… [M]an's supreme honor and real happiness lie in self-respect, in high resolves and noble purposes, in integrity and moral quality, in immaculacy of mind."[21] 'Abdu'l-Bahá

4. "But real thankfulness is a cordial giving of thanks from the heart. When … the heart is happy, the spirit is exhilarated."[22] 'Abdu'l-Bahá

5. "… [L]augh, smile and rejoice in order that others may be made happy by you."[23] 'Abdu'l-Bahá

6. "Joy gives us wings! In times of joy our strength is more vital, our intellect keener, and our understanding less clouded. We seem better able to cope with the world and to find our sphere of usefulness. But when sadness visits us we become weak, our strength leaves us, our comprehension is dim and our intelligence veiled. The actualities of life seem to elude our grasp, the eyes of our spirits fail to discover the sacred mysteries, and we become even as dead beings. There is no human being untouched by these two influences; but all the sorrow and the grief that exist come from the world of matter—the spiritual world bestows only the joy!"[24] 'Abdu'l-Bahá

7. "If the heart turns away from the blessings God offers how can it hope for happiness? If it does not put its hope and trust in God's Mercy, where can it find rest?"[25] 'Abdu'l-Bahá

8. "Abandonment of 'a frivolous conduct' does not imply that a Bahá'í must be sour-faced or perpetually solemn. Humor, happiness, joy are characteristics of a true Bahá'í life. Frivolity palls and eventually leads to boredom and emptiness, but true happiness and joy and humor that are parts of a balanced life that includes serious thought, compassion and humble servitude to God are characteristics that enrich life and add to its radiance."[26] Shoghi Effendi; On behalf of the Universal House of Justice

9. "… [L]aughter should not … be indulged in at the expense of the feelings of others. What one says or does in a humorous vein should not give rise to prejudice of any kind. You may recall 'Abdu'l-Bahá's caution 'Beware lest ye offend the feelings of anyone, or sadden the heart of any person….'"[27] 'Abdu'l-Bahá; on behalf of the Universal House of Justice

10. "It is good to laugh. Laughter is a spiritual relaxation. When [we] were in prison [for our religious beliefs] … and under the utmost deprivation and difficulties, each of [us] at the close of the day would relate the most ludicrous event which had happened. Sometimes it was a little difficult to find one but always [we] would laugh until the tears would roll down [our] cheeks. Happiness … is never dependent upon material surroundings, otherwise how sad those years would have been. As it was [we] were always in the utmost state of joy and happiness."[28] Howard Colby Ives reporting words of 'Abdu'l-Bahá

Whether you are in a relationship or not, and whether you marry or not, it will benefit you to live your life fully, with both happiness and joy—concepts that are often used interchangeably. The Bahá'í quotations above link happiness to how we speak and act, our close connection to God, and goodness in the world. As we contribute to the world's well-being, engage in service to others, pray and meditate, and proceed with our life's purposes, intentions, and interests, we are bound to experience authentic joy. Joyfulness is a spiritual quality that can uplift us even in moments of sadness or difficulty. When challenges arise, our ability to handle them well, and seek gratitude in their midst, can help us feel spiritual joy.

Happy people tend to attract others, so cultivating this quality not only helps us in our own lives but also helps us build relationships and nurture communities. Friendships with others and a romantic relationship founded on spiritual values can also bring joy. A key element of all relationships is the ability to connect through meaningful interactions and conversations. As people share about themselves, tell humorous stories, and invite others to discuss important topics, a connection is built between those individuals.

Throughout the book, we will include perspectives from people who have studied the Bahá'í teachings about marriage. These quotes will help further broaden your view of relationships and marriage. Below are some brief reflections from individuals on their experience of joy.

"I believe gratitude is key to being able to experience joy, and it's especially important to look for opportunities for gratitude during times of difficulty."

"Laughter is a healing medicine for the soul, mind, and heart. Laughter melts away imagined differences and brings to the forefront that we are actually all related in a very real way. It unites us. Joy for me is about detachment from the changes and chances of this world. Joy is a kindness to ourselves and to others. When I am experiencing joy, I have more energy, I find life more pleasing and funnier in general. I'm more compassionate and better able to empathize with others. I'm able to serve others with grace and cheerfulness. I find it easier to think of others' needs and forget my own selfish wants. Others are happier around me when I am happy and joyful!"

"I have been tuning in more to what naturally boosts my level of happiness and joy. Really, I think of it as my 'joy level,' since joy—the joy that comes from accepting the will of God—is stable and always there for me to access. Whenever I feel that joy ebbing (like when I see so much injustice and disunity), I become aware that I am becoming attached to worldly things. Now I have some tools to reconnect my soul to the grace of God! Prayer and reading quotations from the Bahá'í writings and from other faiths, as well as uplifting words of other people, are among these tools. Nature is and has always been a big one for me too. Water is intensely relaxing for me. So are trees and birds."

As we have read, gratitude, laughter, self-respect, and making positive choices in life all contribute to happiness and joy. Having goals and aspirations that uplift us and contribute to others' lives gives us direction and increased gladness.

Reflection

Take time to pause, maybe re-read the quotations, and consider the following questions. Answering them will help you gain insights about yourself. If you get stuck on how to answer a question, consider asking a friend for their insights.

1. What seems to consistently increase my joy and laughter?
   _____
   _____
   _____

2. How do I feel physically when I'm happy and joyful? What is my mental state? How do I feel spiritually?
   _____
   _____
   _____

Starting with Me—Knowing Myself Before Finding a Partner

3. How can I use laughter and humor to create positive outcomes in my interactions and relationships with others?
   _____
   _____
   _____

4. When have I responded to challenges in my life by trying to look at my circumstances from a positive perspective?
   _____
   _____
   _____

5. When have I been thankful during or after a difficulty?
   _____
   _____
   _____

6. How does expressing gratitude affect my feelings and thoughts?
   _____
   _____
   _____

7. Do I joke or tease in a way that seems to uplift others? What do I say?
   _____
   _____
   _____

   Do I ever use humor in a way that may be hurtful to others? How do I know they are hurt?
   _____
   _____
   _____

8. When have I effectively used my sense of humor to deal with problems or imperfections in myself?
   _____
   _____
   _____

9. When have I seen my own happiness affect others? How do they respond? How can I build more of that in my life?
   _____
   _____
   _____

Activities

3. List three activities or occurrences in my life that prompt me to feel happiness or joy:
   a. _____
   b. _____
   c. _____

Choose one and carry it out within the next week. What was my experience like?

_____
_____
_____

2. I am grateful for these three blessings or positive circumstances in my life:
   a. _____
   b. _____
   c. _____

   Please choose one of these and talk about it with someone you meet for the first time in the next week. If possible, ask them to share about something they are grateful for. What was my experience like?

   _____
   _____
   _____

3. Choose a friend and participate with them in an activity that brings you both happiness. Here are some examples: tell each other jokes, watch an uplifting movie or video clip, sing, dance, draw, play with a child, act like a joyful child yourselves, tell each other two qualities you admire in each other, or go for a walk in a naturally beautiful setting. What was my experience like?

   _____
   _____
   _____

Encouraging Reminder: To assist you in tracking and completing all the reflections and growth steps in this book, we have provided suggestions and tools in "Appendix A: Tracking My Action Commitments".

Chapter 2
Learning from Family and Relationships

Now that you have considered the context of your whole life framed within joy and service, let's turn to one aspect of life—your most significant relationships. As you prepare for marriage, it's an opportune time to ponder your interactions with the people you're closest to—particularly family members and anyone you have had an intimate relationship with.

Reflecting on the quality of these relationships can generate learning and self-knowledge. You can see the strengths and gifts you've received from them. You can take these lessons and gifts into a relationship and then into marriage. Since challenges within families are quite common, you can also address anything unresolved. Resolution often facilitates emotional and spiritual healing, which can empower you to strengthen or establish healthy relationships, and then nurture a successful and happy marriage.

The exercises and questions in this chapter are designed to assist your learning, so we recommend you try to complete all of them for maximum benefit and understanding.

Note: If there has been severe abuse or violence in your family, we caution you to consider a more systematic healing process than is in this book, and you may include counseling and medical advice. We address this in further detail in our section at the end of this chapter, called "Healing and Seeking Support".

Key Learning Points

- Learning as a process
- Learning from family and other people
- Working through family experiences
- Gaining insights from past partner relationships
- Healing and seeking support

Learning As a Process

Please consider the quotations below in light of your effort to grow. You are systematically moving from your past to the present, creating an even healthier future.

1. "O ye that have eyes to see! The past is the mirror of the future. Gaze ye therein and be apprised thereof…."[29] Bahá'u'lláh

2. "We note that, as learning accelerates, the friends grow more capable of overcoming setbacks, whether small or large—diagnosing their root causes, exploring the underlying principles, bringing to bear relevant experience, identifying remedial steps, and assessing progress…."[30] Universal House of Justice

3. "… [I]t is only through continued action, reflection and consultation on their part that they will learn to read their own reality, see their own possibilities, make use of their own resources…."[31] Universal House of Justice

4. "When efforts are carried out in a learning mode—characterized by constant action, reflection, consultation, and study—visions and strategies are re-examined time and again. As tasks are accomplished, obstacles removed, resources multiplied, and lessons learned, modifications are made

in goals and methods. The learning process ... unfolds in a way that resembles the growth and differentiation of a living organism."[32] Office of Social and Economic Development at the Bahá'í World Centre

The Bahá'í teachings encourage systematic learning. When we pay attention and summon the required willpower, our lives become a constant learning process of gaining experience, knowledge, and wisdom.

As you prepare to be in a relationship, it will be wise to systematically consider key lessons learned throughout your life. This contributes to making healthy partner choices and accurately assessing the potential of a relationship.

Reflection

1. What is the value of learning from my history?
   _____
   _____
   _____

2. "Learning in action" is a process of taking action and then reflecting on the results. Can it also be helpful and applicable in my life? What about in relationships? If so, in what ways?
   _____
   _____
   _____

3. What is the value of capturing positive lessons I've learned throughout my life?
   _____
   _____
   _____

4. How can I reflect on my past without being overburdened by negative emotions such as anger, self-pity, or shame? Who could help me in this process, if needed?
   _____
   _____
   _____

Learning from Family and Other People

Families are diverse—each one has its own culture and traditions. Single-parent families, stepfamilies, and adoptive families are typical. Whatever the makeup of your family, there is learning available. Many other people from your life experiences are also sources for your learning. Please study the quotations below.

1. "Note ye how easily, where unity existeth in a given family, the affairs of that family are conducted; what progress the members of that family make, how they prosper in the world. Their concerns are in order, they enjoy comfort and tranquility, they are secure, their position is assured, they come to be envied by all. Such a family but addeth to its stature and its lasting honor, as day succeedeth day."[33] 'Abdu'l-Bahá

2. "All the virtues must be taught the family. The integrity of the family bond must be constantly considered, and the rights of the individual members must not be transgressed. ... The injury of one shall be considered the injury of all; the comfort of each, the comfort of all; the honor of one, the honor of all."[34] 'Abdu'l-Bahá

Note: We frequently use the term "parents" in this chapter. If one or more other people raised you, please think of them instead.

In relationships, our words and actions often mirror interactions we've had with others, especially our parents and siblings. Many people choose a partner with attributes similar to one or both of their parents. As a result, interactions with a partner can trigger responses similar to those in the past toward family members. While this is often most obvious and easy to recognize in negative interactions, this mirroring phenomenon can also lead to positive interactions in which one feels at ease with a partner because their way of communicating or making decisions is similar to healthy behaviors experienced during childhood.

Discerning what you appreciate about those who raised you and how they interacted with you—as well as what you would rather not repeat with your own partner and family—will help you be more conscious when choosing a partner and throughout a relationship. It's also a good time to look at whether there are multi-generational patterns in marriages or relationships that cause you concern. Understanding and addressing these may help you create a new pattern.

Related to patterns, one person commented on observing, over time, his perception of his parents:

"In my observation, and I think for many people, the more we age, the more similarities we discover between ourselves and our parents. Perhaps this is because as we approach the age they were when we were children, we take on more of the attributes they manifested at that age and realize our many similarities."

Another person shared this:

"My grandparents divorced, and my parents are each on their third marriage. I was married for two years and divorced. I want to marry again, but this pattern deeply concerns me. I also see it happening in the culture around me. I am starting my own research to better understand these patterns. I am very determined to learn a new way of approaching marriage, so I can be successful next time."

Of course, we also learn about relationships from our siblings, other relatives, friends, and teachers. Essentially, we have the opportunity to learn from every significant interaction we have had. While we focus in this section on parents, you can also consider how other relationships have affected you.

To aid your conscious reflection on and learning from your past relationships, and to help you discern what would be constructive or destructive to continue in your own marriage and family, we encourage you to take the necessary time to complete Worksheet 2A below. This will enhance thorough and systematic evaluation, understanding, and learning.

Starting with Me—Knowing Myself Before Finding a Partner

PrepSheet 2: Understanding Influences from the Past

Date: _____

Purposes:
1. To assess and understand the effect that significant people in my life have had on me and what I learned from them.
2. To see how this learning affects my current relationships and other interactions.

Note: Be aware that you may have changed your attitudes or behavior *because of* people in your past. However, what you learned or a change you made *may or may not* benefit you and the health of a new relationship or marriage. For example, negative feedback from someone who was domineering may have led you to withhold your thoughts and feelings from those close to you. In some relationships, holding back at times may be wise, tactful, and considerate. However, in a different context, not sharing important information can prevent you from building trust and connection with a partner.

Instructions:
A. In the first column of the PrepSheet below, list significant people from your past and present, including family members, close friends, previous partners, and anyone who strongly influenced you. You may want to pay particular attention to what you learned from relationships that could have led to marriage. Use more than one line per person as needed.

B. In the second column, identify the lessons you learned from each person, including what you learned about yourself that might relate to marriage and family life. Think about both positive and negative experiences—which can help you learn more about how you handle relationships. A few examples are provided in *italics*.

Name and Role in My Life Examples	What I Learned Examples
Mother	*How important it is to listen to others and accept them regardless of circumstances.*
Jessica (friend)	*How harmful it is to tell a lie.*
Chen (boyfriend)	*It's good to identify and respect different communication styles.*
Name and Role in My Life	**What I Learned**

Name and Role in My Life	What I Learned (continued)

Reflection

1. What key lessons have I learned that will be useful in building a relationship and marriage?
   _____
   _____
   _____

2. What am I especially happy I gained from my parents or other family members? What skills have I learned from my parents that will be beneficial for building unity? For maintaining a home? For raising children? For carrying out my profession?
   _____
   _____
   _____

3. When have I acted in the same way as my parents? Which aspects of that similarity are positive? Which are not? When has acting like my parents helped me, and when has it hurt me?

___

4. When do my words sound just like one of my parents? Do I want to continue that or learn to curtail it?

___

5. When do I deliberately act differently from the example my parents gave? When has this been positive? When has it had negative consequences?

___

Note: For further insights, you might ask someone who has seen you with your family. In this conversation, focus on learning about yourself and be very careful not to slip into gossip or backbiting about others. Those are habits that the Bahá'í teachings adamantly warn against because of the negative effects on all individuals involved, and due to their tendency to subtly destroy unity within families, groups, and communities.

Working Through Family Experiences

The quotations below illuminate some of the spiritual principles that apply to the family and well-being.

1. "My hope is that your parents may educate you spiritually and give you thorough moral training. May you develop so that each one of you shall become imbued with all the virtues of the human world. May you advance in all material and spiritual degrees. May you become learned in sciences, acquire the arts and crafts, prove to be useful members of human society and assist the progress of human civilization. ... May you be devoted to the love and unity of mankind, and through your efforts may the reality deposited in the human heart find its divine expression."35 'Abdu'l-Bahá

2. "... [I]f you close your eyes to the failings of others, and fix your love and prayers upon Bahá'u'lláh, you will have the strength to weather this storm, and will be much better for it in the end, spiritually. Although you suffer, you will gain a maturity that will enable you to be of greater help to both your fellow-Bahá'ís and your children."36 On behalf of Shoghi Effendi

3. "Your discovery of the Faith, of its healing Writings and its great purposes for the individual and for all mankind, have indeed brought to you a powerful force toward a healthy life which will sustain you on a higher level, whatever your ailment may be. The best results for the healing process are to combine the spiritual with the physical...."37 Universal House of Justice

4. "This is the condition in which we must work in our service to mankind, turning a sin-covering eye to the faults of others, and striving in our own inmost selves to purify our lives in accordance with the divine Teachings."38 Universal House of Justice

5. "'Such hindrances [illness and other difficulties], no matter how severe and insuperable they may at first seem, can and should be effectively overcome through the combined and sustained power of prayer and of determined and continued effort.' That effort can include the counsel of wise and experienced physicians, including psychiatrists. Working for the Faith, serving others who may need you, and giving of yourself can aid you in your struggle to overcome your sufferings."[39] On behalf of Shoghi Effendi; On behalf of the Universal House of Justice

Nearly all of us can identify the benefits of being part of our family of origin, generating gratitude in our hearts. When we recall special memories, we might remember our family sharing fun activities, a parent comforting us after a disappointment, or a grandparent sharing timeless wisdom. As you reflect, you will discover that you gained both positive and negative learning from your family. Even where there are negatives, you may now see how you grew from the difficulties. When we consider our parents in particular, it's wise to recognize that without them, we would not exist, nor would we be who we are.

Each generation learns from the one before, and each one has the opportunity to improve on what happened in the past. Courage, perseverance, and applying spiritual guidance are needed to move toward healing, experience gratitude for blessings, and take thoughtful action to greatly enhance our future happiness. Professional assistance may also be useful.

You may have already addressed and resolved mental or emotional issues resulting from childhood experiences. However, there may still be lingering ones, from which you can learn and grow. For example, many adults are affected by their parents' divorces. If your parents divorced, you may have had to learn that their choice to split up was their decision alone. It was not your fault, nor does it mean there's anything wrong with you.

As we resolve and heal, we are less likely to repeat harmful childhood patterns with our own partner in the future. We may also more readily recognize where we missed observing healthy parental interactions, and we may choose to get to know and observe other couples for more positive modeling.

Gaining Insights from Past Partner Relationships [Skip this section if it doesn't apply to you]

If you've had close relationships that had potential for marriage, or you were in a long-term relationship or married before, you've probably gained some valuable learning and skills from those relationships, even though they eventually ended. In previous relationships, you may have learned certain practices and behaviors that contribute to relationship success. For example:

- Tone of voice is often as important as the information or thoughts someone is sharing
- A homemade gift can be especially meaningful and touch a person's heart
- Communicating face-to-face and by phone typically enhances connection and reduces miscommunication on challenging issues
- For some people, texts and emails help maintain connection and provide valuable information
- Courteous gestures like speaking gently or holding a door open for each other are effective ways to express caring
- Spending time outdoors in activities with a partner is fun and often healthy
- Performing kind acts of service for a partner demonstrates heartfelt interest and caring
- Knowing one another's family can help each partner better understand the other's approach to life

People have also learned what they *don't* want in a relationship, such as:

- Angry words and physical aggression
- Disrespect from a partner, relatives, or friends

- Lies or other untrustworthy behavior
- Critical, overbearing attitudes and remarks

Some people are unconsciously drawn to individuals with these behaviors and attributes, because they are familiar to them from past unhealthy family or relationship patterns. Pay attention if you think this may be true for you. When you are conscious, you can create better outcomes and make improved choices.

Reflection

We encourage you to reflect on and respond to the questions below to learn from your past. You may want to journal or talk to someone you trust about them. In the future, your learning may be important to discuss with a new partner. If a question does not apply to you, please simply move on to the next one.

About Myself

1. What is my history with partner relationships and marriage? How many have I had? Short-term? Long-term?

   _____
   _____
   _____

2. What caused these relationships or marriages to end?

   _____
   _____
   _____

3. What have I learned from building/not building friendships with relationship partners?

   _____
   _____
   _____

4. What did I learn about my character from these relationships? Which of my character qualities or virtues grew through these difficulties? Which ones that I'm now ready to address seemed weak during the relationship?

   _____
   _____
   _____

5. What could I have done to prevent any problems that arose?

   _____
   _____
   _____

6. What have I learned about how my personality or behavior contributed to problems? Where do I need to grow? What actions have I taken to grow?

   _____
   _____
   _____

7. Did I generally use good communication skills? What do I need to improve?
   _____
   _____
   _____

8. What insights have I gained about what motivates me to enter relationships or marriages?
   _____
   _____
   _____

9. What types of help did I seek for any relationship problems? How effective were they?
   _____
   _____
   _____

About My Partner

10. Sometimes people mislead themselves into thinking that someone is the only possible person for them, that there is some mystical reason they are "meant to be together", or that this is their last chance to have a relationship. Did I make any of these mistakes? Did these common misconceptions block me from seeing problems in the relationship? Did they cause me to compromise my values unwisely? In what ways?
    _____
    _____
    _____

11. What attracted me to this person? Were these attributes real or imaginary? In what ways were they beneficial or harmful?
    _____
    _____
    _____

12. What are my experiences with choosing partners who are a good match for me?
    _____
    _____
    _____

13. Have I chosen any partners who negatively affected me, and we were poorly suited for each other? In what ways? Do my partners consistently have major problems, such as addictions, abuse, or other destructive issues? If so, why might I choose partners like that? (examples of some reasons might be: a familiar pattern from childhood, rescuer or hero mindset, or subconscious hope that being a victim will attract attention from others.)
    _____
    _____
    _____

14. What successes and challenges have I had with understanding the character of a potential partner? How accurately have I perceived their personality, attitudes, and behavior? What might I do differently to see these traits in a future partner more clearly?

_____
_____
_____

15. What are a few qualities and attributes I am now certain I should look for in a partner?

_____
_____
_____

Note: Exercises and insights later in the book will help you explore character and describe a future partner more thoroughly.

About the Ending

16. How did I handle the ending of previous relationships or marriages? What were the challenges and outcomes? What did I learn? In what ways was the process of ending a relationship different when I took the initiative to end it compared to when the other person did?

_____
_____
_____

17. Are there outstanding issues from the relationship(s) where healing and forgiveness have not yet been completed? What do I need to accept in myself? Do I need to request forgiveness from God? From someone? What do I need to forgive in someone else's words or actions? What might help me increase forgiveness in these cases? (See the following topic section in the chapter for more about forgiveness.)

_____
_____
_____

18. What will I do with photos, gifts, possessions, and social media connections associated with former relationships?

_____
_____
_____

19. If a previous partner died, how have I gone through the grieving process? Are there any feelings or issues that still need to be healed before I am ready to be in a new relationship or marriage? How much more time do I seem to need?

_____
_____
_____

About the Future

20. How will I talk about former relationship or marriage partners with someone new? What could be helpful to share? Harmful? Why? Are there experiences, issues, or events from previous relationships

that I think I should share with a new partner because they would likely affect the relationship? What might be healthier to keep private, and why?

21. What place do my previous partners' contacts (examples: family, friends, acquaintances, co-workers…) have in my life now? Will that change over time? (examples: participation at events such as graduations, marriages, childbirths, funerals, birthdays…) Is there any healing that needs to occur in my relationships with any of these people?

22. Have I stayed friends with someone after our romantic relationship ended? What made that possible? How have subsequent partners viewed this friendship? Could jealousy be an issue with a future partner? Do I need to let go of contact with someone to help me move toward a new relationship?

23. What might happen, and how might I feel, when a new partner and I are together and a former relationship or marriage partner contacts me or appears unexpectedly?

Healing and Seeking Support

Now that you have identified how your past can help you understand yourself and move forward, we'll briefly address the topic of resolving and recovering from the past. If any harmful issues from the past are still occurring, or you still feel the effects of them, please seek help. A book like this is not suited to addressing the myriad complex issues that may have arisen. We urge you to recognize whether you need assistance to heal and to identify the most useful type of help. This section refers to "family members", but the content could refer to anyone from your past or even currently in your life. Reading the quotations below and reflecting on how they relate to you may empower you to step into action.

1. "Thy generous Lord will assist thee to labor in His vineyard and will cause thee to be the means of spreading the spirit of unity…. He will make thine inner eye to see with the light of knowledge, He will forgive thy sins and transform them into goodly deeds. Verily He is the Forgiving, the Compassionate, the Lord of immeasurable grace."[40] 'Abdu'l-Bahá

2. "… Bahá'u'lláh has ordained that in case of illness we should always consult the most competent physicians. … For the prayer alone is not sufficient. To render it more effective we have to make use of all the physical and material advantages which God has given us. Healing through purely spiritual forces is undoubtedly as inadequate as that which materialist physicians and thinkers vainly seek to obtain by resorting entirely to mechanical devices and methods. The best result can be obtained by combining the two processes: spiritual and physical."[41] On behalf of Shoghi Effendi

3. "As a devoted believer you are urged to strive to develop forgiveness in your heart toward your parents who have abused you in so disgraceful a manner, and to attain a level of insight which sees them as captives of their lower nature, whose actions can only lead them deeper into unhappiness and separation from God. By this means, you can liberate yourself from the anger to which you refer in your letter, and foster your own spiritual development. The peerless example of 'Abdu'l-Bahá merits close scrutiny in your quest for a sense of forgiveness; His abiding love for humanity, despite its waywardness and perversity enabled Him to manifest sincere compassion and magnanimity to those who had brought Him distress and hardship.

    "Such an attitude does not preclude your being prudent in deciding upon the appropriate amount of contact with your parents. In reaching your decision you should be guided by such factors as their degree of remorse over what they inflicted on you in the past, the extent of their present involvement in practices which are so contrary to Bahá'í Teachings, and the level of vulnerability you perceive within yourself to being influenced adversely by them. In the process of reaching a decision, you may well find it useful to seek the advice of experts such as your therapist."[42] Universal House of Justice

4. "There is a clear distinction between, on the one hand, the prohibition of backbiting, which would include adverse comments about individuals or institutions made to other individuals privately or publicly, and, on the other hand, the encouragement to unburden oneself of one's concerns to a Spiritual Assembly, Local or National (or now, also, to confide in a Counsellor or Auxiliary Board member)."[43] Universal House of Justice

5. "Consultation is ... available for the individual in solving his own problems; he may consult with his Assembly, with his family and with his friends."[44] On behalf of the Universal House of Justice

6. "Neither you nor your husband should hesitate to continue consulting professional marriage counselors, individually and together if possible, and also to take advantage of the supportive counseling which can come from wise and mature friends. Non-Bahá'í counseling can be useful but it is usually necessary to temper it with Bahá'í insight."[45] On behalf of the Universal House of Justice

7. "You ask ... for guidance on the implications of the prohibitions on backbiting and more specifically whether, in moments of anger or depression, the believer is permitted to turn to his friends to unburden his soul and discuss his problem in human relations. Normally, it is possible to describe the situation surrounding a problem and seek help and advice in resolving it, without necessarily mentioning names. The individual believer should seek to do this...."[46] On behalf of the Universal House of Justice

Note: "Appendix C: Using Consultation in Marriage Preparation" may assist you, especially if consultation with others is part of what is helpful for you.

As we have discussed, unresolved emotions and harmful thinking patterns tend to resurface in later relationships, potentially causing negative interactions with a new partner. If you have unresolved experiences and difficulties, you may struggle to establish a new and healthy relationship. If the relationship or marriage that ended was long in duration or you were deeply invested in it emotionally, you may need additional support to work through the recovery process.

There are, of course, many ways to heal. Effective healing and personal growth depend on your inner strength, circumstances, and inclination. We have learned that the actions listed below have assisted many people. Assess whether each one is wise for you or not. We encourage you to take any of the actions listed below that are related to family members you think might help you to prepare for the future.

- Pray for the healing of pain or challenges you have
- Pray for unity with them
- Show love to them through your actions, while keeping yourself healthy
- Appreciate the emotional, material, and spiritual gifts you've received from them, and express your gratitude for them
- Initiate positive communication with them, where this is wise and safe, and seek to understand them
- Stop all negative or harmful forms of communication with them
- Spend time with them, if this helps you heal
- If your interactions with them are very unhealthy, it may be necessary to spend time apart from them
- Pray for forgiveness for any of their behaviors that disrupted your life
- In particularly painful situations, search your heart for reasons to be grateful for the learning and growth that resulted from the experiences
- Seek professional help when needed
- Write a letter to them; After reflection and if written with wholehearted effort toward increasing unity, prayerfully read it aloud to them and discuss it, or send it to them—if these actions would be fruitful; Alternatively, write it and then tear it up or burn it, to visualize the resolution of this issue and give you a sense of closure

Even if your family members or others are no longer alive, or you are unable to contact them, you may still benefit from trying some of the reflections and activities above.

Many self-help books, websites, videos, and articles can inform and assist you. Expert relationship professionals also offer a safe, confidential place to express and better understand your thoughts and feelings. Their training, objective perspective, and professional experience with others in similar situations can be highly valuable. Ensure that any professional you rely on is familiar with your beliefs and principles—be they of the Bahá'í Faith or another path—so they don't advise something contrary to your beliefs.

In addition, you may wish to consult Bahá'í institutions, or others familiar with your faith and beliefs. Religious communities and representatives may keep a list of trustworthy, experienced, and competent counselors, or they may offer spiritual counseling themselves.

Reflection

1. Are there any steps I need to take now to heal from past issues?
   _____
   _____
   _____

2. Who can help me on this part of my journey?
   _____
   _____
   _____

Encouraging Reminder: To assist you in tracking and completing all the reflections and growth steps in this book, we have provided suggestions and tools in "Appendix A: Tracking My Action Commitments".

Chapter 3
Observing and Knowing My Character

Part of the purpose of *Starting with Me* is to ensure you know yourself very well before starting a relationship. As you reflected on your past in the previous chapter, we hope you gained a greater understanding of yourself. This chapter will continue the process of building self-knowledge as you now learn more about your character.

This chapter will help you recognize and honor your well-developed character qualities that form part of your "higher nature", as well as discern those that are not yet strengths. Weaker ones can impede our ability to form or sustain a healthy partner relationship. Human character seems to be comprised of different facets or dimensions, each of which involves a range of characteristics.

The most significant and predominant dimension of character appears to be our virtues—our positive qualities of mind and heart, such as truthfulness, forgiveness, kindness, generosity, justice, and mercy. Some people also refer to virtues as spiritual qualities, because they express beneficial attributes of the human soul—and many believe each spiritual quality reflects one of the names and attributes of God, such as the All-Loving, the Most-Wise, the Tender, the Generous, the Ever-Forgiving, the All-Merciful, and so forth.

The 12th course of the Ruhi Institute includes an excellent discussion of 4 virtues particularly helpful to marriages and relationships—and includes an insightful section exploring two other dimensions of character: our attitudes and temperament. The course book states:

> "[Attitudes] are shaped by our culture, upbringing, and our past experiences. Our spiritual qualities ensure that we show forth proper attitudes and eschew harmful ones. The way we think about material comfort, the acquisition and expenditure of wealth, the contributions men and women make to family life—these are examples of attitudes that affect marriage, as are our willingness to learn from one another and the respect we show for others."[47] Ruhi Institute

Following this content are write-in exercises for course participants to consider various stated aspects of the life of a married couple—some of which are mentioned in the quotation above—and reflect on what attitudes would be praiseworthy for each aspect of life. Beyond spiritual qualities and attitudes, the course material addresses a third character dimension:

> "Our temperament includes various traits—for example, whether we are calm and comfortable in most situations or prone to anxiety, whether we are measured in approach or tend to act hastily, whether we are inclined to be sociable or naturally more reserved. While most such traits are not necessarily good or bad, it seems important for two people considering marriage to get to know each other's temperament. Why do you think this is so?"[48] Ruhi Institute

In the following pages, *Starting with Me* focuses primarily on virtues, as the most fundamental and influential dimension of character. However, as the above content from the Ruhi Institute attests, a person's attitudes and temperament also affect how they will think and behave in a relationship or marriage. Therefore, we view this 12th course by the Ruhi Institute—and particularly its first unit, 12.1—as highly complementary to (and mutually reinforcing with) the purposes of *Starting with Me*. Ruhi Institute courses are offered around the world by the Bahá'í community—free of charge to anyone interested, regardless of their background, their beliefs, or any other aspect of their identity. You and any friends or loved ones would be most welcome to participate. Should you wish to learn more about the courses of the Ruhi Institute, and how you can participate in this unique and beneficial learning process, please refer to "Appendix E: Courses of the Ruhi Institute".

Returning to the subject of character, while the exercises in the following PrepSheets often specify virtues—as the main focus of our treatment of character—you are, of course, entirely welcome to also record (perhaps on a separate sheet of paper) your thoughts on any relevant attitudes you notice in yourself, as well as any pertinent aspects of your temperament that you become aware of. In some exercises, such as PrepSheet7B, we have built-in space for you to write your thoughts about attitudes and temperament. We also created space there for any additional character qualities that may not resonate with a virtue, attitude, or temperament; after all, some qualities may not fall neatly into the three categories we covered, and they may suggest additional dimensions of character. Regardless of how you categorize or conceptualize it, what's important is to reflect on yourself (and later, a potential partner) and record any useful observations or insights that may help you prepare for a serious relationship or marriage.

Let's now return to the subject of virtues or spiritual qualities, which every human has the capacity to develop and practice—such as perseverance, optimism, dignity, selflessness, and service (to name a few more beyond those named above). To produce a beneficial outcome, some situations may require the practice of only one virtue. However, in many situations, virtues operate best in collaboration and synergy, with one sometimes moderating or balancing the other. For instance, truthfulness combined with tact helps us provide clear feedback to someone but with gentle words that the person can accept. Showing respect along with helpfulness means we take care to ensure someone wants assistance rather than just assuming they do. Complementary virtues can offset potentially problematic situations. Chapter 4 that follows includes the additional concept of leveraging your strengths to help you further develop your character, including your virtues.

Gaining knowledge on these topics will equip you with the vital skill of discerning a partner's character. Knowing each other's character is a vital part of preparing for marriage. The Bahá'í teachings say that two people considering marriage should "exercise the utmost care to become thoroughly acquainted with the character of the other, that the binding covenant between them may be a tie that will endure forever."[49] ('Abdu'l-Bahá)

Key Learning Points

- Knowing about character
- Appreciating the self-assessment process
- Understanding my character strengths and growth areas
- Balancing my virtues

Knowing About Character

As you study the topic of character, you will come to your own understanding of what it means. You may choose to think about it as the inner collection of positive qualities we develop throughout our lives that guide our choices about how to think, speak, and act in beneficial ways. In addition, the Bahá'í teachings see these qualities as part of the eternal human soul and affirm that virtues are a reflection of God's names and attributes.

When individuals develop their characters, they contribute to the betterment of the world—so much so that Bahá'í communities around the world are prioritizing activities that help children, youth, and adults with this process. To better understand the importance of character, and inspire you to learn more about your character, we invite you to reflect on the quotations below.

1. "The light of a good character surpasseth the light of the sun and the radiance thereof. Whoso attaineth unto it is accounted as a jewel among men. The glory and the upliftment of the world must needs depend upon it."[50] Bahá'u'lláh

2. "Honesty, virtue, wisdom and a saintly character redound to the exaltation of man, while dishonesty, imposture, ignorance and hypocrisy lead to his abasement. ... Man's distinction lieth not in ornaments or wealth, but rather in virtuous behavior and true understanding."[51] Bahá'u'lláh

3. "The purpose of the one true God in manifesting Himself is to summon all mankind to truthfulness and sincerity, to piety and trustworthiness, to resignation and submissiveness to the Will of God, to forbearance and kindliness, to uprightness and wisdom. His object is to array every man with the mantle of a saintly character, and to adorn him with the ornament of holy and goodly deeds."[52] Bahá'u'lláh

4. "Question: How many kinds of character are there in man and what are the causes of the differences and variations among them?
"Answer [from 'Abdu'l-Bahá]: There are the innate character, the inherited character, and the acquired character, which is gained through education.

"As to the innate character, although the innate nature bestowed by God upon man is purely good, yet that character differs among men according to the degrees they occupy: All degrees are good, but some are more so than others. Thus every human being possesses intelligence and capacity, but intelligence, capacity, and aptitude differ from person to person. ...

"As to differences in inherited character, they arise from the strength and weakness of man's constitution; that is, if the parents are of weak constitution, then the children will be likewise, and if they are strong, then the children will also be robust. Moreover, the excellence of the bloodline exerts a major influence; for the goodly seed is like the superior stock that exists, likewise, among plants and animals. For example, you see that children born of a weak and sickly mother and father will naturally have a weak constitution and nerves, will lack patience, endurance, resolution, and perseverance, and will be impulsive, for they have inherited the weakness and frailty of their parents.
...

"As to the differences of character arising from education, they are great indeed, for education exerts an enormous influence. Through education the ignorant become learned, the cowardly become courageous, the crooked branch becomes straight, the acrid and bitter fruit of the mountains and woods becomes sweet and succulent, and the five-petalled flower puts forth a hundred petals. Through education barbarous nations become civilized and even animals take on human-like manners. Education must be accorded the greatest importance; for just as diseases are highly communicable in the world of bodies, so is character highly communicable in the realm of hearts and spirits. ...

"Now, someone might say that, since the capacity and aptitude of souls differ, such difference in capacity must inevitably lead to a difference in character. [That is, that people cannot be held responsible for their own character.] But this is not so, for capacity is of two kinds: innate and acquired. The innate capacity, which is the creation of God, is wholly and entirely good—in the innate nature there is no evil. The acquired capacity, however, can become the cause of evil. For example, God has created all men in such a fashion, and has given them such a capacity and disposition, that they are benefited by sugar and honey and are harmed or killed by poison. This is an innate capacity and disposition that God has bestowed equally upon all men. But man may begin little by little to take poison by ingesting a small quantity every day and gradually increasing it until he reaches the point where he would perish if he were not to consume several grams of opium every day, and where his innate capacities are completely subverted. Consider how the innate capacity and disposition can be so completely changed, through variation of habit and training, as to be entirely perverted. It is not on account of their innate capacity and disposition that one reproaches the wicked, but rather on account of that which they themselves have acquired.

"In the innate nature of things there is no evil—all is good. This applies even to certain apparently blameworthy attributes and dispositions which seem inherent in some people, but which are not in reality reprehensible. For example, you can see in a nursing child, from the beginning of its life, the signs of greed, of anger, and of ill temper; and so it might be argued that good and evil are innate in the reality of man, and that this is contrary to the pure goodness of the innate nature and of creation. The answer is that greed, which is to demand ever more, is a praiseworthy quality provided that it is displayed under the right circumstances. Thus, should a person show greed in acquiring science and knowledge, or in the exercise of compassion, high-mindedness, and justice, this would be most praiseworthy. And should he direct his anger and wrath against the bloodthirsty tyrants who are like ferocious beasts, this too would be most praiseworthy. But should he display these qualities under other conditions, this would be deserving of blame.

"It follows therefore that in existence and creation there is no evil at all, but that when man's innate qualities are used in an unlawful way, they become blameworthy. Thus if a wealthy and generous person gives alms to a poor man to spend on his necessities, and if the latter spends that sum in an improper way, that is blameworthy. The same holds true of all the innate qualities of man which constitute the capital of human life: If they are displayed and employed in an improper way, they become blameworthy. It is clear then that the innate nature is purely good.

"Consider that the worst of all qualities and the most odious of all attributes, and the very foundation of all evil, is lying, and that no more evil or reprehensible quality can be imagined in all existence. It brings all human perfections to naught and gives rise to countless vices. There is no worse attribute than this, and it is the foundation of all wickedness. Now, all this notwithstanding, should a physician console a patient and say, "Thank God, you are doing better and there is hope for your recovery", although these words may be contrary to the truth, yet sometimes they will ease the patient's mind and become the means of curing the illness. And this is not blameworthy."[53] 'Abdu'l-Bahá

5. "Truthfulness is the foundation of all human virtues. Without truthfulness progress and success, in all the worlds of God, are impossible for any soul. When this holy attribute is established in man, all the divine qualities will also be acquired."[54] 'Abdu'l-Bahá

6. "The foundation-stone of a life lived in the way of God is the pursuit of moral excellence and the acquisition of a character endowed with qualities that are well-pleasing in His sight."[55] Shoghi Effendi

Note: You can read other quotations about character from diverse cultures, faiths, and research in "Appendix D: Many Sources About Character".

As the above quotations make clear, knowing and refining your character and striving to develop your positive traits are worthy and meaningful purposes to maintain throughout your life. Your character—who you truly are—is evident in the behaviors you choose. Virtues such as honesty, friendliness, and helpfulness are visible in your words and actions that affect others. Think carefully about your character. Later we will ask you to describe it, how it has affected past relationships, and how it might affect a future partner.

Parents help form the foundation of their children's character through the dynamic power of example, verbal guidance, encouragement, and discipline. Ideally, our parents guided us to understand when our actions were helpful and beneficial—which came from our higher nature—and when they were harmful—which stemmed from our lower nature. Perhaps your father taught you to stay confident and be courteous to teammates after losing a game, instead of becoming angry. Maybe your mother taught you to speak respectfully, instead of rudely, to your grandparents and other elders. There will be more about these concepts in Chapter 4.

Whatever your experiences growing up, you learned how to take what your parents and others taught you and apply it. You continued building your character through new experiences and personal choices. For example, you might have practiced commitment by keeping promises to your friends, and maybe you observed how this virtue strengthened your friendships. Perhaps you were compassionate to a neighbor and noticed the happiness this brought her. You might have learned respect for school property through the guidance of a teacher. A part-time job might have taught you responsibility with time and money.

You observe how the choices people make are influenced by the relative strengths in their characters. If someone applies a strength to a circumstance, the outcome is more likely to be positive. If a virtue is weak, the outcome may not be as positive. We also observe how character strengths and growth areas may be factors in the behavior of people we see in the media, literature, and politics. It's important to discern how exposure to these may influence your behavior; for example, if you observe someone standing up for the rights of others or if you see someone habitually lying.

After studying some quotations about character, an individual offered this personal reflection below.

"Truthfulness is the foundation of all the positive character qualities because it requires us to be honest with ourselves about who we really are, what we think, and what we feel. This is an essential condition for positive change, and it is a process, not something to be achieved all at once. 'Little by little, day by day', as 'Abdu'l-Bahá said. On the other hand, deception—the opposite of truthfulness—is, I think, a defensive reaction to being hurt, criticized, and judged. We try to hide from others, thinking that we are unworthy or defective. However, God knows who we really are and what our character is, accepts us in that condition, and helps us grow. Humbly and honestly sharing with God when we act poorly is essential to allow His healing to reach us. Such honesty is not always easy to achieve. Somewhat counterintuitively, I have found that praying for forgiveness actually helps me know that God is all-Loving and is here to help, not to condemn."

Another person shared this:

"When I'm trying to improve my character, it's really hard to be objective, with all the filters and justifications I can put up. Regardless, part of my growth depends on my being really honest with myself. Prayer and humility help. Reflection on life events and experiences also can be fruitful in understanding myself. The input and comments from friends—and sometimes people who don't even like me—have also been beneficial. Things that get in the way of knowing and growing my own character, like lying to myself, denial, fantasy-driven expectations, and romantic intoxication with somebody, are probably also true of others. I need a heightened awareness and introspection if I want to explore my own or someone else's character. Detachment helps me stay away from judging myself or others and focus instead on discernment."

Reflection

1. On a scale from 1 to 10—with 1 being "I don't know my character at all," and 10 being "I know my character very well"—how do I rate my knowledge of my character? Rating: _____ What are my thoughts about this rating?
   _____
   _____
   _____

2. Is anything preventing me from better understanding my character? If so, what is it, and what might help me overcome that barrier(s)?
   _____
   _____
   _____

Appreciating the Self-Assessment Process

Consider the quotations below that speak highly of us and the gifts from understanding and developing an excellent character.

1. "Regard man as a mine rich in gems of inestimable value. Education can, alone, cause it to reveal its treasures, and enable mankind to benefit therefrom."[56] Bahá'u'lláh

2. "Noble have I created thee, yet thou hast abased thyself. Rise then unto that for which thou wast created."[57] Bahá'u'lláh

3. "… [M]an should know his own self and recognize that which leadeth unto loftiness or lowliness, glory or abasement, wealth or poverty."[58] Bahá'u'lláh

4. "… [M]an's supreme honor and real happiness lie in self-respect, in high resolves and noble purposes, in integrity and moral quality, in immaculacy of mind."[59] 'Abdu'l-Bahá

5. "The root cause of wrongdoing is ignorance, and we must therefore hold fast to the tools of perception and knowledge. Good character must be taught. … The individual must be educated to such a high degree that he would rather have his throat cut than tell a lie, and would think it easier to be slashed with a sword or pierced with a spear than to utter calumny [slander] or be carried away by wrath."[60] 'Abdu'l-Bahá

6. "The importance of 'doing', of arising to serve and to accompany fellow souls, must be harmonized with the notion of 'being', of increasing one's understanding of the divine teachings and mirroring forth spiritual qualities in one's life."[61] Universal House of Justice

It will help you to build self-understanding when you are thoughtful, thorough, and systematic in reflecting on your virtues and other character qualities. Think of your character strengths as gems. You are, in fact, as it says above, "a mine rich in gems of inestimable value". Throughout life, in the mine of your character, you discover beautiful stones or dig out rough-looking rocks that you can clean, cut, and polish into beautiful gems. These gems are gifts you can share with others and use to adorn your relationships. As you know yourself better and share these gifts, you are also more likely to notice and acknowledge the gifts and good character qualities that others express through their words and actions.

Knowing your character will deepen your understanding of what your strengths and growth areas look like as they apply to your own behavior. You may already reflect on this as part of your daily accounting of yourself as Bahá'u'lláh advises. If so, you likely already observe when you align your behaviors with spiritual guidance and when you are off-track and need to address a character growth issue.

As we build our characters through prayer, observation, practice, and reflection, we discover that the growth of every virtue occurs along a continuum. Character qualities are strong, weak, or somewhere in between. While it's unrealistic to expect perfection from ourselves, it's also wise to ensure that our characters are sound before embarking on the serious endeavors of getting married or raising children.

Regular and honest self-assessment is a character development habit that clarifies our progress and enables us to build on our strengths and improve our weaker qualities. We must vigilantly guard against making excuses for why we are the way we are—or why we do what we do. It's ultimately far more empowering to take responsibility for ourselves, our actions, and the resulting outcomes. Honest introspection and correcting our behavior help a relationship or marriage partner to trust us because they see us resist the temptation to justify ourselves or blame others for our words and actions.

A balanced view of ourselves includes appreciating our strengths and how they benefit others. We may not realize or be willing to look at everything about ourselves that is wonderful and worthy of appreciation, but our strengths exist regardless. Perhaps we are trustworthy with others' money, loyal to our friends, or enthusiastic about new ideas. Our positive qualities provide a strong foundation for our lives and likely bring us and others happiness. Recognizing them helps us respect ourselves as valuable, noble human beings—and avoid harsh self-criticism, blame, or dwelling on the negative. We can appreciate our brightly shining gems even as we identify those that need more polishing.

Understanding our characters requires that we step back and observe what we say and do in many situations. This helps us see how our words and actions affect others. When we experience significant interactions in our lives, we can assess ourselves by asking questions such as:

- Were my intentions, words, and actions aligned and consistent?
- What did I do that was effective? What positive effect did my choices have on me and others?
- Which virtues did I practice well?
- Where did I misstep? What would I change if I could do it over?
- Would another virtue have made a difference if I had practiced it instead? For instance, did I practice justice, when mercy might have led to a better outcome?
- Could I have added in a second virtue, such as flexibility or respect, to balance the first virtue and thereby improve the situation?
- Did I behave ineffectively, or did the other person's difficulties or problems contribute to the negative outcome?
- If the interaction didn't go smoothly, what words or actions would I choose instead to elicit a better outcome next time?

Self-assessment is rarely easy. Prayer, reflection, and courageous consultation with a trusted friend or relative can assist us in gaining insights. It helps when we stay focused on our own behavior and responsibilities and exercise care not to compare ourselves to others. These questions can help us dig deeper:

- When friends and family look at me, what do they see in my character?
- What about people that I have less contact with? For example, would a store clerk, teachers or supervisors, or a nearby driver in traffic think that my behavior shows friendliness, patience, respect, and more?

Reflection

1. If I were to develop a more excellent character, how would this affect my life and the lives of others?
   _____
   _____
   _____

2. Am I able to look honestly at my character strengths *and* the qualities that need to be strengthened?
   _____
   _____
   _____

3. Am I able to evenly assess my character, without slipping into strong self-criticism or harsh self-judgment? Am I able to avoid excessive feelings of shame or unworthiness? Alternatively, do I tend to look too highly upon my character and behaviors? What might help me view myself in a more balanced way?

___
___
___

Understanding My Character Strengths and Growth Areas

Reflecting on the quotation below may inspire you to begin your process of self-assessment in the activities that follow.

1. "There is nothing more harmful to the individual—and also to society than false humility which is hypocritical, and hence unworthy of a true Bahá'í. The true believer is one who is conscious of his strength as well as of his weakness, and who, fully availing himself of the manifold opportunities and blessings which God gives him, strives to overcome his defects and weaknesses and this by means of a scrupulous adherence to all the laws and commandments revealed by God through His Manifestation."[62] Shoghi Effendi

As a warm-up exercise before you complete the self-assessment below (PrepSheet 3), we suggest you ask yourself some questions about your virtues. Here are some examples:

- **Compassion:** Do I accurately discern the needs and feelings of family and loved ones and provide them with the proper support? Do I ever ignore requests for understanding or help?
- **Courage and Justice:** Do I courageously stand up for those who are being mistreated, or do I allow fear to keep me from helping those in need?
- **Loyalty:** Am I loyal to friends and family members, or do I let them down when they need me? Do I stand up for them, or do I sometimes backbite about them?
- **Truthfulness:** Am I truthful, or do I often lie? Do I excuse myself for lying? When communicating, am I careful to stick to the facts, or do I make up details?

In addition, researchers Christopher Peterson and Martin E. P. Seligman summarize that people identify their key strengths of character, when they experience the following:

- A sense of ownership and authenticity—that "this is the real me"
- A feeling of excitement while displaying the quality
- A desire to continue learning new ways to use the strength
- Enthusiasm for creating and initiating projects that revolve around the strength[63]

Do any of your strengths fit these criteria? If so, which ones? If you are uncertain, please continue learning about character and return to this reflection later.

___
___
___

For more insights, please complete PrepSheet 3 below. It's an extensive activity, so please pace yourself as you go through it.

Starting with Me—Knowing Myself Before Finding a Partner

PrepSheet 3: Assessing and Understanding My Virtues

Date: _____

Purposes:
1. To gain greater understanding of my character virtues and their relative strength.
2. To identify areas for improvement.

The chart below is an effective way to systematically learn about some aspects of your character. Complete it carefully, thoughtfully pausing to reflect as needed.

Instructions:

A. Read through the definitions of virtues in the table below; these are vitally important for relationships and marriage. Beyond these, you can consider additional virtues as well. There are many more possible ones you could consider though, so fill in any missing ones that are important to you.

B. Rate yourself on each virtue by using the 5-point scale provided. Take whatever time you need to be thorough. You may or may not be able to do this activity all at once, and you may wish to use a pencil to make later revisions easier. Write down the number you think is accurate in the "Rating" column, using the following assessment scale:

   1 – I rarely use this virtue, so my words and actions can often cause problems
   2 – I use this virtue only occasionally, possibly causing problems
   3 – I understand this virtue, and I'm still strengthening it; sometimes resulting in positive outcomes
   4 – I'm becoming more consistent in practicing this virtue, usually with positive outcomes
   5 – I practice this virtue consciously and consistently

C. After you have rated yourself on each, go through the list again and put an "S" next to virtues that are your outstanding **strengths**.

D. Now, go back through the list, and put a "G" next to the virtues that are significant areas where you want to see **growth** and development happening.

E. Next, looking at the list again, circle those 4 virtues you most want to develop or build upon—at least for now. The virtues you rated 1, 2, or 3 may offer good choices if you want to develop those that are currently in a weaker state.

Note: This activity will start you on a development process if you are not doing one currently. You will continue to develop all your virtues throughout your life.

"+" Indicates CharacterYaq™ definitions (see end of table for explanation)

Rating	S or G	Character Virtues
		1. **Acceptance is** a deep, meaningful embracing of who someone is, as well as acknowledging that people and events are as they are or were as they were, rather than wasting time and energy trying to change people, regret the past, or influence events when it is unwise or there is no possibility of success.

Rating	S or G	Character Virtues (continued)
		2. **+Adherence is** following guidelines, rules, agreements, and laws created to protect relationships, safety, and order; stays faithful to promises made to others.
		3. **Assertiveness is** speaking up or acting decisively to improve a situation for the benefit of others and oneself.
		4. **Beauty is** expressing the best of one's inner spirit and demonstrating, seeing, and fashioning attractiveness, loveliness, or order wherever possible.
		5. **Caring is** giving sincere love, attention, consideration, and assistance to others and responding to needy situations in timely and appropriate ways.
		6. **Chastity is** maintaining sexual purity and reserving sexual attraction, thoughts, responses, and intimacy as a special and respectful gift to share with a marriage partner.
		7. **Commitment is** making and keeping a reasonable promise or binding agreement to others or to oneself, including setting and meeting certain goals, standards, or expectations, as well as completing tasks to which one has agreed.
		8. **+Compassion is** demonstrating a unique capacity to listen deeply to others about their situations; understanding others' feelings; caring for others' well-being; and seeking ways to ease someone's pain and suffering in mutually satisfactory ways.
		9. **Confidence is** trusting one's inner value, worthy intentions, capacity to think and act effectively, and ability to accomplish stated goals of oneself and of others.
		10. **Contentment is** maintaining happiness and tranquility in body, mind, heart, and soul, with calm, accepting feelings and actions toward relationships, employment, surroundings, situations, and life in general.
		11. **Cooperation is** working with others in harmony to create or accomplish something that would be more difficult or impossible to accomplish by one person working alone.
		12. **Courage is** taking brave and bold action voluntarily, defending what is right, or facing and completing a worthwhile challenge, even when experiencing fear, resistance, uncertainty, opposition, hardship, or possible danger.
		13. **Courtesy is** showing gracious and warm consideration for others by interacting with polite manners, respectful gestures, thoughtful actions, and positive language.
		14. **+Creativity is** drawing on ideas, inspiration, or imagination from many sources to develop or produce something new; being resourceful, intuitive, and solving problems in unique and beneficial ways; and immersing in a problem or situation, looking broadly for insights and connections, allowing for breakthrough ideas and solutions to emerge.
		15. **+Dependability is** making and keeping commitments, completing agreed tasks, honestly managing resources and money, handling information wisely, and cleaning up after mistakes.
		16. **Detachment is** stepping back to gain a different perspective on what is happening and placing less importance on worldly concerns, while selflessly letting go of one's feelings, hopes, desires, attachments, and need to be in control.

Rating	S or G	Character Virtues (continued)
		17. **Discernment is** perceiving and understanding oneself, others, and situations accurately, deeply, and objectively, including discriminating between what is beneficial and what is harmful, without prejudice or bias.
		18. **Encouragement is** offering sincere, uplifting acknowledgment of the character strengths, effective actions, or good intentions of others and oneself; inspiring or assisting others and oneself to start, continue, or stop doing something; and fostering personal growth and development.
		19. **Enthusiasm is** expressing genuine positive and joyful feelings, often in a high-spirited way, about an occasion, activity, important occurrence, goal, person, or extraordinary situation.
		20. **+Excellence is** achieving high standards and a superior quality of work, effort, appearance, relationships, and personal development; learning and improving from experiences; and continually raising and meeting expectations.
		21. **Faithfulness is** being steadfast and maintaining commitments to others, to a set of beliefs, or to an organization.
		22. **+Flexibility is** being open to change and surprises, adjusting and adapting to life as it happens; being nimble in responding to different people and situations; and considering new and different approaches, methods, ideas, and viewpoints.
		23. **Forgiveness is** accepting pardon from God and pardoning someone else for saying or doing something hurtful or harmful, giving up a desire for revenge, and letting go of anger and resentment.
		24. **Fortitude is** staying brave, resolute, steadfast, and strong mentally, emotionally, physically, and spiritually when facing challenges, difficulties, adversity, danger, pain, or temptation.
		25. **+Friendliness is** demonstrating an outgoing and positive social attitude and reaching out to connect and build relationships with people; and gracious and warm consideration for others by interacting with polite manners, respectful gestures, thoughtful actions, and tactful language.
		26. **Generosity is** giving away or sharing what one has, such as affection, money, time, appreciation, gratitude, encouragement, gifts, celebrations, positive feedback, resources, knowledge, wisdom, possessions, physical abilities, personal energy, ideas, or resources with open mind, heart, and hands.
		27. **Gentleness is** expressing consideration from the heart, honoring the feelings of others and oneself, and using soft and careful physical touch, movement, and words.
		28. **Helpfulness is** taking appropriate interest in and action to address the needs or participate in solving the problems of others or oneself.
		29. **Honesty is** acting and speaking consistently with high and incorruptible moral, ethical, and legal standards.
		30. **+Honor is** having clear principles, beliefs, and positive intentions that guide actions to create beneficial change.

Rating	S or G	Character Virtues (continued)
		31. **+Humility is** seeing and accepting one's whole self, including strengths, imperfections, abilities, accomplishments, failures, and needs in modest and realistic perspective; offering one's time, knowledge, and talents in a self-effacing way; and being willing to accept the knowledge, skills, and help of others.
		32. **Idealism is** envisioning what is possible, thinking beyond what currently exists, and taking action toward or advocating for beneficial change.
		33. **Integrity is** achieving a state of balance and wholeness in life and character, by acting in accord with civil laws and deepest beliefs, highest values and principles, and stated word.
		34. **+Joyfulness is** maintaining a happy, optimistic, and uplifting attitude; energetically celebrating the best in relationships, work, and service; and looking at the positive side of circumstances.
		35. **+Justice is** making careful, independent, and proactive observations of other's actions; initiating decisions, agreements, or actions based on clear facts that are free of bias or prejudice; ensuring fair rewards and appropriate natural consequences or agreed corrective actions occur; and setting appropriate boundaries in relationships.
		36. **Kindness is** considering what is good for others and their needs or wants and acting in a deliberately warm-hearted and empathetic manner to meet them.
		37. **Love is** connecting to others through affection and joining with them to express the powerfully magnetic and caring force that unites and brings life to all.
		38. **Loyalty is** honoring, belonging to, supporting, and remaining devoted and faithful to someone or something beyond oneself, such as a friend, relationship or marriage partner, family, employers, organizations, community, religion, country, or the world.
		39. **Mercy is** treating the mistakes or harmful actions of others or oneself in a forbearing and lenient way.
		40. **+Moderation is** recognizing and avoiding extremes in use of time, words, actions, and other choices; accomplishing variety, balance, and positive outcomes in such aspects as rest, work, reflection, community service, and leisure activities; and effectively applying and adjusting a level of intensity of focus and action to both accomplish goals and protect relationships and well-being.
		41. **+Orderliness is** living and working with a sense of harmony; creating uncluttered, well-organized, clean, and shareable spaces; developing systems that allow for easy finding; and systematically planning improvements, tasks, and projects.
		42. **Patience is** maintaining steady awareness and control of one's thoughts and responses while waiting for or seeking an outcome; and controlling one's words and actions while willingly and calmly taking the time to respond to difficult, inconvenient, hurtful, delaying, or troublesome situations.
		43. **Peacefulness is** being physically, mentally, and emotionally calm and serene; and working to reduce conflict and build harmony between people.

Rating	S or G	Character Virtues (continued)
		44. **+Perseverance is** applying energy, effort, and resources toward worthwhile goals until achievement is attained; being committed to the long-term future benefit of actions done in the present; and using willpower to overcome challenges or adversity as they arise.
		45. **Purity is** maintaining personal physical cleanliness, a clean and orderly environment, uplifting and chaste thoughts, positive words, honest motivations, a loving heart, and a spiritually focused soul.
		46. **+Purposefulness is** pursuing and fulfilling meaningful long-term personal goals, commitments, aspirations, and needs; contributing ideas, words, and actions; and participating primarily in vital activities that contribute to desired outcomes.
		47. **+Reflection is** calm self-awareness, understanding, and assessment; inwardly exploring actions, circumstances, thoughts, feelings, and perceptions; seeking inspiration; and analyzing to learn the best approaches for improving situations.
		48. **Resilience is** accepting, responding creatively and appropriately to, recovering from, and coping with adversity, misfortune, change, or illness; and bouncing back from stressful experiences effectively and in a reasonable amount of time.
		49. **+Respect is** interacting with all people and what they value with fair treatment, dignity, consideration, and esteem; and recognizing the best knowledge, skills, talents, and abilities of others.
		50. **Responsibility is** claiming personal accountability for one's own life, choices, happiness, commitments, work, required activities, and relationships with others, as well as sharing accountability for the quality of life in the communities in which one lives and works and in the global society.
		51. **+Self-Discipline is** maintaining the inner control to perform needed and important tasks in a timely way; consciously responding in appropriate ways; and choosing what is beneficial or productive and resisting what is harmful or distracting.
		52. **+Service is** acting selflessly and often sacrificially, directly or indirectly, and with positive intent; and providing time, knowledge, or resources to benefit others without expecting reward or recognition.
		53. **Sincerity is** being genuine and earnest with one's motives, words, and actions.
		54. **Spirituality is** nurturing your heart and soul through maintaining a close, interactive relationship with God, drawing on spiritual sources for divine guidance, dedicated or devoted service to God or a religion, and acting and speaking in alignment with the teachings contained in the Word of God.
		55. **Tactfulness is** choosing whether and when to act or speak and, when speaking, using gentle and kind words with the intention of not offending others or hurting their feelings.
		56. **Thankfulness is** expressing warm, genuine feelings of praise, appreciation, and gratitude for such aspects of life as loved ones, blessings, benefits, lessons learned, challenges that prompt growth, and warm gestures.

Rating	S or G	Character Virtues (continued)
		57. **Thoughtfulness is** being concerned in a deliberate and genuine way about the well-being and happiness of others, acting in anticipation of and in loving awareness of their expressed and unspoken needs.
		58. **Thriftiness is** managing one's economic situation, expenditures, and resources in a wise and frugal way to meet needs adequately, create prosperity, and successfully plan positive outcomes.
		59. **+Trust is** generously extending confidence; assuming the good intentions and actions of others; accompanying others through learning experiences that build skills and capacities; and giving and expecting appropriate confidentiality.
		60. **Trustworthiness is** handling relationships, tasks, responsibilities, possessions, money, and information reliably and honestly, thereby earning the confidence of others, and it is extending confidence in others to do the same.
		61. **+Truthfulness is** recognizing and accurately communicating facts and feelings; independently seeking knowledge of people, circumstances, issues, and information.
		62. **+Unity is** consciously looking for and strengthening points of commonality, harmony, connection, and attraction; accepting differences; and working with others to build a strong and coherent foundation for oneness, love, fairness, commitment, inclusion, cooperation, and common goals.
		63. **Wisdom is** making good choices based upon knowledge gained from careful listening, observation, education, and experiences, as well as through insights from reflecting that help to determine whether it is best to speak, remain silent, act, or be inactive.
		64.
		65.

Source and Copyright Note: The definitions in this PrepSheet are the copyright of Marriage Transformation® (marriagetransformation.com)—except for those marked with a "+" sign, which are the copyright of CharacterYAQ™ (characteryaq.com) and Susanne M. Alexander, W. Grant Peirce IV, and Johann S. Wong. None of the definitions should be reproduced for any purpose, without express, written permission from the copyright holders. Thank you for your respect toward our work.

Having assessed your virtue strengths and areas for improvement, the reflection questions below can help you further deepen your self-knowledge.

Reflection:

1. What interferes with knowing my character? How can I overcome these challenges?

_____
_____
_____

2. What is easy and wonderful about learning about my character?
   _____
   _____
   _____

3. What specific examples show that I already effectively practice some of my virtue strengths?
   _____
   _____
   _____

4. Which three of my well-developed virtues will likely help me interact well with a relationship or marriage partner?
   _____
   _____
   _____

5. Are there three virtues that I want to use differently or that I want to strengthen, because they might cause problems in my relationships or interactions with others?
   _____
   _____
   _____

6. Who do I trust that knows me well and can help me gain further insights? How and when will I invite them to participate in this self-reflection process?
   _____
   _____
   _____

7. What would help me form the habit of regular self-assessment?
   _____
   _____
   _____

Activities

1. Identify four specific gems you like—for example, diamonds, emeralds, sapphires, and rubies—and locate photos of them in a magazine or on the internet. Choose from PrepSheet 3 (above) four virtues you consider your strengths, and match each of these to one of your chosen gems. As you practice each virtue, visualize the beautiful gem you have associated with it. For example, you could associate a ruby with justice, and then every time you act fairly or fight for justice on behalf of someone else, you could visualize a sparkling red ruby inside of you. You may find it useful to revisit these images monthly, and to consider how consistently you are using this metaphor of gems to guide your words and actions.

2. Create a design that represents your character. For example, you could spread glue over a piece of cardboard and sprinkle different colors of art sand onto the wet surface of the glue. Or, you might draw a picture that reflects your character, or you could use a computer graphics program to build a design. Then you can share your design with someone and discuss your views of it.

3. Select a virtue or another aspect of your character, and use various art supplies, to portray what it represents to you, in its multiple facets. For example, people manifest love through various actions, in many different types of relationships, and using many diverse expressions. Artistically portray this quality or another multifaceted virtue or quality. After completing the project, reflect on these questions:

   a. What new facets of this virtue or quality did I learn about?
   _____
   _____
   _____

   b. How do I practice this virtue or quality now? How might I practice it in the future?
   _____
   _____
   _____

   c. How might this virtue or quality positively affect my future partner?
   _____
   _____
   _____

4. Choose a virtue from PrepSheet 3 above that you want to increase your awareness of. For a week—or some other reasonable timeframe—track how others demonstrate or discuss your chosen quality. Where did you see it happen? How often did it happen? Did the use of it surprise you? What thoughts do you have?
   _____
   _____
   _____

5. Take the free or paid research-based character assessment at viacharacter.org (about 20 minutes). Reflect on whether you learned new information about your character from it. Alternatively, you can take the research-based Character Foundations Assessment with a certified coach; information is available at marriagetransformation.com.

Balancing My Character Qualities

Having enhanced your understanding of character in general, and your own character in particular, you can further expand your knowledge by learning to apply the principles of balance and moderation in how you practice them.

1. "… [E]xercise moderation in all things. Whatsoever passeth beyond the limits of moderation will cease to exert a beneficial influence."[64] Bahá'u'lláh

2. "A good character is in the sight of God … and the possessors of insight, the most excellent and praiseworthy of all things, but always on condition that its center of emanation should be reason and knowledge and its base should be true moderation."[65] 'Abdu'l-Bahá

Moderation is the middle way—an excellent balance. Moderating a character quality *does not mean doing it halfway*. It means recognizing the other complementary virtues and behaviors that lead to wisdom in action. You may think of this as applying "helper" qualities—where one quality helps another quality—to produce a better, more balanced outcome. Here are some examples:

- If you are assertive in requesting information from someone, it could help if you are also patient in allowing time for the other person to respond
- Speaking with open honesty is generally a positive approach, but if it's not balanced with tact and wisdom, the effect can be hurtful and alienating
- When you seek contentment with your life, moderating this quality with purposefulness can save you from perpetual inaction
- Flexibility can be helpful when you are being responsible, because responsibility spurs you to complete tasks, and flexibility reminds you that sometimes circumstances change, resulting in changed tasks
- You have strengths of being purposeful and encouraging; when you collaborate on tasks, you use encouraging words and actions while your collaborator learns to do something for the first time; your purposefulness helps you stay focused on the task so both of you can bring it to completion; and your genuine responses, from the inside out, feel fulfilling, and elicit positive responses from others watching

Reflection

1. When have I balanced a character strength with another character quality to produce a more positive effect? Which pairings have been most effective?

   _____
   _____
   _____

2. When have I relied too much on a character strength and caused harm by not also using a moderating or "helper" quality? What will I do differently next time?

   _____
   _____
   _____

3. What qualities do I avoid using but now see they may be good helper qualities?

   _____
   _____
   _____

Activities

1. With a friend or a group, create a short drama showing someone relying heavily on one character quality, and failing to moderate it with any qualities that could bring balance to the situation. Act out the problems that could arise. Then, create a new version that includes other "helper" qualities that lead the person's words and actions to be more effective and beneficial. Complete the activity by reflecting on and discussing what you observed and learned.

2. Find two photos of anything from any source—one that represents a strong and well-established aspect of your character, and one that symbolizes a different, but also positive, character quality that you practice effectively. Put the two photos next to each other and reflect on how these two qualities cooperate and complement each other in your life. For example, you could pair tactfulness with truthfulness, assertiveness with justice, thoughtfulness with service, and so on.

3. Imagine a recipe for a culinary creation—but the resulting dish is a positive experience in a relationship or marriage. What would be the ingredients? Which character qualities would you add? How would you mix it? What would the result look like?

   Here is an example: Combine a cup of respect, a tablespoon of tactfulness, and a teaspoon of kindness in a large bowl of joy. Stir them with wisdom and let them sit with reflection for an hour. Wait for the patience to rise, and then knead it with love. Get ready to enjoy the outcome of a deliciously beautiful time of connection.

   Your Recipe:

   _____
   _____
   _____
   _____
   _____
   _____
   _____
   _____
   _____
   _____

Encouraging Reminder: To assist you in tracking and completing all the reflections and growth steps in this book, we have provided suggestions and tools in "Appendix A: Tracking My Action Commitments".

Chapter 4
Strengthening My Character

Now that you have completed an initial review of your character in Chapter 3, you likely have a broader picture of your many strengths, as well as a few areas that will be good to develop further. The process of further character growth will include opportunities to practice and strengthen your qualities.

Understanding our characters and appraising ourselves honestly helps us see that we are noble human beings with many gifts. We also see how we want to grow and change. This balanced view shows maturity and empowers us to sustain healthy relationships. Your choices for growth will naturally arise from your vision of who you want to be over time and what you want to do in your life. However, many people are uncertain about the process of self-improvement generally, and character improvement specifically. This chapter offers some ways to proceed.

Changing in superficial ways, with the sole purpose of attracting a potential partner, is unwise, because any change in behavior for that purpose may turn out to be temporary and may not reflect who you truly are. Obviously, it's also not genuine or honest. On the other hand, being confident in yourself, striving for excellence and being of service to others, as well as improving yourself and your character qualities each day through making good choices, will likely lead you toward a healthy marriage.

By studying and further developing your character strengths, you also gain knowledge and skills that help you observe and identify character qualities in a potential marriage partner.

Key Learning Points

- Understanding my dual nature
- Managing my character development
- Striving for excellence
- Drawing on the power of encouragement
- Assessing ongoingly

Understanding My Dual Nature

There is a dynamic within each of us—our dual material and spiritual natures. On the material side is our natural need to eat, find shelter, and fulfill other physical needs. These are perfectly reasonable. However, when the material nature dominates our spiritual nature, it can harm us and others. Our spiritual nature calls us to the divine aspect of ourselves. Expanding our spiritual nature then helps us focus on our character qualities and actions that are beneficial.

1. "In man there are two natures; his spiritual or higher nature and his material or lower nature. In one he approaches God, in the other he lives for the world alone. Signs of both these natures are to be found in men. In his material aspect he expresses untruth, cruelty and injustice; all these are the outcome of his lower nature. The attributes of his Divine nature are shown forth in love, mercy, kindness, truth and justice, one and all being expressions of his higher nature. Every good habit, every noble quality belongs to man's spiritual nature, whereas all his imperfections and sinful actions are born of his material nature."[66] 'Abdu'l-Bahá

2. "If a man is successful in his business, art, or profession he is thereby enabled to increase his physical wellbeing and to give his body the amount of ease and comfort in which it delights. ... But, take heed, lest in thinking too earnestly of the things of the body you forget the things of the soul: for material advantages do not elevate the spirit of a man. Perfection in worldly things is a joy to the body of a

man but in no wise does it glorify his soul. ... It is indeed a good and praiseworthy thing to progress materially, but in so doing, let us not neglect the more important spiritual progress, and close our eyes to the Divine light shining in our midst. Only by improving spiritually as well as materially can we make any real progress...."[67] 'Abdu'l-Bahá

3. "'Abdu'l-Bahá explains that the human being has two natures, the spiritual or higher nature and the material or lower nature, and that the purpose of life is to gain mastery over the limitations and promptings of one's material nature and to cultivate spiritual qualities and virtues—the attributes of the soul which constitute one's true and abiding identity. Worldly desire is not the essence of a human being, but a veil that obscures it. Adherence to the Teachings of the Divine Educator refines the character and develops the potentialities with which each person is endowed; it liberates the individual and society from lower inclinations that give rise to the ills that afflict humanity."[68] On behalf of the Universal House of Justice

To effectively develop our character, we need to assess whether our behavior aligns with our higher or lower nature. Beneficial actions help us feel appreciation and joy. On the other hand, when we have caused harm and recognize that our lower nature dominated us in the situation, this understanding helps us behave differently the next time. For example, we like to do excellent work, which is a higher nature choice. However, suppose our lower nature wants self-serving praise and recognition. In that case, this desire can dominate our higher nature intentions and become more important in our minds than working for high-quality outcomes.

Growth is natural and lifelong. Recognizing both strengths and imperfections offers encouragement and motivates us to continue learning and growing. Consistent reflection, prayer, observation, and striving then help us develop new patterns. We begin to make good choices ahead of time instead of simply seeing our poor choices after the fact. For instance, you may be trying to increase your generosity and find that an instinct is to keep resources for yourself, even when others are in dire need or crisis. As you examine that tendency over time, with compassion for yourself in your struggles, you may become more open-hearted and generous in new situations.

You will also begin to see that you can *leverage* your higher-nature character strengths to help you strengthen weaker qualities. For example, perhaps you are especially good at building "unity" with your coworkers. However, you sometimes struggle with being "purposeful" in completing your work assignments. If you ask two other team members to help you manage tasks and deadlines, your unified effort will help you purposefully meet your goals. This approach of leveraging your strengths to help develop your weaker qualities is often more effective than many other approaches you might try.

Character development results in spiritual well-being, and gives us a joy that is palpable, cleansing, and life-changing. When we engage in negative behaviors, it's as if we drink impure water that poisons our system. When we choose to act according to our higher nature, it's like drinking sparkling clear water from the purest springs. Then we realize what we have been missing—what brings full health and happiness.

Note: If people learned from the adults in their lives that negative behaviors such as backbiting, lying, gossip, cheating, selfishness, or stealing were okay, it may be difficult now to accept that they're not. It can take considerable effort and practice to learn new behaviors, but change is possible.

Activity

1. Identify the names of three people who have influenced your character. For each name, write down a quality or virtue you learned from them—either a strength you adopted and have been consciously

practicing, or a weakness you copied that is not helping you in your life. Having clarified these aspects of your character, reflect on how this knowledge can assist you to develop your character further.

a. Name: _____ Quality: _____
b. Name: _____ Quality: _____
c. Name: _____ Quality: _____
Reflection: _____
_____
_____

Managing My Character Development

Reflect on the quotations below and how they might relate to your process of character development. We hope they will empower you to commit to continuous growth and examine any resistance to change that may arise.

1. "… Bahá'u'lláh … draws our attention to the need to make efforts to develop and demonstrate in action our God-given potential: 'All that which ye potentially possess can, however, be manifested only as a result of your own volition. Your own acts testify to this truth.'"[69] Bahá'u'lláh quoted by the Universal House of Justice

2. "… [I]n this world he must prepare himself for the life beyond. That which he needs in the world of the Kingdom must be obtained here. … That world beyond is a world of sanctity and radiance; therefore, it is necessary that in this world he should acquire these divine attributes. In that world there is need of spirituality, faith, assurance, the knowledge and love of God. These he must attain in this world so that after his ascension from the earthly to the heavenly Kingdom he shall find all that is needful in that eternal life ready for him.

   "That divine world is manifestly a world of lights; therefore, man has need of illumination here. That is a world of love; the love of God is essential. It is a world of perfections; virtues, or perfections, must be acquired. That world is vivified by the breaths of the Holy Spirit; in this world we must seek them. That is the Kingdom of everlasting life; it must be attained during this vanishing existence.

   "By what means can man acquire these things? How shall he obtain these merciful gifts and powers? First, through the knowledge of God. Second, through the love of God. Third, through faith. Fourth, through philanthropic deeds. Fifth, through self-sacrifice. Sixth, through severance from this world. Seventh, through sanctity and holiness."[70] 'Abdu'l-Bahá

3. "As we almost never attain any spiritual goal without seeing the next goal we must attain still beyond our reach, he urges you, who, have come so far already on the path of spirituality, not to fret about the distance you still have to cover! It is an indefinite journey, and, no doubt in the next world the soul is privileged to draw closer to God than is possible when bound on this physical plane."[71] On behalf of Shoghi Effendi

4. "An individual's efforts in this respect [striving to be free from ethnic or racial prejudice] must begin with earnest striving to develop attributes of the soul such as love, truthfulness, kindness, justice, and generosity; to purify the heart of selfishness, envy, and hate; and to align the mind with Bahá'u'lláh's principles of unity. By striving to rid his or her thoughts, words, and actions of ethnic bias, an individual upholds his or her own nobility and the nobility of all of God's children. Freedom from prejudice must then manifest itself in all aspects of an individual's life—in private and public life, in the Bahá'í community, and in the wider society. The home environment must be free of attitudes, tendencies, expressions, and associations that give room for prejudice. In the Bahá'í community, God forbid that

a loyal believer's participation in the electoral processes of the Faith be swayed by narrow ethnic interests or that service on committees, agencies, and institutions be tainted by partiality and favoritism. In society, a believer's freedom from prejudice must be evident in all the social spaces he or she enters—the school, the workplace, the cultural association, the professional organization. A believer's duty at all times is to demonstrate the unifying power of Bahá'u'lláh's Teachings by associating with diverse peoples with a spacious heart, an all-embracing love, and a spirit of true friendship. As was 'Abdu'l-Bahá's injunction, "Let those who meet you know, without your proclaiming the fact, that you are indeed a Bahá'í:'"[72] Universal House of Justice

5. "There are … innumerable examples of individuals who have been able to effect drastic and enduring changes in their behavior, through drawing on the spiritual powers available by the bounty of God."[73] On behalf of the Universal House of Justice

6. "What the friends need to remember in this respect is that, in their efforts to achieve personal growth and to uphold Bahá'í ideals, they are not isolated individuals, withstanding alone the onslaught of the forces of moral decay operating in society. They are members of a purposeful community, global in scope, pursuing a bold, spiritual mission—working to establish a pattern of activity and administrative structures suited to a humanity entering its age of maturity. … This framework promotes the transformation of the individual in conjunction with social transformation, as two inseparable processes. Specifically, the courses of the institute are intended to set the individual on a path in which qualities and attitudes, skills and abilities, are gradually acquired through service—service intended to quell the insistent self, helping to lift the individual out of its confines and placing him or her in a dynamic process of community building."[74] On behalf of the Universal House of Justice

As you develop yourself, it's good to frame your efforts in the context of marriage. Family Life Educator Ana Morante puts it this way:

"To have a healthy couple relationship, it's not as much a matter of *finding* the right person as it is actually *being* the right person. We should ask ourselves, "Am I the type of person that I would like to be married to?" To have a good, solid, healthy couple relationship, we have to start with ourselves. We have to start recognizing who we are, and, within that, we have to see what our gifts are and find the good things within ourselves that strengthen us.

"We all carry baggage from our pasts. Maybe it is from the way we were raised or from the family we came from. When we are not aware of that baggage, it can get in the way of us enjoying our lives and actually performing the way we want to. One of the first things I suggest before even considering entering a serious relationship is take a look at yourself and find out what your strong points are, the things you are proud of. Also, it's important to find some of the areas of challenge that you need to face or work on.

"Difficulties come when people enter relationships and do not feel good about themselves. They want to feel loved and accepted by someone else, yet they cannot do it for themselves! That puts a lot of expectations and pressure on the other person. Most of the time, those expectations lead to disappointment, because nobody can give us what we need to give to ourselves. Therefore, good marriage preparation starts with looking at yourself and seeing the areas you need to work on to feel more content…and you must be willing to do that work."[75]

Sometimes, developing your character will energize you, sometimes you may not want anything to do with it, and sometimes both will show up. Some days you'll feel successful at it, and other times you'll go backward. It's not a linear process, and sometimes it's messy. Change can be difficult, but it can also reward you greatly.

One individual, however, posed an alternative to the word "change":

"Change is the wrong word. What we are really talking about here is moral development. A person committed to moral development, whose commitment is demonstrated by deeds as well as words, is surely a better candidate for marriage than someone who isn't committed, regardless of their current level of development. People have a momentum. We rarely stand still—we either grow or regress. A person who is complacent about themselves and judgmental about others is likely to be on a downward trajectory. Someone humble enough to acknowledge faults may outwardly appear a poor candidate but actually be more likely to be on the right path."

Life is often about the thoughts and behaviors that get in the way of our learning and growth. Consider the list below and respond to the questions about tendencies you may be falling into. This will clarify what may be in the way of your growth.

Yes/No?	Do I Often:
	Deny my need to change and grow?
	Blame others for my behavior and complain about their actions rather than addressing my own?
	Justify, make excuses for, and defend my poor behavior?
	Give up on growth because I feel the change process should be easier?
	Feel lost about how to make changes?
	Refuse feedback about my blind spots?
	Feel pride and satisfaction with how I am, without an intention to continue to grow?
	Hold such high standards of perfection that I give up trying to improve?
	Have an overly strong desire to please others—or to change myself for others?
	Minimize a problem I caused and tell myself that I simply committed a small or isolated offense?
	Justify prior behavior by convincing myself that other people are too sensitive?
	Think no one will ever find out there's a problem with my behavior?
	Lie to myself or others about my behavior?
	React with strong self-criticism when I see my character weaknesses?
	Refuse to forgive myself, ask for forgiveness, or offer forgiveness?

In addition to the thought patterns above, many people also discover *limiting beliefs* about themselves—or their circumstances—that block development. For example, someone might say, "I'll never find a partner", "I don't have enough time to grow", or "I don't deserve to experience happiness." We sometimes insist we are being realistic or logical in our thoughts and perceptions, perhaps telling ourselves that since "all my friends have married", there must be "something wrong with me". However, comparing ourselves to others and being self-critical can be demotivating and prevent growth. At times we may also hear others making similar and discouraging comments about us. Identifying and dismantling false beliefs from these sources can free us to grow and move forward.

As you understand your thinking patterns that can interfere with your development, you can begin to make changes. Practicing moderation will help you start small and organically grow as your ability and capacity expand. If instead you try to address every character issue, or develop every quality simultaneously, you'll typically end up overwhelmed and discouraged. Trying one straightforward improvement before attempting a complex one may increase success. As the Universal House of Justice wrote, "Small steps, if they are regular and rapid, add up to a great distance traveled."[76] Step by step, and day by day, brings progress.

Here are some potential approaches to small successive steps:

- For one day, I will say nothing negative about another person. The following day, I will say something courteous or kind to two people.
- For one week, I will spend fifteen minutes each morning and evening praying and meditating.
- For three consecutive days, I will courageously and consistently do something new, even if it's small.

One person grappling with improving his character described his choices and his process in this way:

"I knew that if I wanted to have a happy and healthy life, I needed to grow. Because of the positive changes I've made, I feel happier, I sleep better at night, I am a better father, and I'm a better friend. I honestly don't think that I know one person who really changed because someone else asked them to and then was genuinely happy. It has to come from inside. I learned mindfulness meditation, I started dance classes (to overcome insecurity issues), I went back to reflection and prayer, and more.

Here is what I learned:

1. *Changing from a personal growth point of view (when the choice is mine, and nobody else is asking me or expecting me to change) required me to leave my comfort zone and take risks. We develop defense mechanisms, and we draw imaginary lines that we're not willing to cross or that we don't let others cross. If we or others get too close to that line, or at the first sign of adversity, we come right back to our comfort zone.*

2. *The hardest thing about changing is admitting that there is something wrong with me. It is as if subconsciously it means that something is broken inside of me and needs to be fixed. If someone else asks me to change, then that feeling gets magnified.*

3. *On the lighter side, I'm discovering that the beautiful thing about change is that ultimately it's a choice. When I am brave enough to go past points 1 and 2, no matter how hard it is, how embarrassing it feels, or how much it hurts, ultimately the choice is mine. Now, if I learn something, fix something, or get any type of benefit from what I do, then the reward is totally worth the risk.*

4. *One hard thing about changing is that by doing so my relationships with a lot of people changed, including some of my best friends with whom I hadn't practiced the best habits. It took me a long time to realize that it was okay, even if it was tough.*

"I still have more growing to do, and more change is coming. Now that I have left my ego behind much more, I have extended my comfort zone way past where it was. I have let some old relationships go, and I now surround myself with people who bring out the best in me. I am looking forward to whatever the future brings—all the new lessons, the new experiences, and everything else that 'change' may bring into my life."

As this person said, when people are used to you behaving a certain way, they may not easily accept your changes as real or even appreciate them. They may not initially trust your commitment to the new actions. It may also take *you* time to accept that you've changed. If someone makes negative comments while you are trying to grow, discern whether the feedback is useful, or whether the person doesn't want you to change. Others may want you to change back, since that's what they're used to. However, hopefully, you can count on many people in your life who encourage and celebrate your growth.

As we grow, sometimes we may slip into judging others around us who aren't making similar improvements. To avoid this, it helps us be aware that an air of superiority would likely alienate people who might otherwise appreciate and encourage our growth.

As you come to know yourself, grow your character, and accept yourself, you will increasingly share yourself honestly and openly with others. This individual's perspective may inspire you to persevere in this process:

"I think we are all on the road toward being better people illumined by the teachings of Bahá'u'lláh. Some seem to be further along the road, and others not so far, but as long as we are striving along this path, there is hope we will continue to improve. People can help us by noticing our small achievements and improvements and overlooking our shortcomings. We should be able to ask for assistance from those in our community, and expect that they will not shun us, discourage us, or backbite about us. But then, if they do, we need to overlook their shortcomings too."

Please respond to the reflection questions below, and then complete PrepSheet 4.

Reflection

1. How do I feel about strengthening my virtues or other aspects of my character? When do I resist?

2. What self-development efforts have I made in the last year? How has that gone?

3. What might I gain by improving my character further? Where do I resist this?

4. What concerns or reactions do I have, if any, about others' responses to my efforts to grow my character strengths?

5. How could I change direction if I feel envious of others who seem to find it easier than I do to develop themselves?

6. What activities can I participate in to give me more significant opportunities to practice and strengthen my virtues or other aspects of my character?

7. How is developing my character a service to others?
_____
_____
_____

8. How do people respond when I apply a virtue in my interactions with them?
_____
_____
_____

Starting with Me—Knowing Myself Before Finding a Partner

PrepSheet 4: My Virtue Development Plan

Date: _____

Purposes:
1. To increase my awareness of my thoughts and actions.
2. To create a character development plan to prepare for being in a relationship.
3. To develop my character qualities with conscious and focused effort.
4. To identify who might be able to assist me in this process.

Instructions:

A. There are many steps in this PrepSheet, so before you begin, it will be helpful to read through them all, and then read the example in the first table below.

B. Go back to the 4 virtues that you circled in PrepSheet 3—the ones you want to develop further—and add these virtues to the top of the 4 forms below. However, although 4 forms are provided, we suggest you **choose only 1 of the 4 virtues to address initially and fully complete only 1 form for now. You can fill out the remaining 3 later.** *Of course, you will also be wise to continue strengthening all your virtues throughout your life.*

C. For your chosen first virtue, note why you want to grow.

D. Identify who you will ask to support you with encouragement, practical suggestions, or gentle feedback, if you want someone to help you.

E. Create a goal. Consider how you will know you have succeeded in growing in this virtue within you. What will success look like for you? Being clear about the desired outcome will help you visualize and track your progress.

F. Write down a few specific actions you will take to lead you toward your desired outcome. For each action, plan and write down the date you will start and the date you will assess your progress. Put these dates in your calendar or reminder system.

The steps below may occur in the future, including returning to assess your progress.

G. When the start date arrives, diligently and systematically begin your actions.

H. When the date arrives to assess your progress, look over your notes, review your behavior, and reflect on your words and actions. Determine how much you have advanced toward your goal. Think carefully about how people responded to you—not only those you consulted with but also those you encountered as you strove to develop and demonstrate the virtue. This assessment process will give you a sense of your progress, which you can note in the "Signs of Improvement" section. If you want feedback in addition to your self-assessment, you can approach people and ask for gentle comments. Is anyone noticing your positive changes? Are you getting enough helpful feedback and encouragement?

I. Having reflected on your progress, note any new actions you want to take, set dates for each, and continue the development process.

J. If you are ready, choose a 2nd virtue from your 4, complete the form below for it, and go through a similar process. This cycle of planning, consultation with others, action, and reflection can empower you on a lifelong journey of personal growth and service to others.

Note: "Appendix C: Using Consultation in Marriage Preparation" may assist you, if someone is helping you.

This is the rating scale that you used in PrepSheet 3, in case it's useful to you here:

1 – I rarely use this virtue, so my words and actions can often cause problems
2 – I use this virtue only occasionally, possibly causing problems
3 – I understand this virtue, and I am still strengthening it; sometimes it results in positive outcomes
4 – I am becoming more consistent in practicing this virtue, usually with positive outcomes
5 – I practice this virtue consciously and consistently

EXAMPLE		
Virtue to Develop: *Perseverance*		
Why? *Because I often fail to finish my personal projects. Too often I allow obstacles or trying to be perfect to discourage me, I lose motivation, and I postpone action until "when I have more time."*		
Who Can Help or Encourage Me with This? *My friend Oscar who told me he found some strategies that helped him develop his virtues of perseverance, "stick-to-it-iveness," and "grit".*		
Development Goal (Desired Outcome): *I currently rank my perseverance at a 2 out of 5. If I could get that quality, when working on my projects, up to a strength of 4, I think I could accomplish much more in life.*		
Development Actions:	**Start Date:**	**Assess Date:**
1. *I will not only create actionable goals but also firm deadlines for when to complete 2 personal growth projects. I will make myself accountable to Oscar or someone else for delivery of these results. I will make sure that at least 1 project is focused on service to others.*	*Date*	*Date*
2. *Talk with Oscar or other friends whenever I feel discouraged, to talk through the obstacle that is discouraging me, so I can keep moving forward.*	*Date*	*Date*
3. *When starting work on each project, I will take 2 minutes to pause to pray for perseverance, focus, and determination.*	*Date*	*Date*
4. *Read inspiring quotations and stories about perseverance as part of my daily practice of reading the Bahá'í writings.*	*Date*	*Date*
Signs of Improvement: *After 1 month of doing this, I completed 1 out of the 2 projects, and I am 75% finished with the second project. The service component of these projects has visibly helped the children in my community.*		
New Actions to Take: *Keep up the accountability, talk to Oscar more often about this—at least once every 2 weeks.*		

My Plan

Virtue #1 to Develop:		
Why?		
Who Can Help or Encourage Me with This?		
Development Goal (Desired Outcome):		
Development Actions:	**Start Date:**	**Assess Date:**
1.		
2.		
3.		
4.		
Signs of Improvement:		
New Actions to Take:		

Virtue #2 to Develop:		
Why?		
Who Can Help or Encourage Me with This?		
Development Goal (Desired Outcome):		
Development Actions:	**Start Date:**	**Assess Date:**
1.		
2.		
3.		
4.		
Signs of Improvement:		
New Actions to Take:		

Virtue #3 to Develop:		
Why?		
Who Can Help or Encourage Me with This?		
Development Goal (Desired Outcome):		
Development Actions:	Start Date:	Assess Date:
1.		
2.		
3.		
4.		
Signs of Improvement:		
New Actions to Take:		

Virtue #4 to Develop:		
Why?		
Who Can Help or Encourage Me with This?		
Development Goal (Desired Outcome):		
Development Actions:	Start Date:	Assess Date:
1.		
2.		
3.		
4.		
Signs of Improvement:		
New Actions to Take:		

Activities

1. Make one small change in your home environment to see how long it takes you to get used to it. You might move a piece of furniture, change the location of a picture hanging on the wall, or put your socks in a different drawer. Then, make a different, more significant improvement in your physical space. Organize a few drawers or a closet, paint a wall, or plant some flowers. How do you feel about the change? What do you think about the amount of effort required for the change?

_____

_____

_____

2. Changing a habit:
    a. Identify a habit you want to modify or replace.
    b. Outline the expected benefits of the change.
    c. Write specific goals for your behavior change.
    d. Make a commitment to another person, and ask that person to hold you accountable and to encourage you.
    e. Plan rewards, for every week or whatever time interval is most helpful.
    f. Set up other reminders or incentives that will help you fulfill your commitment.
    g. Set regular times on your calendar (daily? weekly?) and assess your progress toward your goal.
    h. Celebrate your progress.
    i. Reflect on the questions below.

    What assists me to grow and change for the better?
    _____
    _____
    _____
    _____

    How do creativity and perseverance help me in this effort?
    _____
    _____

Striving for Excellence

Consider the quotations below and allow them to motivate you to continue developing your character.

1. "The more one is severed from the world, from desires, from human affairs, and conditions, the more impervious does one become to the tests of God. Tests are a means by which a soul is measured as to its fitness, and proven out by its own acts. God knows its fitness before-hand, and also its unpreparedness, but man, with an ego, would not believe himself unfit unless proof were given him. Consequently his susceptibility to evil is proven to him when he falls into the tests, and the tests are continued until the soul realizes its own unfitness, then remorse and regret tend to root out the weakness. The same test comes again in greater degree, until it is shown that a former weakness has become a strength, and the power to overcome evil has been established."[77] 'Abdu'l-Bahá

2. "Strive with all your power to be free from imperfections. Heedless souls are always seeking faults in others. ... As long as a man does not find his own faults, he can never become perfect. Nothing is more fruitful for man than the knowledge of his own shortcomings."[78] 'Abdu'l-Bahá

3. "... [T]he fundamental purpose of all religions ... is to bring man nearer to God, and to change his character, which is of the utmost importance."[79] On behalf of Shoghi Effendi

4. "... [E]ffort [is] sustained by earnest desire, not instantaneous perfection. The qualities and habits of thought and action that characterize Bahá'í life are developed through daily exertion. 'Bring thyself to account each day', writes Bahá'u'lláh. 'Let each morn be better than its eve', He advises, 'and each morrow richer than its yesterday.' The friends should not lose heart in their personal struggles to attain to the Divine standard, nor be seduced by the argument that, since mistakes will inevitably be made and perfection is impossible, it is futile to exert an effort. They are to steer clear of the pitfalls

of hypocrisy, on the one hand—that is, saying one thing yet doing another—and heedlessness, on the other—that is, disregard for the laws, ignoring or explaining away the need to follow them. So too is paralysis engendered by guilt to be avoided; indeed, preoccupation with a particular moral failing can, at times, make it more challenging for it to be overcome."[80] On behalf of the Universal House of Justice

No one is perfect at practicing character qualities. Character growth is a process—small transformations can happen each day, through continued practice and through serving others. Be as excellent and consistent as you can—holding high standards for yourself. Sometimes, a nudge of guilt can warn you to pay attention to your words or actions. However, *excessive* guilt or shame can interrupt the self-growth process. Since it doesn't serve you well to ignore areas of concern, accept and forgive yourself when you struggle and slip backward, and strive to do better each day in the future.

Most of us look to people with outstanding character qualities as powerfully positive examples of how we should strive to live. At times in our lives, we no doubt draw on observations of the actions of admirable family members, educators, and personal heroes, and we adjust our lives accordingly. None of these individuals live or did live perfect lives, but they demonstrated essential character qualities.

In the Bahá'í Faith, Shoghi Effendi says that Bahá'u'lláh's son 'Abdu'l-Bahá is regarded as "the perfect Exemplar of [Bahá'u'lláh's] teachings ... the embodiment of every Bahá'í ideal, the incarnation of every Bahá'í virtue...."[81] Bahá'u'lláh's daughter, Bahíyyih Khánum, is respected as one of the most significant heroines of the Bahá'í Faith, with outstanding conduct, spirituality, and character. The following passage pays tribute to Bahíyyih Khánum directly and to 'Abdu'l-Bahá indirectly:

"... [S]he was the living symbol of many an attribute I had learned to admire in 'Abdu'l-Bahá. She was to me a continual reminder of His inspiring personality, of His calm resignation, of His munificence and magnanimity. To me she was an incarnation of His winsome graciousness, of His all-encompassing tenderness and love. ... [I]n Tablets, which stand as eternal testimonies to the beauty of her character, Bahá'u'lláh and 'Abdu'l-Bahá have paid touching tributes ... that proclaim her as an example to their followers, and as an object worthy of the admiration of all mankind."[82] Shoghi Effendi

As you study their lives, it can inspire you to follow their examples and move toward excellence.

Just as physical exercise strengthens the muscles you use, the character qualities you practice most frequently become strongest and form an integral part of your personal identity. For example, perhaps you are good at practicing patience, partly because you had to wait for your sibling every day after school. Now, as a retail store manager, you patiently help customers and consistently practice patience in most circumstances that require it. However, some moments may test you and cause you to become impatient. For example, you might have difficulty waiting in lines or become frustrated when an inquisitive and persistent child repeatedly asks you questions. These experiences remind you that while patience is one of your strengths, your ongoing efforts to further develop it serve you well.

As with our muscles, the less we practice a quality, the less effective it will be, and the more it will weaken and atrophy over time. While building a muscle, initially it can become sore, but it will soon strengthen. For instance, if we consistently quit part way through projects, this is the "muscle" of perseverance lacking exercise. Instead, we need to build its strength more by calling ourselves to account and finishing what we start.

Free will allows us to make whatever character and behavior choices we wish. We have the power to choose how we respond to and treat others. As we choose words and actions that reflect character strengths, our self-respect and happiness will increase and facilitate positive interactions with others. Our behavior does not and should not depend upon the behavior of others, even though it's easy to assume that link.

A somewhat uncomfortable truth about character development is that our problems and poor choices with painful consequences become our most significant learning experiences—if we accept what happened and respond well. In these situations, we can strengthen the character qualities required to address the issue. For example, if we become afflicted with an illness or injury, we can practice patience, compassion, and courage in our response and recovery. Suppose we unintentionally hurt a friend with our words, and they want to cut off contact. In that case, it's a chance to practice responsibility, compassion, and loyalty as we seek to reconnect in friendship.

Sometimes, we may flip back and forth between effectively using a quality or virtue. For example, one week we might show compassion toward a particular family member, and the next week, we might be impatient or pay less attention to that person. Hopefully, in such a situation, we will reflect on the effect of each approach and realize it's essential to show compassion consistently. The positive outcome will be visible. As long as we are alive, we can grow and develop, moving from weakness and ineffectiveness to consistent strength and effectiveness in our behavior.

As we carry out character growth and make mistakes, as everyone does, the gifts of humor and laughter keep us from taking ourselves too seriously. If we can find humor in our efforts and our experiences, we will likely relax and gain more clarity about what to do next. We may even gain more motivation and strength to focus on growth. As we encourage others to laugh along with us—kindly, of course—happiness and joy will lighten our hearts and free us to participate more fully in all areas of life.

Reflection

1. What is my attitude toward myself generally? The prompts below may help you answer this question.
   a. Can I see my positive qualities?
   b. My weaker ones?
   c. Do I respect myself?
   d. Do I think of myself as a success? A failure?
   e. Do I think of myself as a person of worth or "no good"?
   f. Am I able to find the humor in my mistakes and challenges?

2. What am I most willing to change about myself?

3. Is there a part of me that I'm unwilling to change, even though it sometimes causes problems? Why? How can I shift this?

Activities

1. Engage in an inspirational reflection to explore how you can benefit from the examples of 'Abdu'l-Bahá and Bahíyyih Khánum in your character journey, enriching the spiritual standard you strive for in your daily life.

   Instructions:
   A. Read through the small sampling of descriptors below about these two people. If you know of other qualities from studying their lives that you want to include, add them after the "Other" prompts at the bottom of the list.

   B. Focus on two or three descriptors you would like to develop further.

   C. Play some meditative music or simply sit in silence. Visualize yourself practicing a behavior related to the descriptor. What are you doing? What environment are you in? Who are you with? How does it feel to act this way?

   D. After you have completed this visualization with one or two descriptors, reflect on the experience and how you might continue to practice these qualities or behaviors in your life.

   Some Descriptors of Their Exemplary Character Qualities and Behaviors:

   a. Pure, kindly, and radiant heart
   b. Calmness, serenity, and equanimity
   c. Cheerfulness, laughter, and humor
   d. Orderly and well-organized
   e. Quietly influencing others in a positive way
   f. Comforting and helping the sad and the ill
   g. Humbly surrendering to God's will
   h. Generous with personal possessions and money
   i. Providing warm hospitality
   j. Self-sacrificing in the path of the love of God
   k. Staunch and steadfast in faith
   l. Prejudice-free
   m. Unifying
   n. Listening attentively and accepting the other person
   o. Courageous action to change the course of events
   p. Loving and nurturing to children
   q. Respectful and considerate of others
   r. Ongoing prayerful attitude
   s. Patient faith in the eventual beneficial outcome of situations
   t. Simplicity in dress, manners, home, and special occasions
   u. Other: _____
   v. Other: _____
   w. Other: _____
   x. Other: _____
   y. Other: _____
   z. Other: _____

Reflection:

_____
_____
_____

2. Find an activity or design a project that involves cooperating as part of a team with others. Examples: build something, volunteer to serve your community, host a prayer gathering, make a quilt, cook a multi-course meal, beautify a piece of property, or organize an event.

    Before you begin, choose the character qualities you want to improve throughout the project. They may be the virtues you identified in PrepSheet 3. You may choose to share these qualities with your team members and request that they assist with your growth. Invite others involved in the activity to join you by choosing character qualities they can practice. At the end of the activity or project, assess what you learned and how each of you grew. Also, consider how your improved behaviors appeared to benefit others.

Reflection:

_____
_____
_____

Drawing on the Power of Encouragement

As you proceed with the rhythm of observing the need for change, developing yourself, and assessing your progress, you will notice you often make your best progress when you receive encouragement from others and from yourself. Sometimes, self-encouragement helps us maintain self-respect—by reminding ourselves that we are valuable and have gifts, skills, and talents that can contribute to others. Consider the quotations below in this context.

1. "Thou art even as a finely tempered sword concealed in the darkness of its sheath and its value hidden from the artificer's knowledge. Wherefore come forth from the sheath of self and desire that thy worth may be made resplendent and manifest unto all the world."[83] Bahá'u'lláh

2. "We can never exert the influence over others which we can exert over ourselves. If we are better, if we show love, patience, and understanding of the weakness of others, if we seek to never criticize but rather encourage, others will do likewise…."[84] Shoghi Effendi

3. "We must not only be patient with others, infinitely patient, but also with our own poor selves, remembering that even the Prophets of God sometimes got tired and cried out in despair! … He urges you to persevere and add up your accomplishments, rather than to dwell on the dark side of things."[85] On behalf of Shoghi Effendi

4. "… [L]ove each other, constantly encourage each other, work together, be as one soul in one body, and in so doing become a true, organic, healthy body animated and illumined by the spirit."[86] Universal House of Justice

In your path of understanding, assessing, and developing your character, we invite you to be compassionate, kind, and patient with yourself. It's wise and constructive to speak gently to yourself and to avoid negative and critical "self-talk", such as "I am so stupid!" or "Why don't I ever do anything right?!". Reflection will help you see that a person growing their character is not the same as a student trying to earn a good grade, or an employee in a performance review trying to get a pay raise. You are investing in your long-term well-being, your service to the world, your state of happiness, and your prospects for a partner. So, we hope you'll recognize your character strengths and avoid being overly self-critical.

The Gottman Institute's research about couples over decades has shown that successful and lasting relationships need a ratio of five positive interactions to every negative one. That is, we should share five everyday gestures of kindness, affection, and appreciation with our partner for every negative gesture we make[87]. Wouldn't the same then be true with ourselves? We can strive for five positive and encouraging gestures toward ourselves for every piece of negative feedback.

The word "encourage" means to inspire courage, spirit, and confidence. Mutual support, assistance, and encouragement help everyone as they strive to achieve important goals. When people we respect encourage us, it often fills us with energy and happiness. This energy helps us continue our personal development and purposes in life. When someone says, "Well done!" to us, we feel encouraged to persevere. Encouragement helps our spiritual roots go deeper and gives us a positive vision to strive for.

If you practice sincerely encouraging others and yourself, you will gain an appreciation for its power—or perhaps you already do this regularly and are well aware of this power. Encouragement doesn't mean stroking someone's ego, but rather, appreciating the spiritual qualities that shine out from their higher selves—acknowledging the beauty of the soul.

We've listed in the right column of the table below some ways to give and receive encouragement; some of these may be helpful to direct toward yourself. Read each phrase and pause to reflect.

In the left column of the table, indicate your "Status on Practicing" the item, in whatever way works for you. You can consider a method such as this:
- Put a checkmark next to the items that are your common responses
- Put a star (*) or check mark next to the encouragement you give to yourself
- Put a "P" next to the ones you will begin to practice more often.

Status on Practicing	Encouraging Words and Actions
	Dwell on the positive with gratitude
	Share a smile
	Acknowledge someone's best qualities
	Affirm someone's good choices
	Write a note or give a gift
	Offer a hug
	Show enthusiasm
	Express your trust that someone is trying to do their best
	Listen carefully and empathetically
	Demonstrate sensitivity to others and inclusiveness
	Show patience and gentleness
	Spend time together
	Offer to help
	Pray together
	Share laughter
	Offering sincere and honest appreciation
	Be loving
	Say "Thank you"
	Say "Well done!"

Reflection

1. When have I received and appreciated encouragement from another person or myself that helped me move forward or grow?
   _____
   _____
   _____

2. When have I offered encouragement to someone that was particularly effective?
   _____
   _____
   _____

Assessing Ongoingly

Since character development is a lifelong process, daily self-assessment is a useful practice. Consider these quotations:

1. "Bring thyself to account each day ... to give account for thy deeds."[88] Bahá'u'lláh

2. "Noble have I created thee, yet thou hast abased thyself. Rise then unto that for which thou wast created."[89] Bahá'u'lláh

3. "... Every day, in the morning when arising you should compare today with yesterday and see in what condition you are. If you see your belief is stronger and your heart more occupied with God and your love increased and your freedom from the world greater then thank God and ask for the increase of these qualities."[90] 'Abdu'l-Bahá

The more specific, intentional, and diligent we are in developing our character, the greater our success. Some approaches that can help are:

- Choose a quality and focus on strengthening it for a day, week, or longer period
- Spend time with encouraging and supportive people
- Ask a trusted friend or relative to assist in reflecting on behavior
- Review words and actions daily to see how well they reflect character strengths
- Ask direct, in-depth questions about the quality and the situation; for example, "Was I paying attention to others' feelings in this situation, or did I get caught up in my own needs too much?"; "How might I have shown more generosity in that situation?"; or "How did I practice friendliness this week?"
- Keep a journal of growth progress to stay encouraged about steady, ongoing character development
- Use your plans from PrepSheet 4 to participate in ongoing self-assessment

If daily self-assessment feels unnatural or difficult initially, experiment with different approaches and timeframes to determine what works best. It seems people benefit most from reviewing their actions regularly and in enough depth to recall specific details. The balance is not spending so much time and energy that it isn't a sustainable habit.

During a regular review, these are good questions to ask:

- How well did I meet my behavior and character goals today (or yesterday or this week)?
- What character qualities did I practice well?
- When did my actions cause hurt feelings or another negative outcome?
- What could I have done better?
- What did I have control over? What could I not control?
- What do I want to do differently tomorrow?

Close to a mountain, we might see only a handful of rocks and a few trees, but from a mile away, we can see all of it. As we step back and objectively look at a longer vista of our life, the lessons learned over time become more obvious.

Reflection

1. How do I know that I am actively engaged in character growth and development?
   _____
   _____
   _____

2. What do I appreciate about personal changes I've made? How have others responded to these changes?
   _____
   _____
   _____

3. Do I have any significant character challenges or "areas for growth" that could be warning signs that I am not yet ready for marriage?
   _____
   _____
   _____

Activity

1. Create a poster of a quotation or phrase from this chapter to remind you to focus on character development each day.

Encouraging Reminder: To assist you in tracking and completing all the reflections and growth steps in this book, we have provided suggestions and tools in "Appendix A: Tracking My Action Commitments".

Chapter 5
Aligning My Expectations with Reality

We need to carefully examine our expectations before we are generally aware of the *unconscious* ones we have about marriage in general and our own marriage in particular. We also have *conscious* expectations. This chapter helps clarify the many expectations we may hold. Shining a light on our hidden assumptions about married couples' interactions helps prevent us from being surprised and upset after marrying and discovering that our partner doesn't live up to what we imagined, and perhaps that we do not live up to our own hopes either.

Social forces, community, and culture also influence our thinking about marriage. Unrealistic imaginings can form, so these need to be distinguished from achievable and realistic needs that a marriage partner could meet.

Your confidence will grow as you systematically uncover, examine, understand, and re-adjust your expectations. You will be better prepared to share with a potential partner what you look forward to about marriage and what you need from it. This, in turn, will increase your opportunity for clear communication, agreed-upon reasonable expectations, and satisfying each other's needs in a happy marriage.

Key Learning Points

- Clarifying spiritual ideals and realistic expectations
- Understanding the sources of our expectations
- Identifying my expectations and needs

Distinguishing Spiritual Ideals from Realistic Expectations

Please consider the following beautiful quotations and how they impart uplifting ideals based on spiritual behavior. While anyone could only hope to attain these ideals, the quotations present a wonderful vision to strive toward throughout marriage.

1. "In this glorious Cause the life of a married couple should resemble the life of the angels in heaven— a life full of joy and spiritual delight, a life of unity and concord, a friendship both mental and physical. The home should be orderly and well-organized. Their ideas and thoughts should be like the rays of the sun of truth and the radiance of the brilliant stars in the heavens. Even as two birds they should warble melodies upon the branches of the tree of fellowship and harmony. They should always be elated with joy and gladness and be a source of happiness to the hearts of others. They should set an example to their fellow-men, manifest true and sincere love towards each other and educate their children in such a manner as to blazon the fame and glory of their family."[91] 'Abdu'l-Bahá

2. "The news of your union, as soon as it reached me, imparted infinite joy and gratitude. Praise be to God, those two faithful birds have sought shelter in one nest. I beseech God that He may enable them to raise an honored family, for the importance of marriage lieth in the bringing up of a richly blessed family, so that with entire gladness they may, even as candles, illuminate the world. For the enlightenment of the world dependeth upon the existence of man. If man did not exist in this world, it would have been like a tree without fruit. My hope is that you both may become even as one tree, and may, through the outpourings of the cloud of loving-kindness, acquire freshness and charm, and may blossom and yield fruit, so that your line may eternally endure."[92] 'Abdu'l-Bahá

As the above passages indicate, we can—and should—hope and pray for a greatly blessed marriage. Ideally, we would achieve a beautiful spiritual state of friendship, unity, joy, and spiritual delight, as well as bring this harmony and happiness to other souls. However, we will likely be happier in marriage if we view these spiritual ideals as horizons that we always strive to draw closer and closer to. It's much harder if we see these as marital requirements and conditions, or absolute moral standards that must be upheld every moment of every day.

It's better to distinguish between spiritual ideals that we strive for, and our realistic expectations of a partner—both of which are assets in a healthy marriage. If we expect to treat a partner well and if we expect to be treated well, our expectations are more likely to be fulfilled. If we forget this distinction between idealism and realism, our spiritual and other ideals may degenerate into unrealistic expectations of a partner, with our being far too picky to ever get married to a real person. Alternatively, we might marry but be deeply frustrated when our unrealistic expectations are unmet. Instead, we can strive toward the lofty shared state of a beautiful union, while also recognizing that it's two flawed but striving humans who build a healthy marriage day by day.

Spiritual ideals relate to us as individuals striving toward an excellent character and a spiritual state of being—the internal—whereas expectations have more to do with behavior, actions, circumstances, and situations—the external. Expectations can be beneficial or harmful, while striving for spiritual ideals, character strengths, and an uplifted state of being—as individuals or as a couple—can only have positive effects. Expectations are beneficial when realistic and clear, or they can be problematic and potentially harmful when unrealistic. Even realistic expectations are most beneficial when communicated and earnestly agreed upon by the two people involved.

Understanding the Sources of Our Expectations

It takes effort to sort out how we know and believe what we do. There are many influences throughout our lives. The quotation below is a reminder to investigate to determine the truth. In this case, it's learning and understanding the sources of the expectations we have formed.

1. "God has not intended man to blindly imitate his fathers and ancestors. He has endowed him with mind or the faculty of reasoning by the exercise of which he is to investigate and discover the truth; and that which he finds real and true, he must accept. He must not be an imitator or blind follower of any soul. He must not rely implicitly upon the opinion of any man without investigation; nay, each soul must seek intelligently and independently, arriving at a real conclusion and bound only by that reality."[93] 'Abdu'l-Bahá

A mere mention of the word "marriage" can prompt a flurry of mental images and emotional impressions. Observations, experiences, and culture influence our expectations of how things will or should be. For example, suppose you consider the roles and responsibilities men and women often have within relationships, marriages, and families. In that case, you will likely realize you have formed opinions about what you and a partner should or shouldn't do.

Many of your expectations come from childhood observations of your parents. What you grow up experiencing and observing tends to be what you expect to happen in your own marriage and family. As you matured, you also observed other important relationships occurring in your family, friends, and community. Perhaps you have also been married. All these observations and experiences feed into the total of your expectations.

As with character development, positive and negative forces in the broader society also affect expectations. Social media, music, videos, movies, podcasts, photos, books, and articles offer a range of perspectives on what a relationship is "supposed" to be, and these have likely influenced you. Some of these influences are positive and realistic; others are subtly distorted and harmful. Other images are more obviously unhealthy—such as those in pornography.

Many media sources give the impression that love and intimacy are instantaneous events rather than the healthier and more realistic view that they develop organically over time. The media often promotes idealism and romanticism, and it also emphasizes having fantastic sex. Unfortunately, the media also frequently presents the cynical view that a healthy, happy, and lasting marriage is not possible.

In contrast to media images, real couples deepen their feelings of love by sharing many life experiences, and their loving expressions tend to fluctuate over time—rather than always being at the height of romance. At the same time, couples witnessing the failure of marriages can fall prey to the cynical view that enduring marriages are a myth, and they may begin to feel they should give up.

Your age and life circumstances will shape your view of what married life will be like. For example, younger couples are more inclined to imagine and to have expectations around raising children. In contrast, later marriages may have expectations related to companionship and changes in health and income. Expectations can influence behaviors and outcomes in all aspects of a relationship, including these:

- Meals
- Cleaning
- Financial management
- Disciplining and educating children
- Family, spiritual, and recreational activities
- Health and hygiene
- Cultural celebrations

Examining your collection of expectations will empower you to see many that you were unaware of. Then, you can begin to discern which are realistic and identify those that would be wise to discard.

Reflection

1. Who has influenced my expectations of a future marriage partner and married life? In what ways?
   _____
   _____
   _____

2. What other sources have led to my expectations? Which sources are helpful? Which ones might mislead me instead?
   _____
   _____
   _____

Identifying My Expectations and Needs

Read the quotations below to begin discerning how you determine truth for yourself and how this relates to understanding your needs and expectations of yourself and others.

1. "Thou shalt…know of thine own knowledge and not through the knowledge of thy neighbor."[94] Bahá'u'lláh

2. "He must not rely implicitly upon the opinion of any man without investigation; nay, each soul must seek intelligently and independently, arriving at a real conclusion and bound only by that reality. The

greatest cause of bereavement and disheartening in the world of humanity is ignorance based upon blind imitation."[95] 'Abdu'l-Bahá

3. "... [It is] incumbent upon all to investigate reality. What does it mean to investigate reality? It means that man must forget all hearsay and examine truth himself, for he does not know whether statements he hears are in accordance with reality or not. Wherever he finds truth or reality, he must hold to it, forsaking, discarding all else; for outside of reality there is naught but superstition and imagination."[96] 'Abdu'l-Bahá

4. "... [E]ach prospective marriage presents highly individualized relationships, and the decision to marry should preferably be made after acquaintanceship and exploration of each other's character and background and, if necessary, with counsel from trusted friends."[97] On behalf of the Universal House of Justice

5. "A married couple can be a tremendous strength and support to each other, but building a strong, united marriage requires persistence, effort, and the overcoming of many difficulties together. Thus 'Abdu'l-Bahá advises a young couple to get to know each other's characters thoroughly before taking this very important step. They must think not only of the effect on each other but of the effects of their characters on the children who will be the fruit of the marriage."[98] On behalf of the Universal House of Justice

Being reflective and honest with yourself greatly assists you to identify your expectations of relationships and marriage; determine your true, vital needs; and then align your expectations with reality. Disunity and difficulties can result when you don't recognize, share, agree on, or meet key expectations and needs in a relationship—and especially in a marriage.

Your intellect and good judgment are powerful tools for distinguishing unrealistic expectations of a partner from those that are realistic. Consider whether, and how much, your thoughts are supported by evidence. You may sometimes be inclined to follow the ideas and standards of others somewhat blindly. Assess to what degree your expectations are grounded in reality versus imagination.

As you increase your awareness of your thoughts and their effects on your plans and actions, you are independently investigating truth. As you assess previous life experiences and your responses to them, you will likely begin to develop a clear idea—if you have not already—of what works or doesn't work well for you in a relationship or marriage.

Some people expect to be taken care of, to have all the love and affection they want, to always be understood, to have all their problems solved and needs satisfied, or to always be happy. Some people reported the following expectations:

- I will be in a perpetual state of bliss
- I will be loved and respected automatically and all the time regardless of my words and actions
- I will get my own way
- I will be taken care of
- I will be free of parental restrictions
- I will never be lonely
- Marriage will end my miseries, and my partner will be the solution to all my problems
- I will have a perfect marriage partner who will satisfy all my needs
- Love for each other is all we will ever need to see us through problems
- Having children is the answer to improving a relationship

These expectations are unrealistic in anyone's life and certainly not in marriage. Some of your needs will be and should be met, and you may be happy much of the time, but a marriage ceremony is certainly not a guarantee that your life and marriage will be problem-free. Sometimes, married life means you have a supportive partner, and you accompany each other in consulting about and responding to challenges. Sometimes, married life includes navigating through extreme disagreements, hurt feelings, and different vantage points.

Rather than making up your own rules or applying expectations based on media images, a marriage will be strongest when you identify and follow spiritual principles. For instance, if you both believe in God, it *is* reasonable to expect you will both do your best to follow the will of God (as Bahá'u'lláh has stated in the Bahá'í marriage vow, "We will all, verily, abide by the Will of God"[99]). This perspective and orientation can help any marriage, even if neither party is a Bahá'í. Suppose you don't have a shared set of beliefs. In that case, it is realistic—and would no doubt be beneficial—for you to create and agree on some inspiring purposes for your marriage, such as serving others, sharing the beauty of life together, or raising children to be productive and happy citizens of the world.

If an expectation directly contradicts a religious, spiritual, or moral principle you know to be true, there's a good chance your expectation is ill-founded. For example, perhaps you expect your partner to share everything with you, even if it's confidential or constitutes gossip or backbiting. This is not in keeping with Bahá'u'lláh's teaching that recognizes backbiting as error: "backbiting quencheth the light of the heart, and extinguisheth the life of the soul."[100]

Here are some other ways you can assess how viable and realistic an expectation is:

- Read a book about marriage that is grounded in research
- Talk to couples who have been in a happy, healthy marriage for at least three years
- Consult with a trusted friend, advisor, professional, or Bahá'í institution (or its designated representatives) about your expectations for marriage
- Imagine yourself sitting with a future partner and sharing an expectation; visualize your partner responding to your words, and see if it feels realistic for the response to be positive
- Think about your own level of willingness to meet this expectation if your partner held it
- Assess whether fulfilling the expectation would require one of you to know what the other was thinking without asking or speaking it out loud; for example, often, partners are upset when the other doesn't just intuitively know what their partner needs
- Determine whether the expectation and outcome should be automatically present before marriage, or whether the two of you would need to create it or learn how to do it together; for example, you might expect to be able to carry out couple decision-making smoothly, but this may be a skill you learn together instead

Reasonable expectations include being emotionally and sexually faithful to each other, doing one's best to meet a partner's healthy need for affection, and each person continuing their education already begun. Although these expectations are reasonable, they are far more likely to be fulfilled if partners consult and agree upon them, and then mutually commit to making them a reality. As life changes, so do expectations and needs. Therefore, open and respectful communication is a vital tool for every relationship stage.

After one individual assessed his expectations of marriage (see PrepSheet 5A below), he shared what he learned about differentiating realistic from unrealistic expectations:

*"I'm learning there are **expectations**, and then there are **desires** of things I want in a marriage partner—and these are different. Often when I've questioned whether my expectation is realistic, I've considered making a separate list of my wishes or desires. It comes down to what's most essential, what's most fair for me to expect, and what's 'value added'. There are many things I desire in a partner, but all of them would be unrealistic to find in one woman.*

"If I'm honest with myself, one of the main reasons I'm still single is that I've had overly high hopes and expectations of the type of woman I should marry. I've been thinking unconsciously that she will have to be super-amazing for us to be successful in marriage and not get divorced—and therefore for me to be happy being with her. This type of hyper-idealistic thinking then causes me to set the bar unreasonably high.

"Another impediment to marriage has been my thought, at times, that eternity is a very long time to spend with someone, so it needs to be an absolutely perfect match. Perhaps another subconscious reason I want her to be amazing is so that marriage will be easier for me. This is probably the voice of the ego, which always likes things to be comfortable, safe, and easy. Taking the time to write out each hope, expectation, need, or desire I have and then analyze whether or not it's realistic has been a very powerful exercise for me. It is like checking my heart, ideals, fancies, and imaginations against rationality, logic, and the realities of the world we live in."

Even when we hold *realistic* expectations, life and partner circumstances can cause disruptions, and there is no way for them to be fulfilled. Here are some examples:

- An individual could hold an expectation that a partner must be a long-time Bahá'í, and then discover a wonderful loving relationship with a very spiritual person who is not
- A couple could agree that they will live together in a particular location, and a flood has them move right after they marry
- A couple could agree on how they will exercise and maintain their health, and a significant illness or injury could intervene

As you complete the PrepSheets below on your expectations for marriage generally and for a partner more specifically, remember to consider that circumstances could leave you with unfulfilled yet realistic expectations.

Reflection

1. How might the qualities of truthfulness and honesty—both with myself and others—help me with increasing awareness of my expectations and needs, and then communicating them to others?

   _____
   _____
   _____

2. What methods will I use to help me distinguish whether an expectation is realistic or unrealistic?

   _____
   _____
   _____

3. When might it be appropriate for me to practice detachment from a realistic expectation?

   _____
   _____
   _____

We encourage you to complete the two PrepSheets below to clarify your personal expectations, distinguish between realistic and unrealistic expectations, and adjust them as needed.

Starting with Me—Knowing Myself Before Finding a Partner

PrepSheet 5A: My Expectations of Marriage

Date: _____

Purposes:
1. To identify a selection of general expectations I hold about marriage.
2. To distinguish whether these expectations are realistic or not.
3. To strengthen my ability to distinguish between realistic and unrealistic expectations.
4. To identify 5 realistic expectations of marriage.

Instructions:
A. In the table below, list up to 10 expectations you hold *about marriage in general*, regardless of who the partner might be, and note any specifics about them. PrepSheet 5B, further below, will address the expectations *of a partner*.

B. Reflect on how realistic each expectation is and choose "Yes" or "No".

C. Note the reasons for your thinking.

D. Hopefully, you can identify at least 5 realistic expectations.

My Expectations of Marriage	Realistic? Yes	Realistic? No	Reason
Example: We should do all activities together.		X	Occasional time and space apart can strengthen a marriage.
Example: We should be faithful to each other.	*		Follows spiritual guidance; keeps the marriage healthy
1.			
2.			
3.			
4.			
5.			
6.			
7.			
8.			
9.			
10.			

Reflection

1. What do I see as the purpose and value of identifying my expectations about marriage?
   _____
   _____
   _____

2. Was I able to distinguish between realistic and unrealistic expectations? What might help me improve this ability?
   _____
   _____
   _____

3. Can the realistic items I identified help me establish a healthy marriage? If so, in what ways?
   _____
   _____
   _____

Starting with Me—Knowing Myself Before Finding a Partner

PrepSheet 5B: My Expectations of a Marriage Partner

Date: _____

Purposes:
1. To identify my expectations about a marriage partner's words, actions, and character-related behaviors.
2. To distinguish whether or not these expectations are realistic.

Instructions:

A. In the form below, list several of the expectations you hold about the words and actions of a marriage partner.

B. Reflect on how realistic each expectation is and choose "Yes" or "No".

C. Note the reasons for your thinking.

D. Hopefully you can identify at least 10 that are realistic. (See Chapter 8 for more on this topic.)

Note: You may consider some of the items below as possible focus areas for your expectations.

- Character-related behaviors
- Communication frequency and quality
- Religious and spiritual practices and beliefs
- Quality of friendship between partners
- Emotional support from a partner during upsets and disappointments
- Sharing household responsibilities
- Personal cleanliness; Cleanliness of the home
- Orderliness in home; Orderliness in family records
- Philosophies of raising children; Time with children, time with grandchildren
- Time spent together and apart; How partners greet each other when reconnecting
- Managing money
- Socio-economic level; Income
- Frequency for intimate touching and sex
- Standard of clothing at home vs. away
- Time spent on work; Involvement with each other's work
- Specific careers; Changing careers or jobs
- Level of conscious focus on marriage
- Level of involvement in religious, community, or civic activities
- Responding to, and getting help for, marriage challenges and problems
- How to resolve disagreements
- How to build understanding and make decisions
- Time spent with friends, including frequency of contact with them
- Ways that equality is demonstrated
- Eating together; Home and away diets and types of food preparation
- Level of fitness; Frequency and types of sports, recreation, and exercise
- Caring for ill, injured, or aging family members
- Leisure activities
- Adherence to high standards of conduct, such as refraining from the use of drugs, alcohol, and pornography

My Expectations of a Marriage Partner	Realistic?		Reason
	Yes	No	
Example: *Our roles will always be completely equal and the same*		X	*Unrealistic, especially with parenting; Partners in different roles can still be equal*
Example: *Will make all significant decisions together with me*	*		*Follows spiritual guidance; improves understanding and decision-making*
1.			
2.			
3.			
4.			
5.			
6.			
7.			
8.			
9.			
10			
11.			
12.			
13.			
14.			
15.			

Reflection

1. What do I see as the purpose and value of identifying my expectations about a marriage partner?

   _____
   _____
   _____

2. Was I able to distinguish between realistic and unrealistic expectations? What might help me improve this ability?

   _____
   _____

3. Can the realistic items I identified help me establish a healthy marriage? If so, in what ways?
   _____
   _____
   _____

4. Will anyone I meet fulfill my realistic expectations? Or would I have to be flexible and only realistically expect this from someone depending on who they are and the circumstances?
   _____
   _____
   _____

5. Have I created a set of expectations that will cause me to reject a prospective marriage partner who is excellent in many ways?
   _____
   _____
   _____

6. When I reflect on my expectations, have I begun to look for someone "perfect"? Could someone be a good fit for me even if they have some growth areas, as *every* person does?
   _____
   _____
   _____

Encouraging Reminder: To assist you in tracking and completing all the reflections and growth steps in this book, we have provided suggestions and tools in "Appendix A: Tracking My Action Commitments".

Chapter 6
Avoiding Possible Pitfalls on My Journey

At this stage in your marriage self-preparation process, you are growing in self-knowledge and self-development. Now, we invite you to examine some of the mental roadblocks or actions that might be pitfalls while moving forward.

Your experiences, media messages, and stories from people you know, may have left you with some misconceptions or myths about relationships and marriage. We particularly focus on one that says there is only one "soul mate" in the world for you.

In addition, we ask you to more deeply understand your reasons for considering marriage. Some of these may be healthy, and others less so. We also share with you some perspectives on the topic of sex and how it can affect relationships and marriages.

This chapter will hopefully aid you to avoid many common pitfalls and free you to keep advancing toward a healthy marriage.

Key Learning Points

- Debunking the "soul mate" myth
- Exploring reasons to marry
- Navigating sex and chastity
- Addressing fears that arise

Debunking the "Soul Mate" Myth

Read the quotations below and see if they prompt you to recalibrate your current understanding of "soul mates" and destiny.

1. "The love between husband and wife must not be purely physical, nay, rather, it must be spiritual and heavenly. These two souls should be considered as one soul. How difficult it would be to divide a single soul! Nay, great would be the difficulty! In short, the foundation of the Kingdom of God is based upon harmony and love, oneness, relationship and union, not upon differences, especially between husband and wife."[101] 'Abdu'l-Bahá

2. "Bahá'í marriage is the commitment of the two parties one to the other, and their mutual attachment of mind and heart. ... Their purpose must be this: to become loving companions and comrades and at one with each other for time and eternity...."[102] 'Abdu'l-Bahá

3. "With regard to your question as to the value of intuition as a source of guidance for the individual: implicit faith in our intuitive powers is unwise, but through daily prayer and sustained effort one can discover, though not always and fully, God's will intuitively. Under no circumstances, however, can a person be absolutely certain that he is recognizing God's will, through the exercise of his intuition. It often happens that the latter results in completely misrepresenting the truth, and thus becomes a source of error rather than of guidance."[103] On behalf of Shoghi Effendi

4. "There is nothing against a person remarrying, the implication of unity in marriage being meant as a spiritual bond which will be everlasting, and not a sexual thing...."[104] On behalf of Shoghi Effendi

5. "There is no teaching in the Bahá'í Faith that 'soul mates' exist. What is meant is that marriage should lead to a profound friendship of spirit, which will endure in the next world, where there is no sex, and no giving and taking in marriage; just the way we should establish with our parents, our children, our brothers and sisters and friends a deep spiritual bond which will be ever-lasting, and not merely physical bonds of human relationship."[105] On behalf of Shoghi Effendi

6. "The paragraph regarding 'soul mates' [quotation #5 above] simply dismisses the popular idea that there exists only one special person who is preordained for us. Rather, a closeness such as you and your wife achieved can only be realized through a shared life of love and service...."[106] On behalf of the Universal House of Justice

7. "It is suggested that Bahá'í marriage does not automatically 'lead to a profound friendship of spirit, which will endure in the next world'. Further, it would appear that the possibility of such an enduring 'friendship' is not limited to the relationship between husband and wife. Rather, it is dependent on the nurturance and development of 'a deep spiritual bond', which transcends the 'merely physical bonds of human relationship' and is conditional on the establishment of 'unity' in the particular relationship."[107] Memorandum from the Research Department of the Bahá'í World Centre to the Universal House of Justice

It's common for people to think there is only one "soul mate" for each person, only one special person preordained as a partner for them. Often, this concept is linked to "love at first sight"—the notion that we will instantly know if someone will be "the one"—our eternal partner. Being attached to one or both of these myths can strongly interfere with finding a complementary partner and building a harmonious marriage.

Marriages are strongest when built on a foundation of friendship and the ability to be together in unity and harmony. A true spiritual bond naturally develops over time through daily living, shared experiences, and building a family. It strengthens as the couple expresses love to each other, and as they pray and serve others together.

Many people—not just one—can potentially succeed in *this* type of marriage with you—one founded on friendship. This concept is far more realistic than the idea that only one person amongst the billions on this planet is the right match for you. And yet, this notion of the one and only "soul mate" persists, with a large following, and some people struggle to leave it behind.

Considering the matter logically, if soul mates were truly just "found" and this was the only thing needed for a successful marriage, there would be a much lower divorce rate. If, before having an opportunity to know each other's character and share life experiences, two people think they've found their soul mates in each other, the relationship is probably based on emotional needs, physical chemistry, or a temporary feeling of being "in love". Seemingly mystical signs may convince the couple that they are "fated" and "meant to be together"—sometimes despite clear evidence that their relationship has significant problems and potential pitfalls.

Sometimes, people are instantly attracted to each other because they have much in common and seem to understand each other completely. For instance, they may have both survived bad marriages or troubled childhoods and now look for someone to share and heal their hurts and erase their painful pasts. Or maybe two lonely people are overwhelmingly delighted to discover that the other accepts them. Genuine chemistry and complementarity is also possible—but without solid communication skills and true harmony of character, values, and life goals, the relationship is at risk of not achieving long-term viability.

Think about the hazards of trying to sustain a committed relationship or marriage while constantly feeling the *fear of missing out*—"FOMO" for short—wondering whether you made a mistake and the *one* right person, your soul mate, is still out there in the world. Thoughts like, "Maybe he lives across the globe", or "Maybe I took a wrong turn a few streets back, and she is sitting in a different restaurant", are a recipe for the disastrous start of a serious relationship or marriage without total commitment. One foot is "out the door", and parts of the body, mind, and heart are already aiming toward the next person or divorce court.

As we explored in Chapter 1, we are each responsible for our own happiness and joy. The soul mate myth is popular, at least in part, because people believe they'll have guaranteed happiness with that "one special person". However, happiness does not fall upon us or "just happens". Happiness is a spiritual perspective and a choice, and the Bahá'í teachings often encourage us to be happy now—not at some unknown time in the future. Happy couples are created by nurturing a healthy relationship over time, not from simply having the good fortune of finding the perfect other to "complete" them.

Once you experience the freedom of knowing there are many potential marriage partners for you, you can relax and breathe a bit. You can take the time you need to develop your character and get clear on the qualities and attributes that are important to you in a partner. You can strengthen your knowledge and skills related to marriage. You can build friendships and explore the possibility of a relationship with many people. Gone is the hyper-vigilance of having to make sure you do not miss seeing your "only intended partner". You may then more easily identify someone who could realistically become your partner in creating a long-lasting marriage—one that enhances the lives of each of you, your families, and your community.

Consider the following experience an individual shared:

"I've made friends of all types that I'll be attached to my whole life. I have consciously taken the time to observe them in all possible circumstances when we're together. I have done this without thinking about marriage. But once or twice, I did consider a male friend as a potential partner, before changing my mind as I got to know him better and realized our characters weren't well-matched. For someone to be truly considered a friend, there should be several traits that connect you with that person that you've uncovered. Same thing with finding a partner. But something gets in the way of getting to know people—when we focus too much on our own particular vision of a possible future with the other person. I think it's necessary to be detached to a reasonable degree from the feeling that someone is a potential partner to be able to pay close attention to their attitudes, reactions, and character in a good number of circumstances and situations—without trying to force-fit them as a potential partner.

"But on the other hand, finding a great marriage partner isn't impossible, right? Each one needs to focus on getting 'thoroughly acquainted' with the other's character, along with prayer and absolute trust in God's guidance. I think this detachment means leaving aside the common idea of 'soul mates', 'love at first sight', and other unrealistic romantic ideas. This will give us the capacity to identify a person's character qualities in the most ordinary situations.

"There are certainly clues to someone's character in basically everything they do. One just needs to have clear and unbiased vision to see these clues. Of course, it doesn't mean a clear vision would make you able to see all of the person's character. And it's a good thing that's not possible, because that would take away the pleasure of discovering even more wonderful qualities in the other person over time. It also would remove the joy of personal growth when facing, with the right attitude, the less pleasant traits of a partner."

Note: You may also find the discussion about soul mates on this webpage helpful in further understanding this topic: http://what-if.xkcd.com/9/.

Reflection

1. How might believing that there's only one soul mate in the world for you affect your relationships and your search for a marriage partner?
   _____
   _____
   _____

2. What are your thoughts now about the concept of soul mates?
   _____
   _____
   _____

Exploring Reasons to Marry

The quotations below help us see that marriage is a divine institution designed to be beneficial—a view upheld by many religious and cultural traditions. Suppose this view does not align with your particular beliefs. In that case, you may wish to reflect on aspects of marriage—or long-term committed relationships—that can be considered sacred or beautiful, and which transcend the interests of the two individuals (examples: by benefiting extended family or friend networks; serving the community; fostering professional accomplishments that serve humanity; raising children or empowering youth to contribute positively to society…)

1. "And when He [God] desired to manifest grace and beneficence to men, and to set the world in order, He revealed observances and created laws; among them He established the law of marriage, made it as a fortress for well-being and salvation … He saith, great is His glory: 'Enter into wedlock, O people, that ye may bring forth one who will make mention of Me amid My servants. This is My bidding unto you; hold fast to it as an assistance to yourselves.'"[108] Bahá'u'lláh

2. "And then the voice of the Divine Lote-Tree sounded, calling aloud and saying: 'Praise be unto God Who hath ordained marriage to be a portal for the appearance of the manifestations of His Name, the All-Merciful, and adorned by its means the cities of His mention and praise.' Verily, it is the key to the perpetuation of life for the peoples of the world, and the inscrutable instrument for the fulfillment of their destiny. Through it the water of life hath streamed forth unto the people of certitude. Praised be God, Who hath made marriage a means for propagating His Cause amongst His servants and proclaiming His Word throughout the world….

   "All loving-kindness is Thine, O Thou Who art the Object of the adoration of all humankind, inasmuch as Thou hast ordained marriage to be a cause of unity amongst Thy creatures and of the exaltation of Thy Word amidst Thy people. Through its agency, Thou hast bound together the hearts and revealed the manifestations of Thy Name, the Best-Beloved. By its means, the hidden mysteries have been disclosed from behind the mount of Thy power, and earth and heaven have been illumined with the light of Thy loving-kindness."[109] Bahá'u'lláh

As we dismantle false beliefs about soul mates and how we are supposed to meet our future marriage partner, it becomes easier to think clearly about the benefits of being in a relationship and marriage. Probably most of your motivations for marriage are healthy and useful, but some of them, if they go unchecked, could land you in trouble. Unhealthy factors often lead to unhappy breakups or divorces later or keep people trapped in bad relationships.

Below are two tables that will help you explore some of your motivations for marrying. You may notice that some beneficial and some less healthy motivations are part of your thinking and choices. Please read through all the items and note next to each one whether it seems to be motivating you. Add in any that are missing. If you find that you have any unhealthy motivations, a reflection question at the end will help you think through how to address them.

Beneficial:

Motivating Me?	Some Beneficial Reasons to Marry Are To:
	Express a deep love and appreciation for someone and to receive these in return
	Share a close, meaningful, and lifelong friendship
	Develop a spiritual connection with another soul, help each other draw closer to God, and build an eternal relationship
	Have children and share the joys and responsibilities of parenthood and family life
	Collaborate with a partner and support each other in serving humanity in our families, neighborhoods or towns, religious communities, work…
	Learn and grow with someone
	Share mutual life purposes and goals
	Share and communicate with someone special
	Establish a safe, trusting relationship where both parties can be emotionally vulnerable, physically intimate, and express their deepest feelings, their sexuality, their creativity…
	Continue personal healing work by being in a safe, healthy relationship
	Build a place of refuge and well-being

Potentially Problematical:

Motivating Me?	Potentially Problematical Reasons Are Because a Person:
	Feels desperate; thinks that any relationship would be better than being alone
	Wants someone to fill an internal emptiness and "fix" them, so they don't have to do their own personal and spiritual development
	Hopes to change, "fix", or rescue someone else
	Feels guilty because their parents, other family members, or friends want them to get married and are pressuring them
	Feels guilty that they haven't given their parents grandchildren and feels pressure to do so
	Worries about getting older and being unable to have/raise children
	Wants a parent for their children more than a partner for themselves
	Wants a partner's children or family more than the partner
	Hopes the sacred institution of marriage will purify them from the damaging effects of pornography use or other poor choices
	Runs away from problems or wants someone else to handle their problems
	Feels fed up with restraining their sexual appetites

Motivating Me?	Potentially Problematical Reasons Are Because a Person: (continued)
	Wants to enjoy sex without feeling guilty (if sex has been happening outside of marriage and they feel conflicted because this contradicts beliefs or personal standards)
	Is afraid of hurting the other person if they end the relationship
	Is afraid that they or a partner may do something drastic or tragic if the relationship ends
	Wants to have someone to take care of them emotionally, financially, and/or physically

Taking time to examine why you want to marry will help you determine whether your reasons will propel you toward a healthy, lasting marriage—or might land you in an unhealthy relationship.

Reflection

1. What will I do to adjust and correct any of my unhealthy motivations?
   _____
   _____
   _____
   _____

Navigating Sex and Chastity

We address the topic of sex here to help you navigate this complex topic, which often ignites many emotions and has aspects that become a pitfall for many. It also generates varying opinions, so we've changed the format in this section, by integrating quotations throughout the text. This topic is addressed in more depth in the authors' dating, courtship, and marriage books; this section is simply an introduction.

We want to make a key point at the outset. Since sex before marriage is discouraged or prohibited in many faiths, and religions often try to help people transcend their physical nature, some religious people have come to believe that sex is somehow "dirty" or sinful, not only before marriage but for some, even within marriage. The Bahá'í Faith offers a different perspective: that couples should be "free of the old attitude that sex is despicable"[110] (Research Department of the Bahá'í Faith's World Centre) and that sex is a normal part of marriage—and one of the reasons marriage exists.

"The Bahá'í Faith recognizes the value of the sex impulse…. The proper use of the sex instinct is the natural right of every individual, and it is precisely for this purpose that the institution of marriage has been established."[111] Shoghi Effendi

"Outside of their normal, legitimate married life they should seek to establish bonds of comradeship and love which are eternal and founded on the spiritual life of man, not on his physical life. This … [will] lead the way to a true human standard of life, when the soul of man is exalted and his body but the tool for his enlightened spirit. Needless to say this does not preclude the living of a perfectly normal sex life in its legitimate channel of marriage."[112] On behalf of Shoghi Effendi

"The primary purpose of sexual relations is, clearly, to perpetuate the species. The fact that personal pleasure is derived therefrom is one of the bounties of God. The sex act is merely one moment in a long process, from courtship through marriage, the procreation of children, their nursing and rearing, and involves the establishment of a mutually sustaining relationship between two souls which will endure beyond life on this earth."[113] On behalf of the Universal House of Justice

Physical intimacy, including sexual touch and intercourse, is the norm in dating relationships in many parts of the world, for people of all ages. When two people care for each other, the desire to express their affection physically pulls strongly on their hearts, often speeding them toward each other. In such situations, personal moral standards and religious beliefs can act as an internal braking system that empowers them to wisely wait until the ideal time for physical intimacy.

Of course, you will want to know there's a spark of attraction between you and a potential marriage partner. For some people, this attraction becomes obvious even in early encounters. However, for others, it becomes more evident after getting to know and appreciate someone's mind, heart, and soul. In either case, the Bahá'í teachings indicate that having sex before marriage actually hinders, rather than helps, two people assessing how suitable they would be as marriage partners.

Sex within marriage is a gift and a sacred means of bonding marriage partners together. If couples have sex before marriage, this physical relationship can bond them before they have any idea of their ability to harmoniously sustain a marriage. Sexual connection can, and often does, blind a couple to significant sources of problems. It can override clear-sighted discernment about other equally important determinants of future marriage success, such as character.

Popular media in the Western world usually shows sex early in a relationship, and as a normal, positive behavior. This implies that making very fast decisions about the long-term viability of a relationship based on intense physical attraction is a reasonable route to take. This social climate—and the risks that come with relying too much on physical passion—are described in the passages below:

"The world today is submerged, amongst other things, in an over-exaggeration of the importance of physical love, and a dearth of spiritual values. In as far as possible the believers should try to realize this and rise above the ... over-emphasis on the purely physical side of mating."[114] On behalf of Shoghi Effendi

"He realizes your desire to get married is quite a natural one, and he will pray that God will assist you to find a suitable companion with whom you can be truly happy and united in the service of the Faith. Bahá'u'lláh has urged marriage upon all people as the natural and rightful way of life. He has also, however, placed strong emphasis on its spiritual nature, which, while in no way precluding a normal physical life, is the most essential aspect of marriage. That two people should live their lives in love and harmony is of far greater importance than that they should be consumed with passion for each other. The one is a great rock of strength on which to lean in time of need; the other a purely temporary thing which may at any time die out.

"He will pray for your true happiness and the solution of all your problems, as well as for the progress of the noble work you are carrying on..."[115] On behalf of Shoghi Effendi

As you prepare for marriage, consider carefully and conscientiously the potential negative effects of sexual activity on a relationship, as well as its intended unifying role within marriage. The Bahá'í teachings encourage us to make respectful choices that protect our future, so naturally, we wish to share these teachings with you. However, please be assured that we know and respect that many people have different opinions on this matter, and if you are not a Bahá'í and do not agree with these teachings, no judgment is intended from us. Our only intention is to convey what the Bahá'í teachings propose and allow our readers to exercise their own discernment.

In light of that, we feel we would be doing our readers a disservice if we didn't mention that, like other topics explored in this chapter, sexual experiences at the wrong time or stage can be a pitfall. It often causes many problems that can, and often do, jeopardize a happy, healthy, and lasting marriage. We have seen time and again, throughout our personal and professional lives, the harmful consequences of couples choosing to engage sexually too early in relationships. For example, we've seen these decisions result in attachments and commitments that are not sustainable and do not undergird a lasting relationship.

Sex is, of course, an intimate physical act, but it also has mental, emotional, and spiritual components and effects. Sexual interaction releases chemicals and hormones that cause feelings of emotional bonding. In this way, physical intimacy can set up the illusion in your mind that you and a partner are very close to each other, when you actually are not. One of you may think that having sex means you're in a committed relationship, while the other could be focused only on enjoying the physical experience and a temporary connection. If the relationship then ends and you feel bonded to that person, you may feel quite betrayed and, at the same time, may still want intimate physical affection. This desire could be a trap and unwise cycle in subsequent relationships. There could be a strong draw toward physical contact without knowing a partner well, and unhappiness is the likely result.

Sexual intimacy while you and a partner are getting to know each other, or as a method of getting to know each other, increases the difficulty of objectively assessing a partner's character. According to Dr. Mark Laaser, an expert on sexual addiction, sex releases a chemical cocktail—which includes adrenaline, dopamine, serotonin, and oxytocin.[116] These neurotransmitters produce very powerful emotions and feelings of pleasure, which cloud people's ability to clearly see each other's character, and to notice incompatibilities and future problems that would threaten the health of a long-term committed relationship or marriage. Sometimes, the fact that a couple is sexually involved creates a false perception that "If I'm this close to this person, I must be making a good partner choice." Sexual intimacy shifts the focus onto physical attraction rather than exploring and developing the other far more important dimensions of a friendship-based relationship—dimensions that sustain a marriage when a physical connection is not enough.

One of the most helpful strategies for preventing untimely sexual experiences is to avoid situations that arouse passion and cause temptation. It can be helpful to spend time in groups, avoid being alone with another person in private places, and be prepared to call someone when temptations arise.

Even using pornography to masturbate, which doesn't involve a relationship partner, can cause habits of thought that can get in the way of a healthy, loving relationship and/or marriage. Use of pornography—especially online—has become widespread, in many cases causing problems for the individual and relationships—such as multiplying misconceptions about sex, increasing demeaning attitudes toward women, and reducing the ability to function sexually.

Our Bahá'í readers—and anyone wanting to learn about Bahá'í views on this topic—may be interested in the following guidance (provided in response to a question about pornography):

"There is nothing in the Bahá'í writings that specifically addresses the questions you have raised. As you well know, Bahá'ís are called to exemplify the high standards of a chaste and holy life, a subject discussed in depth by the beloved Guardian [Shoghi Effendi] in *The Advent of Divine Justice*. Indeed, the Faith calls for an exalted standard of behavior which 'can tolerate no compromise with the theories, the standards, the habits, and the excesses of a decadent age', condemns 'all manner of promiscuity, of easy familiarity, and of sexual vices', and 'demands daily vigilance in the control of one's carnal desires and corrupt inclinations'. Thus, the standard expected of Bahá'ís is clear. In addition, the House of Justice has stated that it is neither possible nor desirable for it to set forth a set of rules determining what would be appropriate behavior for a Bahá'í in various circumstances. Indeed, a believer cannot fulfill his or her true mission in life as a follower of the Blessed Perfection merely by living according to a set of rigid regulations. Rather, it is the task of the individual believer to determine, according to his or her own prayerful understanding of the writings, precisely what his or her course of conduct should be in relation to situations he or she encounters in daily life. Every believer must continually study the Sacred Writings and the instructions of the Guardian, striving always to attain a new and better understanding of the import of the teachings to him- or herself and to society, and orient his or her life towards service to Bahá'u'lláh, praying fervently for divine guidance, wisdom, and strength to do what is pleasing to God."[117] On behalf of the Universal House of Justice

Regardless of your worldview or beliefs, if pornography use is a problem affecting your life—as it has become for many people—you have many options to help free yourself from problematic patterns, compulsive behaviors, or its negative effects. These options include: praying and meditating; studying the quotations in this chapter; consulting with supportive friends and relatives, and/or trusted advisors; and seeking appropriate medical and/or psychological resources. The following additional options from an author may also help (for men or women):

"Some men will need to go to Sex Addicts Anonymous (SAA) meetings in addition to therapy. Some may have to check themselves into rehab, and some may be able to use online tools…to beat it. The key is just being willing to recognize that you have an issue in the first place and that you need assistance."[118] Justin Baldoni

In this connection, anyone seeking out support resources online should practice the virtue of discernment and exercise caution, because some online influencers and male-driven communities around pornography dependency and masturbation can quickly lead one to spaces that have espoused misogyny, toxic masculinity, conspiracy theories and fringe partisan ideologies and political movements. While appearing to only want to help the struggling individual, some such entities are driven solely by a profit motive and are taking advantage of these individuals.

While pornography (most used without a partner) can cause feelings of guilt or shame, these feelings can also result from sexual acts *with* a partner, when they happen outside of the proper context. Such acts can also present other pitfalls, such as increasing the risk of contracting sexually transmitted diseases, and/or resulting in an unplanned pregnancy. Although some claim that people can't control their sexual urges, in fact, every person has the capacity to make conscious choices about sex and to use self-discipline to restrain these impulses.

"The Bahá'í youth should…be taught the lesson of self-control, which, when exercised, undoubtedly has a salutary effect on the development of character and of personality in general…."[119] On behalf of Shoghi Effendi

A breakthrough in scientific research in recent years is challenging the myth that sex is an uncontrollable drive—a myth that influences many of the sexual patterns we see in society. Dr. Emily Nagoski distinguishes desires from drives:

"A drive is a biological mechanism whose job is to keep the organism at a healthy baseline—not too warm, not too cold, not too hungry, not too full. … Appetite is the classic example of a drive. Hunger for food drives foraging and eating, and then when you feel full, you stop eating. … Hunger and thirst are motivational systems that push you to do the things you have to do in order to avoid dying. The uncomfortable ('aversive') internal states of thirst, exhaustion, and cold push you out into the world, to go meet a need, so that you can return to a baseline, and that baseline is all about staying alive. When you hear 'drive,' think 'survive.'"[120] Emily Nagoski

Nagoski goes on to say that no one ever died from not having sex: "There is no baseline to return to and no physical damage that results from not 'feeding' your sexual desire." Instead, the human reproductive system motivates us by pulling us toward an external attraction. She says that when we conceptualize sex as a need that must "be fed" for survival, it "fosters men's sense of sexual entitlement," which reinforces a culture in which they commonly sexually assault women. But in reality, sex is not a human need—it is a wish or want that we can consciously choose to regulate and control.[121]

Many of the problems described in this section are prevented when individuals preserve sex for marriage. For these reasons, and many more beyond the scope of this section, the Bahá'í teachings advise restricting sex to the "fortress for well-being" that is marriage.

We believe that the Bahá'í principles and laws are designed to benefit all of humanity, so we view these teachings as advisable for anyone to follow, if they see the wisdom of them and choose to benefit from them. However, we have no intention of telling others how they should live. As the Universal House of Justice wrote, "the Bahá'í community does not seek to impose its values on others, nor does it pass judgment on others on the basis of its own moral standards. It does not see itself as one among competing social groups and organizations, each vying to establish its particular social agenda."[122] (On behalf of the Universal House of Justice)

Having said that, our humble understanding as Bahá'ís is that preserving sex for marriage has many positive effects on the marriage bond between two people, and it makes for a better sex life within marriage. This view is also supported by scientific studies which found that couples who have a "secure attachment" have "more positive emotions during sex, more frequent sex, higher levels of arousal and orgasm, and better communication about sex."[123] (Emily Nagoski, PhD)

The decision of a couple to *wait until marriage* involves not only refraining from sexual behaviors but also cultivating in their bodies, minds, and hearts the character quality of chastity. In the Bahá'í teachings, chastity means not only refraining from sex outside of marriage, but also from any other actions, thoughts, or words that we might, in prayerful consideration and good conscience, conclude are impure or unchaste.

Within marriage, chaste actions include faithfulness to one's chosen partner and keeping one's thoughts and words pure and focused on each other rather than outside to others. As we've said, sexual intimacy is a natural part of marriage.

The passages below offer more explanation and insight into chastity. Since the language and concepts may be different than what you're accustomed to, please read the entire first quotation below carefully. Change is underway in the standards and character needed for the world. The standards in this passage are very high, but they are also balanced with reason.

As with any high moral standard, we benefit from striving, with sincere motivation, to reach the standard, while also having compassion and understanding for ourselves and others when we may fail to reach it. It's the sincere, daily effort to strive for the standard that results in long-term spiritual and moral growth, which often happens gradually.

"A chaste and holy life must be made the controlling principle in the behavior and conduct of all Bahá'ís, both in their social relations with the members of their own community, and in their contact with the world at large. ... It must be upheld, in all its integrity and implications, in every phase of the life of those who fill the ranks of that Faith, whether in their homes, their travels, their clubs, their societies, their entertainments, their schools, and their universities. ... It must be closely and continually identified with the mission of the Bahá'í Youth, both as an element in the life of the Bahá'í community, and as a factor in the future progress and orientation of the youth of their own country.

"Such a chaste and holy life, with its implications of modesty, purity, temperance, decency, and clean-mindedness, involves no less than the exercise of moderation in all that pertains to dress, language, amusements, and all artistic and literary avocations. It demands daily vigilance in the control of one's carnal desires and corrupt inclinations. It calls for the abandonment of a frivolous conduct, with its excessive attachment to trivial and often misdirected pleasures. It requires total abstinence from all alcoholic drinks, from opium, and from similar habit-forming drugs. It condemns the prostitution of art and of literature, the practices of nudism and of companionate marriage, infidelity in marital relationships, and all manner of promiscuity, of easy familiarity, and of sexual vices. It can tolerate no compromise with the theories, the standards, the habits, and the excesses of a decadent age. ...

"It must be remembered, however, that the maintenance of such a high standard of moral conduct is not to be associated or confused with any form of asceticism, or of excessive and bigoted puritanism. The standard inculcated by Bahá'u'lláh seeks, under no circumstances, to deny anyone the legitimate right and privilege to derive the fullest advantage and benefit from the manifold joys, beauties, and pleasures with which the world has been so plentifully enriched by an All-Loving Creator."[124] Shoghi Effendi

"… [T]he Bahá'í conception of sex is based on the belief that chastity should be strictly practiced by both sexes, not only because it is in itself highly commendable ethically, but also due to its being the only way to a happy and successful marital life. Sex relationships of any form, outside marriage, are not permissible therefore…."[125] On behalf of Shoghi Effendi

"Chastity in no way implies withdrawal from human relationships. It liberates people from the tyranny of the ubiquity of sex. A person who is in control of his sexual impulses is enabled to have profound and enduring friendships with many people, both men and women, without ever sullying that unique and priceless bond that should unite [husband] and wife."[126] On behalf of the Universal House of Justice

"As to chastity, this is one of the most challenging concepts to get across in this very permissive age, but Bahá'ís must make the utmost effort to uphold Bahá'í standards, no matter how difficult they may seem at first. Such efforts will be made easier if the youth will understand that the laws and standards of the Faith are meant to free them from untold spiritual and moral difficulties in the same way that a proper appreciation of the laws of nature enables one to live in harmony with the forces of the planet."[127] On behalf of the Universal House of Justice

"… [T]here is nothing in the Bahá'í Writings which relates specifically to the so-called dating practices prevalent in some parts of the world, where two unmarried people of the opposite sex participate together in a social activity. In general, Bahá'ís who are planning to involve themselves in this form of behavior should become well aware of the Bahá'í Teachings on chastity and, with these in mind, should scrupulously avoid any actions which would arouse passions which might well tempt them to violate these Teachings. In deciding which acts are permissible in the light of these considerations, the youth should use their own judgment, giving due consideration to the advice of their parents, taking account of the prevailing customs of the society in which they live, and prayerfully following the guidance of their conscience. It is the sacred duty of parents to instill in their children the exalted Bahá'í standard of moral conduct, and the importance of adherence to this standard cannot be over-emphasized as a basis for true happiness and for successful marriage."[128] On behalf of the Universal House of Justice

We are all responsible for our own choices and lives, and the last quotation above points to the need for us to use mature judgment, draw on the advice of those we trust and who know us well, and look at the greater context of our society. We live with the consequences of our choices—whether they relate to sex or anything else.

In the Bahá'í Faith, sex and sexuality are not "impure" or "unholy"; sex is a natural impulse, but it belongs in a certain context: within a healthy marriage. Marriage is a divine institution, within which sexual intimacy serves as a unifying factor for a married couple. Sexual intercourse, of course, can also lead to creating a new life—another human being with both a body and a soul. This is a powerful, humbling, and meaningful reality with both physical and spiritual ramifications. Lovemaking within marriage can strengthen couples' spirituality by enhancing their unity. They can also enrich their sexual experiences by consciously practicing respect, love, and generosity.

The guidance on sex and chastity also does not negate the role that sensuality can play in a marriage:

"'Sensuality' covers a wide range of meanings, all related to the pleasures to be obtained from the physical senses or sensations. Again, it is the extremes of this quality that are reprehensible. To renounce all sensual pleasures, or even to go beyond this and to inflict pain upon oneself falls in the region of asceticism, which … [Bahá'u'lláh] prohibits. On the other hand, to be self-indulgent in regard to food, drink, and sexual enjoyment, giving oneself up to the gratification of one's appetites, becomes the licentiousness which is, likewise, forbidden in the Faith. As in the case of passion, individuals vary in the sensuality of their natures; some may need to restrain this quality, others may need to foster a greater warmth of feeling. … Undoubtedly each couple will approach the matter differently, in accordance with the characters of the two people involved, but it is certainly here that passion and sensuality can play an important role, if accepted as normal qualities of a human being and if properly controlled and balanced by the reason and will."[129] Research Department of the Bahá'í World Centre

The Bahá'í teachings affirm the importance of sex in marriage, and the wisdom of living a well-rounded, multifaceted life in many spheres, without sex or sexual thoughts dominating one's mind, heart, or behavior. This relates back to Chapter 1, which talks about living a coherent life filled with happiness, joy, a profession, and marriage.

As suggested in the quotations above, "the proper use of the sex impulse" (within marriage) and the practice of chastity to help maintain "profound and enduring friendships" are topics at the heart of building a long-term relationship. Regardless of your personal views or beliefs about sex and sexuality, we hope you'll consider the profound benefits that gradually incorporating these standards into your life might bring—if you are not already practicing them. We hope you'll include these reflections and considerations in your ongoing coherent preparation for marriage.

We close this section with a quotation about the spirit in which we should strive to follow spiritual principles and laws—which, at times, may be challenging. We think this may offer some valuable perspective to our Bahá'í readers who are striving to uphold the Faith's teachings—and of course, to all our readers, who are most welcome to glean from it any insights you find useful in your life.

"The duty to obey the laws brought by Bahá'u'lláh for a new age, then, rests primarily on the individual believer. It lies at the heart of the relationship of the lover and the Beloved; 'Observe My commandments, for the love of My beauty,' is Bahá'u'lláh's exhortation. Yet what is expected in this connection is effort sustained by earnest desire, not instantaneous perfection. The qualities and habits of thought and action that characterize Bahá'í life are developed through daily exertion." …

"The friends should not lose heart in their personal struggles to attain to the Divine standard, nor be seduced by the argument that, since mistakes will inevitably be made and perfection is impossible, it is futile to exert an effort. They are to steer clear of the pitfalls of hypocrisy, on the one hand—that is, saying one thing yet doing another—and heedlessness, on the other—that is, disregard for the laws, ignoring or explaining away the need to follow them. So too is paralysis engendered by guilt to be avoided; indeed, preoccupation with a particular moral failing can, at times, make it more challenging for it to be overcome."[130] On behalf of the Universal House of Justice

Reflection

1. What do I think about the role of sex in relationships and marriage?

2. What do I agree with in the previous section?

   _____
   _____
   _____

   What do I feel uncertain about or disagree with?

   _____
   _____
   _____

3. How have my experiences affected my view of sex? Do I have anything to resolve from previous experiences?

   _____
   _____
   _____

4. How can I help myself practice purity and chastity before marriage?

   _____
   _____
   _____

5. What do I look forward to about sex in marriage?

   _____
   _____
   _____

6. What can I do, even when I'm married, to strive that my thoughts are always as pure as possible?

   _____
   _____
   _____

7. When impure thoughts do arise in my mind, how can I ensure they pass through and quickly leave my mind, rather than becoming fixated—or worse, expressed in improper acts?

   _____
   _____
   _____

Note About Sexual Abuse: It is not within the purview of this book to fully address this issue, but we would be remiss not to mention that sexual abuse experiences are widespread in society, and Bahá'ís are also affected by this grave moral failing. Trauma from such abuse can disrupt a healthy sex life in marriage. Therefore, it's vital to the well-being of the individual and the marriage for any abuse victims to heal, often with professional assistance, ideally before marriage and potentially during marriage as well.

It's also important to note that many people who have experienced sexual abuse have gone on to have happy, healthy marriages. They often benefit from personal healing work, self-acceptance, forgiveness, and a compassionately loving, patient, and caring marriage partner.

Addressing Fears that Arise

Commitment is vital to creating healthy relationships and marriages, helps to balance fears that arise, and is beneficial in life in general. Consider these quotations below.

1. "... [S]ay not that which thou doest not."[131] Bahá'u'lláh

2. "He should not ... promise that which he doth not fulfill."[132] Bahá'u'lláh

3. "In all matters, great or small, word must be the complement of deed, and deed the companion of word: each must supplement, support and reinforce the other."[133] Shoghi Effendi

4. "I wish to assure you, in particular, of his supplications for your guidance in connection with your proposed plan to unite in marriage with.... May the Beloved help you in forming the right decision, and spare you the anxiety and suffering which too hasty action in such matters inevitably produces. You should give this question, which is of such vital concern to your future, the full consideration it deserves, and examine all its aspects carefully and dispassionately. The final decision rests with you and ... [the proposed partner]."[134] On behalf of Shoghi Effendi

5. "There is no doubt about it that the believers in America, probably unconsciously influenced by the extremely lax morals prevalent and the flippant attitude towards divorce which seems to be increasingly prevailing, do not take divorce seriously enough and do not seem to grasp the fact that although Bahá'u'lláh has permitted it, He has only permitted it as a last resort and strongly condemns it. The presence of children, as a factor in divorce, cannot be ignored, for surely it places an even greater weight of moral responsibility on the [husband] and wife in considering such a step. Divorce under such circumstances no longer just concerns them and their desires and feelings but also concerns the children's entire future and their own attitude towards marriage."[135] On behalf of Shoghi Effendi

If you notice you are wary of making a relationship or marriage commitment, pause and reflect carefully on your doubts, hesitations, and fears. As you reflect, you can determine which of these concerns have validity and which do not—and what you can do to shift your perspective. You can also consider the commitments people in your life have kept or not kept and understand how their behaviors have informed your attitudes and concerns.

Pause and reflect for a few minutes. Note below your thoughts about commitments.

_____
_____
_____
_____
_____

If you, your parents, other relatives, or close friends have cohabited or gone through divorces, you may be skeptical or fearful about your ability to sustain a marriage commitment. You may want to avoid repeating history, or you may struggle at times with feeling resistant to the idea of marrying or marrying again. Perhaps you wonder how you can succeed at marriage when many don't. If you haven't seen models of happy and healthy unions, you may feel unsure about how to pattern your life.

If you've been on the receiving end of many broken promises, strive to understand how that has affected your faith in others. How have broken promises influenced how you follow through on commitments? You may find it difficult to trust others and nearly impossible to trust a person who has repeatedly broken his or her word with you. However, suppose you are suspicious of everyone because of the actions of one person. In that case, this can negatively affect your ability to develop friendships and a close relationship with a potential marriage partner who is worthy of your trust.

In addition, you may not understand that you already have the skills and experience to make a commitment. Looking back over your life, you will probably see at least one regular commitment you've made and successfully upheld: your commitment to your own mental, physical, emotional, or spiritual well-being. For instance, you may be committed to:

- Pray regularly
- Eat healthy food
- Read more and watch television less
- Pursue your education
- Read the Bahá'í writings or another sacred scripture every morning and evening
- Exercise regularly
- Participate in a religious community
- Be involved in purposeful group activities
- Meditate regularly

When kept, these commitments increase self-respect and well-being. Take a moment to reflect on your history of keeping—and breaking—commitments. What are three commitments you made in the last year? How have you fared in keeping them? Maybe it was to begin an exercise program, pay your bills on time, or keep all your appointments. Try to recognize where you have succeeded, even if you've also encountered difficulties keeping your commitments.

If you are challenged with a fear of committing to marriage, studying and learning what helps relationships and marriages thrive is especially important. You can also identify positive role models and mentors to guide you. It may help if you:

- Understand and honestly acknowledge your fears (consider expressing them in writing if helpful)
- Resist basing your current choices solely on past difficulties and experiences
- Recognize that you are not doomed to repeat the mistakes of others
- Apply sustained effort and attention to learn what makes marriages function well
- Seek professional support if needed

Taking steps such as these makes it possible to heal, move forward, and create a thriving, excellent marriage—regardless of your history and the examples in your past. It's up to you to decide what type of relationship and marriage you want and then to strive systematically toward that goal.

Reflection

1. On a scale of 1-10—with 1 being low and 10 being high—how certain am I that I want to find a partner and marry? Rating: _____

2. What scares me, even slightly, about being in a relationship? A marriage?
   _____
   _____
   _____

3. What does it mean to me to give my word and honor it—or to make a promise about something?
   _____
   _____
   _____

4. In what ways are trust and commitment connected?
   _____
   _____
   _____

5. In what ways are commitment, marriage, and divorce prevention connected?
   _____
   _____
   _____

6. When I make scheduling commitments, do I keep them? Do I generally begin them on time?
   _____
   _____
   _____

7. How do I handle broken commitments or promises, both my own and those of others?
   _____
   _____
   _____

8. Do I intentionally seek short-term sexual encounters? Does this help me avoid being in serious relationships or marrying?
   _____
   _____
   _____

9. Do I pursue someone—romantically, sexually, or otherwise—only to drop the relationship after achieving the initial goal?
   _____
   _____
   _____

10. How can I strengthen my confidence in my ability to have a successful marriage?
    _____
    _____
    _____

Encouraging Reminder: To assist you in tracking and completing all the reflections and growth steps in this book, we have provided suggestions and tools in "Appendix A: Tracking My Action Commitments".

Chapter 7
Describing Myself and a Potential Partner

You already know a significant amount about your character from your efforts in previous chapters. In this chapter, you'll explore concepts about your maturity level and begin to think about the maturity level of a future partner. You'll also round out your self-description with information to share as you meet potential partners.

These encounters may naturally arise through such examples as community activities, social gatherings, your workplace or school, conferences, or service endeavors. Alternatively, you could meet someone through social media, online services, dating apps, intentional introductions from friends and family, or other means.

In addition, you'll complete an initial exercise to help you consider what to look for in a marriage partner. At this stage, you'll identify only a few key elements. You'll likely refine these elements as you meet more people of interest.

Your age, experiences, and maturity will influence how you describe yourself and what you seek in a marriage partner. This chapter will be a starting point for some, while others may already know what's important to them.

Key Learning Points

- Being an adult—Mature life management
- Describing myself
- Describing a potential partner

Being an Adult—Mature Life Management

Every person's journey toward maturity is unique to that person in the way it unfolds. Yet, we all tend to go through the same broad stages of the maturation process. One of the key influences that matures us is the appearance of tests and challenges and our response to them. The quotations below address the path of maturity and the difficulties that occur along the way.

1. "From the beginning to the end of his life man passes through certain periods or stages each of which is marked by certain conditions peculiar to itself. For instance during the period of childhood his conditions and requirements are characteristic of that degree of intelligence and capacity. After a time he enters the period of youth in which his former conditions and needs are superseded by new requirements applicable to the advance in his degree. His faculties of observation are broadened and deepened, his intelligent capacities are trained and awakened, the limitations and environment of childhood no longer restrict his energies and accomplishments. At last he passes out of the period of youth and enters the stage or station of maturity which necessitates another transformation and corresponding advance in his sphere of life-activity. New powers and perceptions clothe him, teaching and training commensurate with his progression occupy his mind, special bounties and bestowals descend in proportion to his increased capacities and his former period of youth and its conditions will no longer satisfy his matured view and vision."[136] 'Abdu'l-Bahá

2. "The mind and spirit of man advance when he is tried by suffering. The more the ground is plowed the better the seed will grow, the better the harvest will be. Just as the plow furrows the earth deeply, purifying it of weeds and thistles, so suffering and tribulation free man from the petty affairs of this worldly life until he arrives at a state of complete detachment. His attitude in this world will be that

of divine happiness. Man is, so to speak, unripe: the heat of the fire of suffering will mature him."[137]
'Abdu'l-Bahá

Relationships proceed best when both partners consciously demonstrate a level of mature responsibility. This maturity is not necessarily correlated with a person's age, but rather has to do with how we choose to act as responsible and functional adults who keep our healthy commitments. The ability to successfully and maturely manage the details of everyday life is part of a strong foundation that can facilitate connection and carry relationships through rocky times. The difficult times then may also contribute to our maturation process. This ability to operate with maturity is sometimes humorously called "adulting".

Dr. Paul Coleman, PsyD, in his essay "Are We Mature Enough for Marriage?" writes the following:

> "*Psychological maturity* is a broad term that defines how well and in what manner a person copes with life and is able to relate well to others and the environment. There are numerous factors that determine your current level of maturity and adjustment, most notable being the quality of your early family life, the types of losses or challenges you've had to face so far in your life, your degree of optimism or pessimism, and even biology (some people have a nervous system that makes them more or less vulnerable to stress). It is wise to assess how mature you both are and whether you are mature enough to handle the responsibilities of marriage. If you are not mature enough, then assess whether you have the support structure in place with family and counseling to help you as your marriage progresses through challenges. ...
>
> "Ideally, for each of you as human beings, your personal goal is to try to grow to the highest level of maturity and adjustment that you can. In your relationship and marriage, a related goal is to support your partner's efforts to grow. It doesn't matter where you start from—it is still wise to raise your maturity and adjustment levels before marriage. Ensure that you are choosing a partner who will become a spouse that encourages you to be the person you were meant to be within a relationship that fosters growth, trust, and love."[138]

Stress is highly disruptive, and problem-solving is difficult for people of all ages who are not emotionally mature. As people mature, they improve their ability to work through difficulties—although under stress, any of us can revert to less mature functioning. At higher levels of maturity, people are likely to listen well with open minds, have a strong sense of who they are and what they believe, handle disagreements well, cooperatively consult through plans with a partner, and avoid the tendency to blame others for their difficulties.

In PrepSheet 7A below, we share with you our understanding of some of the factors that tend to indicate a person's maturity level in various areas of life.

Starting with Me—Knowing Myself Before Finding a Partner

PrepSheet 7A: Assessing My Level of Maturity

Date: _____

Purpose: To explore various aspects of maturity and assess my current maturity level.

Instructions:
A. In the table below are some aspects of living a balanced, mature life that represent mature behavior (words and actions). Review and reflect on each of them, considering how important they are in yourself or for you to find in a partner. Consider how mature behaviors might affect a future marriage as well.

B. You may see aspects that don't seem to be a fit for you. You may also add ones that are more applicable to your life or culture. Blank lines are provided for this purpose.

C. On a scale of 1 to 5, rate how often you currently carry out each activity using the scale below.

   N/A = Not applicable
   1 = Never
   2 = Rarely
   3 = Sometimes
   4 = Usually
   5 = Always

Rating	Aspects of My Life
	Maturity in Daily Living and Well-Being
	Eat regular, balanced, and nutritious meals
	Practice healthy self-care, including exercise, cleanliness, dental care, and medical exams and treatments
	Get enough sleep each night
	Clean and maintain personal living space/home, ensuring it is safe and well-functioning
	Organize home or living space in an orderly way
	Arrange reliable transportation
	Maturity in Education, Work, and Financial Management
	Go to work and/or school; complete appropriate tasks in a timely manner with a positive outlook and an attitude of service
	Take the necessary steps to be self-supporting
	Pay bills on time, manage debts, and maintain savings
	Maturity in Intellectual Matters
	Learn about the world at large, staying informed about current events
	Participate in ongoing learning experiences

Rating	Aspects of My Life (continued)
	Maturity in Intellectual Matters (continued)
	Engage in problem-solving discussions as needed
	Express thoughts openly and honestly
	Maturity in Handling and Expressing Emotions
	Recognize feelings as they arise
	Manage feelings with balance and wisdom
	Effectively express feelings
	Address and heal issues from the past, and as needed in a timely way in the present
	Practice joyfulness and confidence, even when life is difficult
	Handle challenges effectively and in cooperation with others
	Take personal responsibility rather than blaming others or making excuses when something doesn't go smoothly
	See and interact with other adults as equals, not as a parent-substitute or as a child
	Maturity in Social and Community Interactions
	Interact well with family members
	Interact positively with friends
	Practice friendliness and courtesy with strangers
	Engage with others in community activities and service
	Build knowledge and skills for a future relationship and marriage
	Manage activity levels to accommodate natural energy (example: If I am an introvert and need time alone to recharge, or if I am an extrovert and need time with others to recharge)
	Relate well and solve problems peacefully with parents, family members, friends, neighbors, and co-workers
	Maturity in Spiritual Matters (where applicable to your belief system)
	Believe in and have faith in God
	Pray regularly, both during difficulties and in times of ease; say prayers according to my beliefs or religion
	Turn to wise and spiritual sources for insight and help
	Meditate and reflect to achieve deeper understanding, fulfill spiritual teachings, and share insights with others
	Regularly read sacred scriptures or other books with spiritual content—with reverence, attention, and thoughtfulness
	Participate in spiritually-based activities
	Demonstrate respect for self and others
	Strive to improve the world
	Recognize opportunities to be of thoughtful service to others, and then do so joyfully
	Observe, reflect on, and improve the quality of thoughts, words, actions, and character
	Regularly feel and express gratitude for blessings

Rating	Aspects of My Life (continued)
	Maturity in Spiritual Matters (continued)
	Share insights and beliefs with others

Reflection

1. When do I handle my responsibilities maturely? Which ones do I particularly struggle to fulfill? How might I address these?

   _____
   _____
   _____

2. What three areas do I want to demonstrate more maturity in? Write them in the chart below, along with the associated actions, notes, and assessment dates for each focus area.

Focus Area	Specific Actions to Take	Progress Notes
1.	1. 2. 3.	
2.	1. 2. 3.	
3.	1. 2. 3.	

It's helpful to reflect on and assess overall progress. I will review my growing maturity on these dates:

1. _____
2. _____
3. _____

Describing Myself and My Experiences

The quotations below will help clarify why knowing yourself is valuable and wise.

1. "… [M]an should know his own self and recognize that which leadeth unto loftiness or lowliness, glory or abasement, wealth or poverty."[139] Bahá'u'lláh

2. "The All-Knowing Physician hath His finger on the pulse of mankind. He perceiveth the disease, and prescribeth, in His unerring wisdom, the remedy. Every age hath its own problem, and every soul its particular aspiration. The remedy the world needeth in its present-day afflictions can never be the same as that which a subsequent age may require. Be anxiously concerned with the needs of the age ye live in, and center your deliberations on its exigencies and requirements."[140] Bahá'u'lláh

3. "Each individual is unique and has a unique path to tread in his lifetime. In espousing the Bahá'í Faith you have defined the direction of that path, for … your devotion to His Message provide[s] the spiritual

and ethical basis for all aspects of your life of service to mankind, while the continuing guidance that He has provided for the community of His followers enables you to know the directions in which the most effort is required at the present time. … It is … the precious privilege of the individual human being to direct the course of his own life. Through exercising this privilege while striving always to conform his conduct to the divine Teachings and devote his talents in the best possible way to the service of the Cause and mankind, a soul deepens his understanding of God and His will."[141] On behalf of the Universal House of Justice

4. "When two believers begin to investigate each other's character with the possibility of marriage in mind, they must establish between them a level of openness and close communication. They will themselves determine if, when and how they will share past and personal experiences. In this process, it is necessary to reconcile a variety of spiritual principles and obligations. Truthfulness and trustworthiness are essential of course, yet other aspects of the teachings must be weighed, such as Shoghi Effendi's guidance that while a believer may choose to acknowledge to another a wrong or fault of character, one is not obliged to do so. In connection with preparation for marriage, 'Abdu'l-Bahá explains:

   'Bahá'í marriage is the commitment of the two parties one to the other, and their mutual attachment of mind and heart. Each must, however, exercise the utmost care to become thoroughly acquainted with the character of the other, that the binding covenant between them may be a tie that will endure forever. Their purpose must be this: to become loving companions and comrades and at one with each other for time and eternity….'

   "As this sensitive interaction unfolds, generally, it is not the business of others to interfere. It is understandable that family or friends may feel a desire to contribute to a particular outcome, but they must not overstep the bounds of the explicit guidance provided in the teachings.
   "There is a distinction to be made between speaking about the mistakes and shortcomings of others, which is backbiting, and protecting someone from the harmful or evil intentions of an abuser, a chronic liar or a sociopath. Serious concerns can, of course, be brought to the attention of the relevant institution of the Faith should circumstances require."[142] On behalf of the Universal House of Justice

Writing a self-description will help you understand yourself better. It will also help you see how to introduce yourself to others, including how to share about yourself in person or through social media, dating apps, or relationship websites. Practicing introducing yourself in different situations will likely boost your confidence when you first meet someone.

The more you clarify your description and practice using it, the better you'll know what is useful to share early and what you'll wisely refrain from divulging until you are in a closer friendship or relationship. Your sense of whether you're ready to discuss certain topics will help you gauge how close you feel to someone and whether you've built adequate trust for that conversation.

You may also realize you're already in the process of building a relationship, one that might eventually blossom into a happy and successful marriage. If so, introductory information is unnecessary, and you'll move right into building a deeper connection and trust.

Sharing about what you value most and what you see as your life purposes are key facets of building a friendship that could become a marriage. Your choices about education, work, community service, and marriage all speak to those values. Your core, or most important, values and the principles you want to live by, guide how you strive to fulfill your life purposes.

If you are unsure what your purposes or guiding principles are, this is worthy of reflection and consultation with others who know you well and are a positive influence on you. Below is a list of items you may resonate with and that are central to your sense of purpose. Each person is unique, so we provide these examples simply to begin your process.

- Knowing and worshiping God
- Helping others laugh and be happy
- Showing equality and respect for others, including a partner
- Following through on every commitment I make; being in communication if the commitment needs to be adjusted
- Enjoying and preserving the natural habitat
- Ensuring that my choices align with the Bahá'í writings
- Putting family as a priority
- Turning to God for guidance rather than feeling forlorn when problems arise
- Sharing my artistic works and talents with others
- Establishing and maintaining a healthy marriage and family
- Excelling in my career; using my talents in my profession to build on my skills, follow my passion, and serve my community
- Guiding children and youth to strengthen their characters
- Sharing spiritual insights with others in a gentle and loving way
- Being generous to those in need
- Steadily building wealth and using it for positive purposes

Someone preparing herself for marriage described her values and principles in this way:

"I've begun to realize one of the most impactful things I can draw on in this process is the power of commitment. First, I commit to myself, to recognize, honor, and hold steadfast to what is important to me. Second, I commit to uncovering, improving, and feeling confident in what I have to offer in a marriage relationship. And third, I commit to looking at what is essential, what is important, and what is an absolute 'no' in a partner. I'm discovering it's very helpful to be able to stand my ground when I realize that no matter how nice and kind the man, if we do not have the same core values and some similar purposes, we will not be paired well. And that relationship will never grow into a happy, enriching friendship and marriage."

Write your answers to these reflection questions below (Again, discussing them with someone you trust and who has your best interests at heart can be helpful.):

1. What are some of my guiding principles or core values that lead me to make the choices I make in my life?

   _____
   _____
   _____

2. If my choices are out of alignment with my values, what would I like to change?

   _____
   _____
   _____

3. What other values would I like to enhance?
_____
_____
_____

4. What are some of my strengths and interests?
_____
_____
_____

5. What spiritual guidance do I resonate strongly with?
_____
_____
_____

6. If I picture myself a few years from now, and I am looking back, given the direction I'm taking now in my life, what will I have accomplished? Would the choices I made fill me with joy and satisfaction?
_____
_____
_____

7. When I think about my friends and family, which of their needs do I want to fulfill? Which of them am I able to meet?
_____
_____
_____

8. What about the needs of my community? The world? Is there a need or issue that draws me to it? (examples: taking care of the environment, eliminating racism, helping the elderly, educating children...)
_____
_____
_____

Given my reflections and responses above, as well as a general sense of how I would like to live my life, how would I now describe my life purpose or purposes?
_____
_____
_____
_____

Please complete PrepSheet 7B below.

Starting with Me—Knowing Myself Before Finding a Partner

PrepSheet 7B: Describing Myself

(Part of this PrepSheet was influenced by the Prepare-Enrich Report that helps couples assess marriage readiness; prepare-enrich.com; marriagetransformation.com)

Date: _____

Purposes:
1. To develop the ability to introduce myself, with clarity and confidence, to someone I want to get to know better. (examples: in-person, by video chat, through text/chat, in an email...)
2. To develop the capacity to share in a helpful, timely, and appropriate way, more personal aspects of myself with a serious relationship or potential marriage partner, when wisdom and discernment indicate the relationship has developed sufficient trust, closeness, and openness for more vulnerable or personal conversations.
3. To clarify which information, for me, is fine to share openly in an initial encounter and which should wait until my relationship has developed more mutual trust and closeness.

Instructions:
A. Read through column 1 to get a sense of the types of information you might share. You will not necessarily use all of them. We've also provided blank spaces, in case you want to add more.

B. Look at the examples provided in italics in columns 2 and 3, and then begin to think about what you might say about the various aspects of your life in introductions or initial conversations (in column 2), and later on as a friendship and relationship develop (column 3).

C. Begin to complete the table in whatever way works best for you—perhaps moving horizontally first, completing both columns for each aspect, or moving vertically first, completing all of column 2 before moving to column 3. Whichever method you choose, we encourage you to complete both columns.

D. **Note:** The more personal conversations considered in column 3 are likely best suited for sharing with a close friend, serious relationship partner, or potential marriage partner with whom you've developed an open, trusting, and supportive relationship. However, you know yourself best, and you can decide the pace at which you build trust and share information.

1 - ASPECTS OF MY LIFE	2 - SELF-DESCRIPTION: (initial conversations)	3 - SELF-DESCRIPTION: (later, deeper conversations)
Example: *Favorite physical and recreational activities*	*I enjoy swimming and walking.*	*Sometimes I like to exercise, and sometimes I resist the idea and skip it.*
Example: *Number of children*	*I have two children from a prior marriage*	*I am very close with my daughter. My son had trouble with drugs for a while, but he is healthier, and we have a fairly good relationship.*
PERSONAL		
Where I live and my current living arrangement		

1 - ASPECTS OF MY LIFE (continued)	2 - SELF-DESCRIPTION: (initial conversations)	3 - SELF-DESCRIPTION: (later, deeper conversations)
Current employment status, place of work, and role at work		
Educational background and experiences		
Spiritual or religious path; Religious beliefs and background		
Favorite volunteer or community services		

PHYSICAL

Note: In column 2, you might share objective descriptions that anyone could observe. In column 3, for when you know someone better, you might share about your past sexual experiences and how they affected you and your partner, or you could share details about your and your family's medical history, including any ongoing illnesses.

Physical description (examples: height, build, fitness level)		
Favorite physical and recreational activities		
How often I like to be involved in physical activities each week		
Medical history (of myself and perhaps my family)		
Sexual history (see later in this PrepSheet for related difficulties)		

Starting with Me—Knowing Myself Before Finding a Partner

1 - ASPECTS OF MY LIFE (continued)	2 - SELF-DESCRIPTION: (initial conversations)	3 - SELF-DESCRIPTION: (later, deeper conversations)
MENTAL		
Favorite types of reading materials, sources for listening and learning, or types of shows/movies to watch		
How frequently I read, listen to, or view substantive content		
News sources and other types of media I consume		
Favorite hobbies and leisure activities; Artistic interests		
Daily mental habits, such as tracking goals and priorities		
Favorite subjects to learn or talk about		
CHARACTER		
My 5 strongest virtues (from PrepSheet 3)		
My 4 developing virtues (from PrepSheet 4)		
My attitudes in 5 areas (examples: money, gender equality, health, hardship, volunteer service, parenting duties, decision-making in the family…)		

1 - ASPECTS OF MY LIFE (continued)	2 - SELF-DESCRIPTION: (initial conversations)	3 - SELF-DESCRIPTION: (later, deeper conversations)
My temperament in 3 areas (examples: calm or anxiety-prone, hasty or methodical, introverted or extroverted, thick-skinned or easily offended...)		
My other character qualities		

MAJOR LIFE FOCUS

Note: In column 2, you might share the basic facts; in column 3, you might share how each aspect has affected your life.

Core values		
Life purposes or goals		
Profession, occupation, craft, or trade		

EMOTIONAL AND SOCIAL

Note: In column 3, you could include details such as how your personality affects others, how you prefer to give and receive love, what causes you the most stress and how you deal with it, how you handle change, and what you are like to live with.

What makes me laugh		
How often I spend time with friends; Types of activities		
What makes me a good friend		

1 - ASPECTS OF MY LIFE (continued)	2 - SELF-DESCRIPTION: (initial conversations)	3 - SELF-DESCRIPTION: (later, deeper conversations)
5 personality traits (examples: adventurous, fun-loving, formal, impulsive, intense…)		
How I recharge my batteries (examples: alone, for introverts; with people, for extroverts)		
5 most common expressions of feelings in response to change or disappointment (examples: anxious, angry, excited…)		
3 things that tend to result in me feeling moderate to high levels of stress		
Cultural heritage or identity; ethnicity and race; languages spoken (example: aspects of your culture or background that you enjoy, or have struggled as a result of, perhaps including experiences—on either side—of privilege, bias, prejudice, or discrimination, be it racial or otherwise…)		
SPIRITUAL		
Belief in God/Higher Power		
Beliefs that influence life choices and actions		

1 - ASPECTS OF MY LIFE (continued)	2 - SELF-DESCRIPTION: (initial conversations)	3 - SELF-DESCRIPTION: (later, deeper conversations)
Personal prayer, meditation, and other spiritual practices		
Group worship practices and frequency		
Spiritually-based community building and service		

FAMILY EXPERIENCES

Note: Consider in column 3 sharing about the quality of your relationships and specifics of experiences, while also taking care not to backbite or mention negative things about others. This can often be done by not using specific names. As you begin to share with others, be judicious as to whether you are simply speaking negatively about someone, which could be quite harmful, or whether your intent is to help someone get to know important aspects of your life or consult for problem-solving. If there has been a history of abuse of any type, please ensure your sharing is with a safe person, and seek professional guidance as needed.

Who raised me; My relationship with them; How it affected me		
Number of children in my birth family, and my birth position (example: second of four); Relationship with my siblings and half- or step-siblings		
My birth family's closeness and connectedness (example: whether the quality of the relationship is one you would want with your own children)		
My parents' marital status and its effect on me (example: whether you would want to emulate it)		

1 - ASPECTS OF MY LIFE (continued)	2 - SELF-DESCRIPTION: (initial conversations)	3 - SELF-DESCRIPTION: (later, deeper conversations)
If I've been married before, how many times, and for how long		
Number of children, stepchildren, or grandchildren I have or would like to have; Relationships with them, if relevant		

PROBLEMS AND DIFFICULTIES		
Early after meeting someone, most people are unlikely to share about the sensitive subjects listed in column 1, so you will probably leave column 2 blank. Instead, please focus on completing column 3. You could list any experiences or struggles you've had in these areas, or in any other areas of your life—for which we've provided extra spaces below. If there has been a history of abuse of any type, please ensure your sharing is with a safe person, and seek professional guidance as needed.		
Addictions (specify type)		
Alcohol or drug use or abuse		
Physical, mental, or emotional abuse		
Mental illnesses		
Pornography use and/or promiscuity		
Maintaining steady work		
Truthfulness, trustworthiness, and other moral behavior		

Reflection

1. What do I now see more clearly about myself?
   _____
   _____
   _____

2. What is easy to share about myself? What is more difficult?
   _____
   _____
   _____

3. What challenges did I experience in deciding what to share early on, and what's better to share later in the friendship or relationship when significant trust is present?
   _____
   _____
   _____

4. What are three very important aspects of me that I think someone should know about soon after meeting me and/or starting to build a relationship with me?
   _____
   _____
   _____

Note: Chapter 8 may assist you with searching for and developing a connection with someone through electronic apps and websites. Online encounters can be excellent, but they can also have difficulties. Some precautions are provided as well.

Activity

1. Write a summary or a specific list of what you might say when you first introduce yourself to someone.

2. Ask a friend, family member, or other person you trust to describe what they think is important about you. They could use the following guide:

Aspect	Comments
Character	
Personality	
Habits	
Talents	
Life Skills	

Aspect (continued)	Comments
Readiness for Being in a Relationship or Marriage	

Describing a Potential Partner

Now that you've begun the process of learning how you might introduce yourself to someone, we suggest you start identifying what's vital and what's less important to you in a partner. *As you do this, please include the essential matter of character.* Determining the elements that would create complementarity between you will be an ongoing process that requires discernment and wisdom. The inspiration and guidance in the passages below can help on this journey.

1. "Above all else, the greatest gift and the most wondrous blessing hath ever been and will continue to be wisdom. It is man's unfailing protector. It aideth him and strengtheneth him."[143] Bahá'u'lláh

2. "… [T]he happiness and greatness, the rank and station, the pleasure and peace, of an individual have never consisted in his personal wealth, but rather in his excellent character, his high resolve, the breadth of his learning, and his ability to solve difficult problems."[144] 'Abdu'l-Bahá

3. "Every imperfect soul is self-centered and thinketh only of his own good. But as his thoughts expand a little he will begin to think of the welfare and comfort of his family. If his ideas still more widen, his concern will be the felicity of his fellow citizens; and if still they widen, he will be thinking of the glory of his land and of his race. But when ideas and views reach the utmost degree of expansion and attain the stage of perfection, then will he be interested in the exaltation of humankind. He will then be the well-wisher of all men and the seeker of the weal and prosperity of all lands. This is indicative of perfection."[145] 'Abdu'l-Bahá

4. "He realizes your desire to get married is quite a natural one, and he will pray that God will assist you to find a suitable companion with whom you can be truly happy and united in the service of the Faith. Bahá'u'lláh has urged marriage upon all people as the natural and rightful way of life. He has also, however, placed strong emphasis on its spiritual nature, which, while in no way precluding a normal physical life, is the most essential aspect of marriage. That two people should live their lives in love and harmony is of far greater importance than that they should be consumed with passion for each other. The one is a great rock of strength on which to lean in time of need; the other a purely temporary thing which may at any time die out."[146] On behalf of Shoghi Effendi

5. "There is a difference between character and faith; it is often very hard to accept this fact and put up with it, but the fact remains that a person may believe in and love [the Bahá'í Faith]—even to being ready to die for it—and yet not have a good personal character, or possess traits at variance with the teachings. We should try to change, to let the Power of God help recreate us and make us true Bahá'ís in deed as well as in belief. But sometimes the process is slow, sometimes it never happens because the individual does not try hard enough."[147] On behalf of Shoghi Effendi

6. "A couple should study each other's character and spend time getting to know each other before they decide to marry, and when they do marry it should be with the intention of establishing an eternal bond."[148] On behalf of the Universal House of Justice

7. "In contemplating the choice of a future marriage partner, it is suggested that you study the Writings on marriage and family life to glean general principles to guide you. Your Local or National Spiritual Assembly could undoubtedly recommend sources of material on the subject. There are several steps you could consider should you contemplate marriage at some time in the future and if you would like advice on your choice of a marriage partner: turn to the Blessed Beauty in prayer for guidance and assistance; weigh carefully the character of the person according to the guidelines on marriage you find in the Holy Writings; and consult with your Local Spiritual Assembly, family or trusted friends to obtain their views. Ultimately such a decision rests with you, and depends also on the consent of parents; however, the above may provide the support you require in taking such an important step in your life."[149] On behalf of the Universal House of Justice

8. "As to qualities a man should look for in seeking a life partner, no universal guidelines can be set forth as whatever characteristics or conditions one considers essential are, of course, subjective and relative...."[150] On behalf of the Universal House of Justice

In this section, we ask you to explore with your mind, heart, and soul, some descriptors of what might make a person complementary to you in marriage. PrepSheet 7C, later in this section, offers a systematic structure for writing these and determining which of them are essential, which are important—but not essential, and which are good and preferable—but not essential or as important.

Many relationships succeed or fail due to character strengths that energize the relationship or character weaknesses that sabotage it. It will be valuable, then, to seriously consider what character qualities in a partner would be most important to you and complementary to your character. The goal is for there to be harmony that enables you to live, build a healthy family, and serve others together in unity.

Two people described what they value in a partner:

"In my mind, truthfulness and trustworthiness are two fundamental qualities that I want to discover are present in a partner. They lead to faith, hope, and love. In our personal lives, these are tested daily. We only see others' qualities in context, such as when they are involved in service, recreation, or work. But physical attraction often gets in the way of our clear vision of character; it clouds our inner sight. If we are realistic, we need tools to help us think and act differently."

"I used to think I had to have it all together before marriage and then look for someone, but I'm realizing I'll never have it all together (not in a bad, defeating way), but rather that I'm looking for someone who will be on the journey of growth with me. This shift in perspective changed the way I view weaknesses, and now I see them as just areas for growth."

Another person expressed the importance of knowing what you're looking for in a relationship or marriage partner:

"Let's say you go to an area with lots of stores and have NO IDEA what you are looking for. Then you spend hours trying on many, many things—most of which don't fit or that you don't even like. But if you know exactly what you are looking for, you skip a lot of stores and pointless visits to the dressing room, and you are purposeful and get exactly what you want. I guess that's why making a shopping list is helpful. I dated aimlessly for a long time. It wasn't until I actively stopped dating that I learned more about myself and who I was. Now I feel more prepared to actually be open to finding a partner, because I don't have to 'try on random hats' anymore!"

It's interesting to reflect that as we consider the mix of possibilities before us, we tend to filter them through our own experiences, perspectives, and priorities. We may automatically make judgments or jump to conclusions about how someone's behavior would affect us. Therefore, sometimes it's helpful to pause and allow some time to learn more about the whole person before reaching definitive conclusions about whether or not you would make a good match.

One person reflected on what's important for them to look for in a potential partner and identified these priorities:

- A willingness to abide by the Will of God
- An understanding that marriage is a journey, not an event
- An understanding that there will be bumps and potholes along the way
- An ability to endure hardship
- An agreement that divorce is not an option except in very extreme circumstances
- A willingness to seek help when unity and harmony seem difficult to achieve (such as from a Spiritual Assembly, or from a relationship professional)
- An understanding that marriage is a solution only if both people invest in making it so
- Self-respect, and a refusal to allow oneself to be trampled on
- A realization that love is not only a feeling but also a deliberate behavior
- A willingness to search the Bahá'í writings for answers

Another person described their most important requirements as follows:

- Willingness to forgive and leave the past in the past and not dwell on previous problems
- To be joyous and happy under all conditions (even if not all the time)
- A commitment to service as a basis for life
- Generosity (not only contributing money and possessions, but also generous acts, such as inviting people into your home, serving them, and so on)
- Humility in consultation (and in general)
- Flexibility and willingness to grow and learn always
- Lightheartedness
- Devotion
- A radiant countenance!

A third person made this comment:

"The list of what to look for in a potential marriage partner should include a willingness and ability to genuinely accept someone else's love. It may be that the need 'to love' is as strong as, or stronger, than the need 'to be loved'. Being in any relationship, particularly marriage, where the other refuses to accept your love is very frustrating. The refusal to receive love blocks the development of spiritual qualities in a person. Such refusal is often experienced as rejection by the other partner. It can happen that the one not accepting the love thinks it's somehow selfish to allow another person to meet her or his needs. It can also happen when they feel the need to protect themselves by not showing any weakness or need that the other person can meet. Marriage requires reciprocity, and it needs an honest acknowledgment of interdependence, so each person has to both give and receive love."

In addition to the character strengths you wish for in a partner, it's wise to think about what behaviors or traits you might want to *avoid* in a partner. We encourage you to also write these down, in the second table of PrepSheet 7C below. Clarifying the attributes to avoid in a partner helps prevent divorce. Someone may have bad habits or personal attributes that would make it difficult for you to sustain a relationship with them.

For instance, you might not be able to cope with someone who is always messy and is unwilling or unable to change this behavior. On the other hand, you might find it challenging to live with someone who demands that the home always be completely organized and tidy. At a more fundamental level of character, if you are involved with someone who constantly lies, this behavior should prompt you to seriously question continuing with that relationship, and to identify dishonesty as a characteristic you will avoid in the future.

Generally, aside from actions like lying and stealing, which are almost universally to be avoided, most items to avoid vary from person to person. What is important and relevant for one individual may not be for another. You'll also need to determine how much your efforts, influence, and consultation as a couple can change a situation. Sometimes people think it will not matter if a partner has a lot of problems, because they believe it will be good for their personal growth. They may even harbor the hope that they can change their partner once they're married. Remember that life and marriage will provide enough opportunities for growth without setting up a marriage with significant problems from the beginning. You can also develop the capacity to identify when someone is unlikely to change, a valuable skill. Discernment is needed to determine what works best for you. Here are some balancing perspectives:

"I believe that the direction a partner is moving in might be more important than where he or she is at. Someone may be very virtuous but moving in the 'wrong' direction; whereas, another might not have as many virtues, but is moving in the direction of developing more all the time. Someone could have many virtues absorbed from their environment without any real effort, and when put to the test of colliding with the real world, they crumble because they are not strong. Someone else may have developed fewer virtues because of an unfavorable environment, but the ones they have are strong because they were developed through hard work and testing."

"When it comes to choosing a marriage partner, of course you'll want to understand his or her past, just as they'll want to know about yours, but what we are looking for are signs of development, change, and improvement, of having begun to try to live by the laws and teachings of Bahá'u'lláh, and of striving along that road. Some things are more difficult than others for people to overcome—such as addictions or a propensity for violence and abuse—those will need professional assistance and the support of others to overcome. All this would be a subject for consultation between prospective marriage partners."

In a healthy marriage, you have the gift of a very dear friend and partner to build a life with, and then together you both grow, consult, and adjust as you live together. It's wise to choose someone who can adjust to meet life's challenges with you, where you can accompany each other through whatever happens as you *create a marriage together*, and who can build a family with you—if this fits your life goals and circumstances. Happy, healthy marriages are built through an organic, creative process; they don't simply happen because a wedding occurs.

Clearly, everyone is unique, and we'll never be able to design our perfect partner. We will marry another human, with their strengths and flaws—never perfectly aligned with our own. We must all be cautious about this desire for some *perfect partner*, as it feeds into the unrealistic and magical thinking that one person will meet all our needs. (For further information, refer back to Chapter 5 about unrealistic expectations and Chapter 6 about "soul mates".) It's not possible to live intimately with another person without making adjustments. The goal is to choose someone with the qualities that will help both of you establish a happy marriage and family life.

Rúhíyyih Rabbaní—the wife of Shoghi Effendi and a dynamic, influential Bahá'í in her own right—shared her perspective on marriage, which may assist you as you go forward:

"Marriage must be viewed in its correct relation to the individual and to the community at large. You will never get the most out of anything unless you understand its proper function. Marriage should be looked forward to, primarily, for the lifelong comradeship it provides. It is likely that your life partner is going to outlast all your other intimate relationships. Your parents will most probably die before you do, your children will grow up and make lives for themselves, your brothers and sisters and friends will have their own intimate relationships in life which will perforce have to take first place. But your partner, your wife or husband, will be there with you always. Joys and sorrows will have to be shared, the home, the children, the income, to a great extent your interests and diversions, will be a common holding. Before you marry you have to realize this, you have to ponder whether you two can go through all that together satisfactorily.

"Do not expect too much of marriage, or too little. ... Your union cannot produce more than you two contribute to it. If you are full of imperfections, intolerant, impatient, exacting, dictatorial, suspicious, short-tempered, selfish, do not imagine that these characteristics are going to make your marriage happy or that by changing your partner a new union will be more successful! Marriage, like all our other relationships in life, is a process which, among other things, serves to grind the sharp edges off us. The grinding often hurts, the adjustment to another person's character is difficult at first, that is why love is needed here more than in any other relationship. Love, being essentially a divine force, binds; it leaps like a spark the gaps between people's thoughts and conflicting desires, between perhaps widely different temperaments. It heals the wounds we all inflict on each other whether inadvertently or in moments of rage, jealousy or spite. To the influence of love in marriage is gradually added another powerful catalyst: habit. The common home, the daily association, produces a common framework, and habit, one of the most powerful forces in life, begins to knit husband and wife together. It acts as a wonderful stabilizer; if love is allowed to fail, habit itself may be strong enough to preserve the union."[151]

Keeping in mind these themes and ideas, we encourage you to now complete the PrepSheet below. Remember, your first series of answers to these prompts is simply the beginning of a gradual process. Determining what you are looking for and want to avoid will take time, action, and more reflection—you will gain clarity and refine your answers as you go.

PrepSheet 7C: What to Seek—and Avoid—in a Potential Marriage Partner

Date: _____

Purposes:
1. To begin identifying some aspects of a potential marriage partner that would be beneficial for me, and to consider the level of priority of each.
2. To begin determining likely incompatible character weaknesses, habits, and personality traits in my potential partner.

Note: This marriage preparation process is about creating a strong marriage, so please try to keep your initial possibilities realistic, focused, and limited. The attributes you write down will evolve as you learn, grow, and experience a variety of relationships and observe others. Each involvement with another person will inform you, and you will refine your list as needed. Chapter 8 will continue to help you think about a potential partner.

First, a few cautions:

- If you alter what you *say* you are looking for to fit a particular, pre-identified person you are already thinking about for a relationship or marriage, you may end up misleading yourself. The person may not be a good fit for you, despite your efforts to make the descriptors fit.

- Avoid being too specific. For example, if you list physical attributes like height or hair color, or a requirement that someone must live in your area, you may exclude people that would otherwise be very suitable, if you were to widen your list of what's possible. It's also wise to keep in check any strong attachments you have to your future marriage partner having a particular lifestyle or profession, or to their being engaged in specific ways of serving their community—since all of these can change over time. We suggest striking a balance of being specific enough to discern a complementary match but not so particular that you eliminate in your mind someone who might, in fact, be a good partner for you.

- Stay aware of any prejudices or biases that might lead you to either identify one possibility to the exclusion of others or to completely exclude a group of people as possibilities.

- Use the list you create to begin your learning journey, rather than to create such high standards or hopes that you end up closing your mind to most of the population and many viable candidates for marriage.

The priority you place on each item on your list will evolve over time and with experience. You will expand your ability to discern whether someone is a good complement for you, or whether the two of you differ too much to live in harmony. Be careful not to devalue and give up on something essential to you to accommodate someone who interests you. Strive to be wise and cautious, as this is a common trap.

Instructions:
A. In the first column of Table 1 below, list a few attributes of a potential marriage partner. It will be difficult to identify a small number of them that will be particularly important to you, but do your best. Begin with choosing 5 character strengths you would most like your partner to have. You may wish to review the list and your answers in "PrepSheet 3: Assessing and Understanding My Character Virtues". Then write down a few other factors besides character.

B. Think carefully about what partner traits would be complementary to yours. For example, a very creative person with many fluctuating emotions throughout each day might benefit from having a partner skilled with the practical side of life who is emotionally supportive of their life work. Or, a creative person may feel the need to have someone who brings passion and zest rather than steadiness. You will not find a perfect fit, but being specific will help calibrate your thinking as you meet people. Prioritize each characteristic with check marks or stars (*) in the adjacent columns.

Table 1: What to Look for in a Potential Marriage Partner

Complementary Attributes	Essential	Important, But Not Essential	Good and Preferable, But Less Important
1.			
2.			
3.			
4.			
5.			
6.			
7.			
8.			
9.			
10.			
11.			
12.			
13.			
14.			

In contrast to the attributes above—which you think would likely complement yours—Table 2 below can help you identify those aspects of a person and their habits which, if your partner had them, would likely make the two of you a *poor* match. Please complete this table with what you would find very difficult in a partner.

Table 2: Incompatible Habits and What to Avoid in a Partner

Personality Traits/Habits/Attributes/Lifestyle I Would:

Find Almost Impossible to Live With	Prefer Not to Live With
1.	1.
2.	2.
3.	3.
4.	4.
5.	5.

Reflection:

1. What insights have I gained about what I want and do not want in a partner? These prompts may help:
    a. Did I identify any patterns? Were there any surprises?
    b. Did I discover any areas where my "wish list" is unreasonable or overly idealistic, such that it significantly limits my choices? If so, which areas?
    c. Did I discover any prejudices? If so, what are they?

    _____
    _____
    _____
    _____
    _____
    _____

2. Have I completed Table 1 or Table 2 with a particular person in mind? Did I complete them when I was with other people—or in a particular environment—that influenced my answers? If so, in what way was I influenced? And now that I realize this, what adjustments should I make to the tables?

    _____
    _____
    _____

3. Which trusted person in my life, who knows me well, should I discuss this PrepSheet with?
   a. Name: _____
   b. By what date do I commit to having this conversation? _____
   c. Return later to record the insights from your discussion:
   _____
   _____
   _____

   d. As a final step, return to the PrepSheet to make any necessary changes based on the reflections and insights that resulted from your conversation. Remember, however, that you will adjust what you've written and refine it with time and experiences. You might consider re-looking at this PrepSheet every 3 months or so to determine if any edits, additions, or deletions are needed.

Activities

1. If you are ready, and it appeals to you, prayerfully reflect on what you wish to communicate about yourself online—such as on social media platforms or online relationship websites—and then create and post it. You could also ask a friend if they know someone they might want to introduce you to. Discuss with this friend how the two of you would describe who you are. Then you can explore together whether the person your friend has in mind might be a good fit for you. This may help you begin to describe what's important to you in a potential partner.

   Note: Chapter 8 may assist you with searching for and developing a connection with someone through electronic apps and websites. It includes cautions about actions to increase your safety when in encounters that begin with interacting online and long-distance.

2. Create two collages, one illustrating the complementary attributes you've identified you want *to have* in a partner, and the other showing aspects you want *to avoid having* in a partner. After completing the collages, assess whether to add or change anything on PrepSheet 7C. [**Note:** If you're new to collages, here's how to create one: Cut out photos and/or words relating to a particular topic or theme from magazines or other sources. Glue them onto a large piece of paper or cardboard. You can also use markers to add your own artwork or words to the collage.]

Encouraging Reminder: To assist you in tracking and completing all the reflections and growth steps in this book, we have provided suggestions and tools in "Appendix A: Tracking My Action Commitments".

Chapter 8
Creating My Future

As you know, this book focuses on preparing you for a healthy, happy marriage and empowering you to avoid choices that could land you in divorce court. In this chapter, we begin with helping you to strengthen your spiritual practices that will assist you with significant decision-making.

We invite you to deepen and clarify your understanding of why marriage is important to you, as well as to reflect on whether or not you want to marry. If you decide to go forward, then we ask you to determine your readiness.

In creating your future, it will benefit you to summon courage—and perhaps develop it further if needed—to help you make new friends, seek new experiences, learn new skills, and share information about your life with others. It will take time to find and get to know several people before you discover someone special. Chapter 9 will also help with these topics.

When the process of finding a relationship or marriage partner takes longer than we would like, we may feel discouraged. At such times, it's good to remind ourselves to be patient, even as we persevere toward our goals. Determined efforts attract God's guidance and assistance, as do prayers, meditation, and wisdom. The process requires that you continually seek balance in your life—and be flexible as life changes.

Key Learning Points

- Expanding my spiritual practices
- Revisiting the importance of marriage
- Reflecting on whether to marry
- Considering my readiness to marry
- Being practical in how I seek to find a marriage partner

Expanding My Spiritual Practices

In this section, we suggest enhancing your knowledge of and experience with spiritual practices such as prayer, meditation, consultation, and involvement in community activities and service. These can help you develop skills for making major decisions and for creating a healthy marriage. The quotations below clarify and illustrate the value of such practices.

1. "It is an axiomatic fact that while you meditate you are speaking with your own spirit. In that state of mind you put certain questions to your spirit and the spirit answers: the light breaks forth and the reality is revealed. ... The spirit of man is itself informed and strengthened during meditation; through it affairs of which man knew nothing are unfolded before his view. Through it he receives Divine inspiration, through it he receives heavenly food.

    "Meditation is the key for opening the doors of mysteries. In ... that state man withdraws himself from all outside objects; in that subjective mood he is immersed in the ocean of spiritual life and can unfold the secrets of things-in-themselves. To illustrate this, think of man as endowed with two kinds of sight; when the power of insight is being used the outward power of vision does not see. This faculty of meditation frees man from the animal nature, discerns the reality of things, puts man in touch with God.

    "This faculty brings forth from the invisible plane the sciences and arts. Through the meditative faculty inventions are made possible, colossal undertakings are carried out; through it governments can run smoothly. Through this faculty man enters into the very Kingdom of God."[152] 'Abdu'l-Bahá

2. ['Abdu'l-Bahá] "... said guidance was when the doors opened after we tried. We can pray, ask to do God's will only, try hard, and then if we find our plan is not working out, assume it is not the right one, at least for the moment."[153] On behalf of Shoghi Effendi

3. "It is not sufficient to pray diligently for guidance, but this prayer must be followed by meditation as to the best methods of action and *then action itself*. Even if the action should not immediately produce results, or perhaps not be entirely correct, that does not make so much difference, because *prayers can only be answered through action and if someone's action* is wrong, God can use that method of showing the pathway which is right...."[154] On behalf of Shoghi Effendi (*italics* are in the original text)

4. "Bahá'u'lláh has stated quite clearly in His Writings the essential requisites for our spiritual growth, and these are stressed again and again by 'Abdu'l-Bahá in His talks and Tablets. One can summarize them briefly in this way:

   1. The recital each day of one of the Obligatory Prayers with pure-hearted devotion.
   2. The regular reading of the Sacred Scriptures, specifically at least each morning and evening, with reverence, attention and thought.
   3. Prayerful meditation on the Teachings, so that we may understand them more deeply, fulfill them more faithfully, and convey them more accurately to others.
   4. Striving every day to bring our behavior more into accordance with the high standards that are set forth in the Teachings.
   5. Teaching the Cause of God.
   6. Selfless service in the work of the Cause and in the carrying on of our trade or profession.

   "These points ... represent the path towards the attainment of true spirituality that has been laid down by the Manifestation of God for this age."[155] Universal House of Justice

5. "Responding to the inmost longing of every heart to commune with its Maker, they carry out acts of collective worship in diverse settings, uniting with others in prayer, awakening spiritual susceptibilities, and shaping a pattern of life distinguished for its devotional character. As they call on one another in their homes and pay visits to families, friends and acquaintances, they enter into purposeful discussion on themes of spiritual import, deepen their knowledge of the Faith, share Bahá'u'lláh's message, and welcome increasing numbers to join them in a mighty spiritual enterprise. Aware of the aspirations of the children of the world and their need for spiritual education, they extend their efforts widely to involve ever-growing contingents of participants in classes that become centers of attraction for the young and strengthen the roots of the Faith in society. They assist junior youth to navigate through a crucial stage of their lives and to become empowered to direct their energies toward the advancement of civilization."[156] Universal House of Justice

6. "To follow a path of service, whatever form one's activity assumes, requires faith and tenacity. In this connection, the benefit of walking that path in the company of others is immense. Loving fellowship, mutual encouragement, and willingness to learn together are natural properties of any group of youth sincerely striving for the same ends, and should also characterize those essential relationships that bind together the components of society. ... You know well that the habits of mind and spirit that you are nurturing in yourselves and others will endure, influencing decisions of consequence that relate to marriage, family, study, work, even where to live. Consciousness of this broad context helps to shatter the distorting looking glass in which everyday tests, difficulties, setbacks, and misunderstandings can seem insurmountable. And in the struggles that are common to each individual's spiritual growth, the will required to make progress is more easily summoned when one's

energies are being channeled towards a higher goal—the more so when one belongs to a community that is united in that goal."[157] Universal House of Justice

Your ability to turn to and draw inspiration from God and from spiritual practices, can powerfully benefit your life in general and your marriage preparation process in particular. Prayer, meditation, and reading spiritual and sacred materials help tune us into God's will for us. They align our minds and hearts to God's guidance and will for humanity, as well as to our individual life purposes. We can also use prayer to ask God for help with deciding whether to marry, preparing us for marriage, and preparing our future partner. Meditation can lead to insights about marriage, why it's important, how we can grow, and ways to find a partner.

Some people have found the following personal suggestions from Shoghi Effendi about prayer useful:

"... [U]se these five steps if we have a problem of any kind for which we desire a solution, or wish help.

"Pray and meditate about it. Use the prayers of the Manifestations, as they have the greatest power. Learn to remain in the silence of contemplation for a few moments. During this deepest communion take the next step.

"Arrive at a decision and hold to this. This decision is usually born in a flash at the close or during the contemplation. It may seem almost impossible of accomplishment, but if it seems to be an answer to prayer or a way of solving the problem, then immediately take the next step.

"Have determination to carry the decision through. Many fail here. The decision, budding into determination, is blighted and instead becomes a wish or a vague longing. When determination is born, immediately take the next step.

"Have faith and confidence, that the Power of the Holy Spirit will flow through you, the right way will appear, the door will open, the right message, the right principle or the right book will be given to you. Have confidence, and the right thing will come to meet your need. Then as you rise from prayer take immediately the fifth step.

"Act as though it had all been answered. Then act with tireless, ceaseless energy. And, as you act, you yourself will become a magnet which will attract more power to your being, until you become an unobstructed channel for the Divine Power to flow through you."[158] Shoghi Effendi

In addition, Bahá'ís around the world have been learning collaboratively and systematically through a rhythmic process of studying the Bahá'í teachings, consulting with each other, forming plans to serve their communities, taking action on these plans, reflecting on what they've learned, and repeating these elements to continually generate new insights and understanding. This process of learning through study, consultation, action, and reflection can also be applied to our personal lives with great results—if we are consistent.

As indicated in a quotation earlier in this section, some Bahá'í community-building activities include groups that gather to pray, study, build fellowship, educate children, and empower youth. These collective efforts may provide opportunities that can help you with marriage preparation. You can meet new people, build friendships, and serve alongside others. These experiences can help you learn about character, advance your personal growth, develop communication skills, acquire parenting capabilities, and more.

Reflection

1. What spiritual practices do I draw upon to make decisions and to guide my actions?
   _____
   _____
   _____

2. How could I enhance my use of these practices?
   _____
   _____
   _____

3. What spiritually-based activities will I include as part of my coherent life and my marriage-preparation process?
   _____
   _____
   _____

4. What skills do I want to gain or strengthen to better prepare myself for marriage?
   a. _____
   b. _____
   c. _____
   d. _____

   To develop these skills, I will take the following action steps:
   a. _____ By when: _____
   b. _____ By when: _____
   c. _____ By when: _____
   d. _____ By when: _____

Revisiting the Importance of Marriage

The theme of the importance of marriage is woven throughout this book. At this stage, we invite you to gather your thoughts on this theme and determine how important it is for you to marry, and whether you wish to do so. With this in mind, please consider the quotations below.

1. "Regarding the question of marriage, know thou that the command of marriage is eternal. It will never be changed or altered. This creation is divine, and it is not possible for that which is created by God to be changed or altered."[159] 'Abdu'l-Bahá

2. "… [T]he importance of marriage lieth in the bringing up of a richly blessed family, so that with entire gladness they may, even as candles, illuminate the world."[160] 'Abdu'l-Bahá

3. "The true marriage of Bahá'ís is this, that husband and wife should be united both physically and spiritually, that they may ever improve the spiritual life of each other, and may enjoy everlasting unity throughout all the worlds of God."[161] 'Abdu'l-Bahá

4. "O Thou kind Lord! Make Thou this marriage to bring forth coral and pearls."[162] 'Abdu'l-Bahá

5. "He realizes your desire to get married is quite a natural one, and he will pray that God will assist you to find a suitable companion with whom you can be truly happy and united in the service of the Faith. Bahá'u'lláh has urged marriage upon all people as the natural and rightful way of life. He has also, however, placed strong emphasis on its spiritual nature, which, while in no way precluding a normal physical life, is the most essential aspect of marriage."[163] On behalf of Shoghi Effendi

6. "… [Y]oung women and men become acutely conscious of the exhortations of the Supreme Pen to 'enter into wedlock' that they may 'bring forth one who will make mention of Me amid My servants'….

... This generation of youth will form families that secure the foundations of flourishing communities. Through their growing love for Bahá'u'lláh and their personal commitment to the standard to which He summons them will their children imbibe the love of God, 'commingled with their mother's milk', and always seek the shelter of His divine law. Clearly, then, the responsibility of a Bahá'í community towards young people does not end when they first start serving. The significant decisions they make about the direction of their adult lives will determine whether service to the Cause of God was only a brief and memorable chapter of their younger years, or a fixed center of their earthly existence, a lens through which all actions come into focus."[164] Universal House of Justice

7. "Bahá'ís should be profoundly aware of the sanctity of marriage and should strive to make their marriages an eternal bond of unity and harmony. This requires effort and sacrifice and wisdom and self-abnegation."[165] On behalf of the Universal House of Justice

8. "You may be assured that in the Bahá'í Teachings, family unity goes far beyond the married couple themselves, and is of critical importance. In the Bahá'í Faith marriage is regarded as both a spiritual and a social institution which affects not only the couple and their children, but also the parents, grandparents, grandchildren and other collateral relations. Indeed, it affects (or, in a healthy society, should affect) all other community associations that surround it."[166] On behalf of the Universal House of Justice

Marriage has been a well-researched topic for several decades, and with time, we are likely to see an increasing number of studies that align with the guidance on marriage contained in the Bahá'í writings. At present, several reliable studies offer clear evidence for conclusions that corroborate many of the Bahá'í teachings on marriage. These studies have found that happy, connected marriages generally bring these benefits to couples:

- Increased mental and physical health and fewer injuries, illnesses, and disabilities
- A higher quality of relationship
- Less partner abuse and violence
- Greater financial well-being and prosperity
- Longer life expectancy

In their book, *The Case for Marriage*, Linda J. Waite and Maggie Gallagher observed that "Marriage actually changes people's goals and behavior in ways that are profoundly and powerfully life enhancing."[167] They also concluded that:

Marriage makes you better off, because marriage makes you very important to someone. When you are married you know that someone else not only loves you but needs you and depends upon you. ... Spouses expect to be able to trust each other, financially, sexually, and emotionally, not only because of their individual personal qualities but because being married means that most of their goods are jointly owned. The trust implicit in marriage reduces the need for spouses to monitor the behavior of each other closely....[168]

Marriage benefits individuals both because of what they receive and the ways in which it requires each person to grow and give. The final quotation from the Bahá'í writings above outlines some vital attributes for a successful marriage: effort, sacrifice, wisdom, and self-abnegation.

Good marriages require both partners to invest effort, time, and energy. With sacrifice and self-abnegation, their actions focus on the greater good, a positive outcome for the couple and the family, and also often for others as well. Wisdom grows as the couple makes appropriate sacrifices. It also offers a balance, so the health and well-being of the individuals and the couple are not also sacrificed. Wisdom is also developed and applied continually as partners get to know one another, strive to serve each other and the wider world, and seek to grow spiritually.

Reflection

1. What do I see as the potential benefits of marriage? What benefits have I seen in any marriages I've experienced or observed?
   _____
   _____
   _____

2. What do I see as the downsides of marriage? What problems have I witnessed?
   _____
   _____
   _____

3. What attracts me to the idea of marrying?
   _____
   _____
   _____

   What, if anything, do I resist about the idea of getting married?
   _____
   _____
   _____

Reflecting on Whether to Marry

Intellectually, you can assess the benefits of marrying, and you may feel this is important for you to do. However, marriage is not a life requirement, and you may choose not to marry. Regardless of the decision you arrive at, we encourage you to consider the matter—wisely, consciously, and deliberately—then decide your direction and align your actions with your choice. You can, of course, review and change this decision later, but for now, making a decision puts you in motion. The perspectives offered in the quotations below may help inform your decision.

1. "… [M]arriage is by no means an obligation. In the last resort it is for the individual to decide whether he wishes to lead a family life or live in a state of celibacy."[169] Shoghi Effendi

2. "The Bahá'í Teachings do not only encourage marital life, considering it the natural and normal way of existence for every sane, healthy and socially-conscious and responsible person, but raise marriage to the status of a divine institution, its chief and sacred purpose being the perpetuation of the human race—which is the very flower of the entire creation—and its elevation to the true station destined for it by God."[170] On behalf of Shoghi Effendi

3. "… [A]lthough to be married is highly desirable, and Bahá'u'lláh has strongly recommended it, it is not the central purpose of life. If a person has to wait a considerable period before finding a spouse, or if ultimately, he or she must remain single, it does not mean that he or she is thereby unable to fulfill his or her life's purpose."[171] Universal House of Justice

Marriage and parenting are two of the most important choices we can make, with significant implications not only for our life in this world, but also for the eternal journey of our souls. One's relationship with a marriage partner, and with one's children, constitute a connection between eternal souls—a bond that can likewise continue forever. This concept may draw you toward the idea of marriage, or it may scare you away from it. But you can rest assured in the knowledge that preparing for marriage eases fears that arise.

As you consider whether to marry, imagine your future marriage. Begin to create a picture in your mind and a feeling in your heart of what marriage could be like for you. While your vision may be somewhat realistic at this stage, this visualization exercise will help you clarify your goal. Sharing a clear picture of the type of life you would like to live will also aid your communication when you are in a relationship. It could help you gauge whether the two of you have complementary views of the future.

As you think about marriage and your potential partner, consider what is *most* important to you emotionally, spiritually, mentally, and physically. As you do this, we suggest trying to stay reasonable and balanced in the vision you create for your future marriage. Striking this balance may not be easy or straightforward for everyone, but doing so is well worth the effort, as it will likely bring good results.

As you envision sharing your life with someone, consider your shared values, beliefs, and attributes, as well as anything you feel you must have in common. Also, consider whether you would enter a relationship with someone who doesn't seem to have the essential attributes you identified in PrepSheet 7C. If you would make this choice, assess the potential consequences or outcomes.

Once a couple marries, they begin a lifelong process of communication and adjustment, centered on love, growth, and flexibility. Sharing a mutual vision of a healthy, fulfilling marriage helps couples create such a marriage. PrepSheet 8A below can assist you to create a draft vision for your marriage—which can be refined as you go forward.

Starting with Me—Knowing Myself Before Finding a Partner

PrepSheet 8A: Creating a Vision of My Marriage

Date: _____

Purposes:
1. To envision what my marriage could look like and what elements it could include.
2. To help me discern whether to marry.

Instructions:
A. Go to a quiet, private place where you can do a visualization without interruption.

B. Do something to help you relax, focus, and feel inspired. (examples: breathe calmly, pray, meditate, read inspiring verses, listen to music, gentle stretching, exercise…)

C. Create your vision.

Visioning Activity:

Once you are calm and focused, imagine being in a marriage over a long period of time. The prompts below may help:

- What do I imagine my marriage to be like?
- How do I feel?
- How am I speaking to and acting toward my partner?
- What am I saying?
- What is my marriage partner saying?
- How is my partner speaking to me and acting toward me?
- What are we doing together?
- How do we express love between us?
- How often, and when, do we consult?
- How are we handling disagreements?
- How is the household being managed?
- Are there children? Grandchildren?
- If so, what are they doing?
- What does time with friends look like?
- What spiritual activities are taking place?
- What community service activities are happening?

Based on the images that come to you in response to the questions above, and thinking of any other aspects of married life that are important to you, note some of the key parts of your initial vision here:

_____
_____
_____
_____
_____
_____
_____
_____

Think about how else you would like to express your vision. This can be done creatively—by composing a poem or song, by drawing or painting pictures that illustrate it, or through music, dance, or video. Consider expressing yourself in any other way that helps you further enliven your vision or strengthen your connection to it.

Reflection

1. What would enable me to feel happy and unified with a partner?
   _____
   _____
   _____

   What might cause regular disunity between us instead?
   _____
   _____
   _____

2. What concerns and fears do I still have about being married?
   _____
   _____
   _____

3. Do I feel courageous enough, and sufficiently committed to marrying, to keep preparing myself?
   _____
   _____
   _____

4. What is my current attitude toward and level of openness to the idea of finding a marriage partner? How proactive do I want to be in seeking a partner?
   _____
   _____
   _____

Considering My Readiness to Marry

If you choose to continue preparing for marriage, it will be wise to consider what else, if anything, you need to learn and do to be ready. The advice in the quotation below may be instructive.

1. "I wish to assure you, in particular, of his supplications for your guidance in connection with your proposed plan to unite in marriage with.... May the Beloved help you in forming the right decision, and spare you the anxiety and suffering which too hasty action in such matters inevitably produces. You should give this question, which is of such vital concern to your future, the full consideration it deserves, and examine all its aspects carefully and dispassionately. The final decision rests with you and ... [the proposed partner]."[172] On behalf of Shoghi Effendi

Ahead of you on the way to marriage are potential new friends, dates, courtship, shared service, and more. As you think about these activities, assess whether you have the skills and knowledge to help you successfully navigate the experiences. These could include communication skills, character refinement, friendship building, and more.

These quotes below will help you reflect on your own readiness to marry and the process you might choose to follow.

"Life is, in part, about finding a partner with good character who I can be in harmony with, knowing where I want to go, and making a realistic plan for how to get there. It's also about deciding what dreams I am not going to chase, so I can make time for the dreams I am going to chase. Faith and spirituality are essential to this. Flexibility is too. For I have to learn how to be happy and make do with things the way they are, even when it's not how I thought things would work out. It's also essential to remember that in making others happy, I'll make myself happy."

"I have found that many of my acquaintances have taken years and years to try to get to know someone. They think they need to know every single part of that person and be sure of EVERYTHING before committing. I think there is value in seeing that a partner meets certain criteria, and in my being sure we each have a sound character, but then I think you have to take the rest on faith. We'll never know everything about anyone, and part of the magic of marriage is that we continue to learn things about each other, and overcome challenges within the marriage framework, instead of endlessly using challenges to determine whether they are worthy partners or not. A partner will grow with me, serve with me, make me better, be devoted to family and God, and will overcome obstacles and trials with me. We will have a blast doing it together."

There are many possible ways you can increase your relationship and marriage readiness. You can gain knowledge through courses, read research-based sources, and enjoy thoughtful books, videos, or podcasts on the subject. You might also learn by spending time with or interviewing people in marriages you would like to learn from and pattern your own marriage after. Along those lines, please do PrepSheet 8B below.

Starting with Me—Knowing Myself Before Finding a Partner

PrepSheet 8B: Learning About Marriage by Interviewing Married Couples

Date: _____

Purposes:
1. To help me increase my understanding of love and marriage.
2. To equip me to interview married couples and reflect on the insights and learning I gain from the process.

Instructions:

A. Recognizing that no marriage is perfect, nor are the people in it, invite a couple that seems to be in harmony and who has been married for less than 3 years to let you "interview" them—to learn important lessons and insights for your potential marriage. Ask them the designated questions in Section 1 below.

B. Meet with a second couple that you think is a good role model and that has been married for a long time, preferably more than 15 years. Ask them the questions in Section 2 below that is designated for this more experienced couple.

C. After you have interviewed both couples, use the "Interviews Reflection" section to consult about how you can use the insights gained from the interviews to form and maintain a harmonious, unified, strong, happy marriage. Identify specifics that will assist you with this once married.

Section 1: Complete the following for a couple married for a short time (less than 3 years):

1. What is their level of community service? How are they balancing service and marriage/family?
   _____
   _____
   _____

2. What are their favorite ways to connect with one another?
   _____
   _____
   _____

3. What communication challenges and successes are they experiencing?
   _____
   _____
   _____

4. What other factors are contributing to the strength of their marriage?
   _____
   _____
   _____

5. What difficulties have they experienced over time, and how have they addressed them?
   _____
   _____
   _____

6. What advice do they offer to people considering being married or to newly married couples?
   _____
   _____
   _____

7. What else did you observe?
   _____
   _____
   _____

Section 2: Complete the following for a couple married a long time (more than 15 years):

1. What is their level of community service? How are they balancing service and marriage/family?
   _____
   _____
   _____

2. What are their favorite ways to connect with one another?
   _____
   _____
   _____

3. What communication challenges and successes are they experiencing?
   _____
   _____
   _____

4. What other factors are contributing to the strength of their marriage?
   _____
   _____
   _____

5. What difficulties have they experienced over time, and how have they addressed them?
   _____
   _____
   _____

6. What advice do they offer to people considering being married or to other couples who have been married for a longer amount of time?
   _____
   _____
   _____

7. What else did you observe?
   _____
   _____
   _____

My Reflections on the Interview:

1. What did I hear and observe that I want to include in my relationship/marriage?
   _____
   _____
   _____

2. What did I hear and observe that I do not want to include in my relationships/marriage?
   _____
   _____
   _____

3. What further actions will I take to expand my knowledge of how marriages succeed?
   _____
   _____
   _____

4. What knowledge or skills do I need to strengthen? (examples: communication, cooking, home maintenance, raising children...) How can I do this?
   _____
   _____
   _____

5. Do I think I am generally ready to be in a relationship and seriously consider marrying?
   _____
   _____
   _____

6. When do I use "not being ready" as an excuse to avoid moving forward?
   _____
   _____
   _____

Being Practical in How I Seek to Find a Marriage Partner

We naturally have romantic thoughts, feel attracted to others, and want to be with certain people. The quotations below remind us to stay focused on reality and be engaged in the process as a way to balance our romantic thinking and attractions with our long-term well-being.

1. "... [M]an and woman should truly be friends and should be in sympathy with each other. Their understanding should have a basis in reality and not be based upon passion and desire...."[173] Provisional translation from a talk by 'Abdu'l-Bahá

2. "Man must cut himself free from all prejudice and from the result of his own imagination, so that he may be able to search for truth unhindered."[174] 'Abdu'l-Bahá

3. "... [I]mplicit faith in our intuitive powers is unwise, but through daily prayer and sustained effort one can discover, though not always and fully, God's will intuitively. Under no circumstances, however, can a person be absolutely certain that he is recognizing God's will, through the exercise of his

intuition. It often happens that the latter results in completely misrepresenting the truth, and thus becomes a source of error rather than of guidance."[175] On behalf of Shoghi Effendi

4. "Change … be it swift or hard won, flows neither from a formulaic approach nor from random activity; it proceeds to the rhythm of action, reflection, and consultation, and is propelled by plans that are the fruit of experience."[176] Universal House of Justice

5. "Armed with the strength of action and the cooperation of the individual believers composing it, the community as a whole should endeavor to establish greater stability in the patterns of its development, locally and nationally, through sound, systematic planning and execution of its work—and this in striking contrast to the short-lived enthusiasms and frenetic superficialities so characteristic of present-day American life."[177] Universal House of Justice

6. "God has endowed human beings with more than one way of receiving guidance in the decisions we have to make, as 'Abdu'l-Bahá has explained. There are the Holy Writings, in which are clear directions for the way in which we should live; if an inner voice prompts us to act contrary to the explicit teachings we can be sure that, far from being an inspiration from God, that inner voice is the expression of our own lower nature, and should be disregarded. There is also the gift of intelligence and good judgment—the faculty which distinguishes man from the animal kingdom; God intends us to use the faculty, which can be a powerful instrument for distinguishing between true inspirations and vain imaginings. There is the power of prayer through which we strive to purify our motives, to seek the Will of God and to implore His guidance and assistance. There is also the law of consultation, one of the distinguishing features of this great Revelation."[178] On behalf of the Universal House of Justice

Throughout *Starting with Me*, we have proposed many practical ideas. The perspectives below from several individuals express their interpretations of some of the principles shared in the quotations above. They address the practical aspects of a marriage partner's qualities, the importance of balancing ideals with reality, and the components of service that are central to a healthy family and community.

"Thoroughly knowing someone's character means I do more than assess what it would be like to live with someone or lay out my 'top ten qualities' as if that's 'all I need to know.' Instead, I am also assessing how that person will treat my parents, how they'll be as a parent themselves, how they'll be as a host to our friends and community, how they'll treat animals and pets, how they'll interact with people who are serving them, how they'll be of service to humanity, how they'll deal with tests, difficulties, and illnesses that they and others experience, and more. And I need to consider whether they have the qualities and strengths necessary for building family unity, weathering the dark and stormy times, fulfilling their roles in the marriage and family, managing family finances, and so on."

"I feel like we all have a list of things we are looking for: security, stability, spirituality, commitment, sense of humor, good looks, and more. Whatever those items may be, we should be honest with ourselves and know ourselves well enough to understand that we can ask for these things—and we can try to find them in a potential partner—and we also have to be realistic. Some things we can learn from observation—and others we can't. Is this person going to be an amazing father to my children? I have no idea. I have never seen him interact with my potential children. What I do know is that he supports my spiritual practices, is kindhearted, energetic, intelligent, well-read, and devoted to his family. To me, those things add up to a great father. All that is to say that we must get to know the person fully, to the best of our abilities. If that person is the one we select, all parties involved must then enter the union with the understanding that they are unequivocally devoted to one another. They will accept the faults of the other.

They will work through tests together. And they are committed to learning and growing together. After that, you communicate, compromise, practice flexibility, and genuinely hope for the best."

Making Connections Electronically

As you're no doubt aware, millions of people worldwide now seek to build connections and meaningful relationships through social media, online dating and relationship services, mobile apps, video services, and other forms of electronic communication. All these offer opportunities to share information about yourself.

A relationship is decidedly more likely to succeed when both partners possess character strengths and truly complement each other. The Bahá'í teachings encourage couples to "study each other's character and spend time getting to know each other before they decide to marry", and they suggest that "when they do marry it should be with the intention of establishing an eternal bond."[179] (On behalf of the Universal House of Justice) Therefore, it's vital to start learning about a person's character strengths and growth areas early in the friendship and before becoming seriously involved in a relationship or considering marrying them.

Electronically Describing Myself and a Potential Partner

In many situations, you'll need to describe yourself—and what you're looking for in a partner. Generally, people don't share about their character in their descriptions of themselves. However, if you do your part by articulating your character strengths and the qualities you seek in a potential partner, you will distinguish yourself, and your act of open sharing may encourage others, in turn, to share their strengths. Being transparent around character may even increase your pool of interested contacts, since many people find self-knowledge and clarity of purpose attractive. This clarity may prevent interactions with people who do not consider strength of character a priority, thereby making your process clearer from the beginning.

When getting to know others, we suggest you share some of your stronger virtues—in a way that doesn't seem awkward or boastful. You identified these in PrepSheet3, and the character strengths you hope for in a potential partner in PrepSheet 7C. Of course, you may also choose to talk with a potential partner about the areas you want to grow in. If you haven't yet completed these exercises, we encourage you to do so before sharing about yourself with others so you can be clearer about how you see your own character strengths and areas to grow.

Sharing About Yourself

Having identified in your efforts throughout the book many of the relevant character strengths and virtues—those belonging to you and your desired qualities in a partner—next comes the task of deciding whether and how to convey this information. (Please see PrepSheet 3 for a list of virtues and their definitions.)

Many people feel uncomfortable saying positive things about themselves. For example, one profile we read said, "I'm not really inclined to dwell at length on myself." This is, of course, entirely understandable—whether it's due to shyness or to humility, which is, after all, a virtue. However, character is so vital in a couple's relationship that this is not the time to hide your light. Knowing what's good about yourself and sharing it may help each of you discern more clearly. Simply put, truthfulness and honesty are crucial in this process. This awareness of your strengths never negates the beauty and strengths of others. It only allows you to share candidly how you believe you uniquely show up in this world.

Your Electronic Presence and Profiles

Of course, any of the above information can be shared in a live conversation—perhaps with someone you are getting to know as a potential partner in a long-term relationship or marriage. At the same time, your valuable self-knowledge around character can also be shared more broadly through online profiles as part of your honest and powerful online presence.

To offer an example of candidly sharing one's virtue strengths, here's an online description someone posted: "I am honest, funny, kind of handsome, well-dressed, faithful, and fun. Almost always in a great mood and laughing! Also opinionated, passionate, loyal, outgoing, shy at times (until I relax), spontaneous, and romantic."

If, in the end, you still cannot overcome this barrier of talking about yourself, we suggest you at least say some version of "Others say I'm....". For example, based on the feedback you receive from others, you could write something like, "Friends have said I'm warm, insightful, compassionate, strong, and a good listener, while being gently assertive", or "I've been told I'm generous, kind, and a gentleman." If you are not able to share about yourself, reflect on whether that indicates others may have difficulty getting to know you. This reticence to be open may lead you to unwittingly pass over opportunities to make friends and meet people who may eventually be potential marriage partners.

Additionally, in your introduction of yourself, rather than merely listing your strengths, we suggest you round them out a bit. If you demonstrate them in a sentence, it helps people understand what you mean. Here are some examples of self-descriptions:

- It took **courage** for me to (climb a mountain, restart my career, recover from my wife dying in a car accident, or any other example).
- I like to have fun, but I prefer doing things in **moderation**. I am not a big risk-taker.
- I strive for **excellence** in my work, especially when **helping** my co-workers with projects.
- When I face challenges, I tend to be **patient, persevering**, and **resilient**.
- When friends tell me their difficulties, I do my best to be **compassionate** and **caring**.
- My friends say that I'm **gentle** and **loving**, especially with children and pets.
- I believe in **cooperating** with my partner, not competing with each other.
- I tend to be **enthusiastic** about new activities and adventures.
- I've been told that I speak **confidently** in front of groups.
- I like to do **spontaneous, thoughtful**, and **kind** things for my friends.
- **Truthfulness** is vital for me—both giving it (being truthful with others) and receiving it (knowing others are being truthful with me).
- I'm very **loyal** and deeply value my family and friendships.
- I'm **hardworking** and am **responsible** in paying my bills on time.

Describing What You're Looking For

Character qualities that grow into strengths tend to endure throughout a person's life. In contrast, physical attributes and lifestyle interests are subject to change. For example, today a desired partner might be riding motorcycles around the country, but that may be impossible next year; today they might have beautiful black hair, but over time become bald or gray. Unlike these changing external aspects of a partner, inner qualities tend to endure, so be clear about what's very important to you. As with your self-description, be specific. The examples below show how you could describe desired qualities in a partner:

- I seek a partner who is **honest**, fun, and **trustworthy**.
- I prize **kindness, compassion**, and a desire to make a positive difference for others.
- You are **responsible**, but do not take yourself too seriously.

- You have a nice balance of **humility** and **confidence**.
- Because I'm not much of a risk taker, I would like someone who balances that out with **courage** and would help me take a few (reasonable) risks.
- You are a friendly, caring, spiritual person.
- I'm passionate about people who show **kindness** and understanding where it's needed.
- I'm looking for honesty, caring, trust, dependability, a sense of humor, and integrity.
- My ideal match would be a **caring**, sensitive person.
- I'm super tidy and need a partner who is similar in being **orderly**.
- What excites me is **kindness**, **compassion**, intelligence, a great sense of humor, and a smile that radiates sunshine.

Whatever phrasing you choose, the clarity will likely help you in your search for a suitable partner. On the other hand, if you start your introduction, profile, or first communication with wording that makes it clear you aren't serious or committed to finding a relationship partner, most people will not respond. If you focus on what is true about your character and on what you most appreciate in a potential partner, a match will be far more likely.

Online Risks: Some Words of Caution

When you're looking for, or have found, a potential partner through online sites, you should take care to know the other person's character and intentions before making any decisions about courtship or marriage. This is important in all circumstances, particularly with interactions on the internet, which has unfortunately made it easier for people to misrepresent themselves and potentially cause harm.

People who meet online often must get to know each other from afar, often through social media, video chatting, phone calls, and emails. This can enhance openness by removing some of the pitfalls of being near each other, such as overemphasis on physical traits, early sexual desires, and social pressures. Virtual communication also reduces expenses.

However, distance makes it harder to observe specific behaviors and interactions that indicate character strengths and weaknesses. In addition, individuals can lie about their background, beliefs, affiliations, and other aspects of who they are, with less chance of being caught than if you frequently saw each other in person.

Therefore, when you are communicating online and/or virtually, please exercise vigilance and caution to avoid any scams that ask for money or personal information. We strongly recommend not loaning any money or sharing any personal details that could make you vulnerable to fraud, identity theft, hacking, scams, and so on. In addition, if you meet this person through some community or network that you share, you may wish to reach out to a contact in that network who might know this individual and be able to serve as a character reference for their trustworthiness, honesty, and integrity.

If and when you decide to meet in person, please continue being cautious and safe, and take good care to protect your body, money, and possessions—as well as your heart. While courage is necessary to meet new people, you must also be wise in how you get to know them. One important guide is to do so gradually.

After a period of virtual communication, meeting in person is, of course, an important way to observe real-life behaviors. However, again, please be cautious and ensure safeguards, such as:

- Meeting in public
- Bringing someone else with you
- Ensuring you have your phone

- Some loved ones have your phone number and know where you are
- Checking in with someone before and after any encounters
- Arranging for friends or community members to provide a comfortable setting in which to meet.

In addition, again, it would be wise to refrain—at least in your early in-person interactions—from financial transactions such as giving or loaning money to this person—even if they have appeared thus far to be sincere and trustworthy.

Being clear with yourself on how to be wise and stay safe will increase your confidence and free you up mentally to enjoy this new potential friendship and relationship!

Reflection

1. What approaches to finding a marriage partner would serve me well?

   _____
   _____
   _____

   What am I unwilling to participate in?

   _____
   _____
   _____

2. How possible does it seem for me to discover a potential marriage partner while living a full life and being involved in acts of service?

   _____
   _____
   _____

   What else might I do? How might I utilize electronic methods?

   _____
   _____
   _____

3. In the past, have I made lists of requirements for a potential marriage partner? If so, how did I use these lists? What is my view of such lists and how I used them?

   _____
   _____
   _____

4. How long have I usually taken to get to know someone before committing to being a relationship partner? How long have I been in a relationship before deciding with them about marriage? Do these amounts of time seem healthy and reasonable? Why or why not? What length of time would work well for me going forward?

   _____
   _____
   _____

5. If I am often nervous a relationship will not work out, what would I need to understand about my history or see in the other person or in the relationship to be able to relax and make a long-term commitment?

_____
_____
_____

Encouraging Reminder: To assist you in tracking and completing all the reflections and growth steps in this book, we have provided suggestions and tools in "Appendix A: Tracking My Action Commitments".

Chapter 9
Completing This Stage of My Journey

By this point in the book, you've taken many preparatory steps toward marriage, and you're expanding your ability to live a full, coherent life. Naturally, different people will focus to varying degrees on finding a partner, and that focus may change at various stages of life. If marriage and building a family are among your key life purposes, that will affect how much time and energy you put toward this goal. This chapter offers some ways you can move in that direction, if you want that to be part of creating your coherent life.

We encourage you to actively participate in your life and the life of the community, rather than simply observe what's happening from the sidelines. Therefore, if you struggle with this, we offer a few suggestions for living an involved and purposeful life, such as participating in service and community-building activities, expanding the social and community activities you participate in, and widening your friendship circle.

Building relationships is usually a gradual process, and the friendships you grow along the way can be valuable in and of themselves—even if they never evolve into a relationship, or they return to a friendship after an attempted relationship. It would be unwise to be so single-minded about finding a marriage partner that you neglect other important aspects of your life or other important relationships. After all, a relationship sometimes grows out of a friendship—at times unexpectedly.

As you engage fully in life, with the goal of a relationship and then marriage in your mind and heart, possibilities will open. Some of them may be surprises, so your self-preparation efforts will serve you well. Sometimes, what seems like a roadblock, problem, or bad relationship turns out to be a person or event that sends you in new and exciting directions, so it's always wise to keep an open mind.

As you make activity and relationship choices, please stay attuned to your well-being. When you need to moderate your level of activity, then you may wish to pray, seek counsel, spend a day in a beautiful natural setting, or revive and rejuvenate your spirit or body in some other way. You can also draw on the strength of those who encourage and support you—resources this chapter will help you to build.

Key Learning Points

- Building my encouragement and support "team"
- Creating friendships
- Orienting myself toward marriage
- Continuing my marriage preparation process
- Reflecting on the whole-book experience and next steps
- Closing inspiration

Building My Encouragement and Support "Team"

This section aims to prompt ideas about who among your family, friends, community, and other social circles can be part of your support system as you stay open to finding a partner. The quotations highlight some spiritual and practical reasons for creating a support system for moving toward marriage. They may also prompt ideas about what type of support would benefit you the most, who might be able to offer it, and how. At the end of this section, you can write down names and ideas that come to mind.

1. "The question of consultation is of the utmost importance, and is one of the most potent instruments conducive to the tranquility and felicity of the people. For example, when a believer is uncertain about his affairs, or when he seeketh to pursue a project or trade, the friends should gather together and

devise a solution for him. He, in his turn, should act accordingly. Likewise in larger issues, when a problem ariseth, or a difficulty occurreth, the wise should gather, consult, and devise a solution. They should then rely upon the one true God, and surrender to His Providence, in whatever way it may be revealed, for divine confirmations will undoubtedly assist."[180] 'Abdu'l-Bahá

2. "If thou wouldst show kindness and consideration to thy parents so that they may feel generally pleased, this would also please Me, for parents must be highly respected and it is essential that they feel contented...."[181] 'Abdu'l-Bahá

3. "Youth also support each other ... coming together in groups to engage in further study and discuss their service, to reinforce one another's efforts and build resolve, looking to ever extend the circle of friendship more widely. The encouragement offered in this way by a network of peers provides young people with a much-needed alternative to those siren voices that beckon towards the snares of consumerism and compulsive distractions...."[182] Universal House of Justice

4. "Although a Bahá'í may, if he chooses, seek his parents' advice on the choice of a partner, and although Bahá'í parents may give such advice if asked, it is clear from the Teachings that parents do not have the right to interfere in their children's actual choice of a prospective partner until approached for their consent to marry. Therefore, when discussing the issue of courtship with your sons, it would be best to discuss it on the level of principle without reference to individuals."[183] On behalf of the Universal House of Justice

5. "... [The Universal House of Justice] suggests that you consult your Spiritual Assembly or an Auxiliary Board member or, if you have close friends whose judgment you respect, consult with them and pay careful attention to their advice...."[184] On behalf of the Universal House of Justice

6. "... [T]he House of Justice feels it most essential for your husband and you to understand that marriage can be a source of well-being, conveying a sense of security and spiritual happiness. However, it is not something that just happens. For marriage to become a haven of contentment it requires the cooperation of the marriage partners themselves, and the assistance of their families...."[185] On behalf of the Universal House of Justice

Note: "Appendix C: Using Consultation in Marriage Preparation" may also assist you.

The more you live a full life, involved with diverse people in a variety of places and situations, the more likely you are to find a complementary partner. This may not be easy. Being courageous and gaining support from friends and family can help. Those who support your efforts can invite you to new experiences where you are likely to meet new people. You can let a few trusted individuals know you're thinking about marriage and share some key aspects you're looking for in a partner (PrepSheet 7C). Your helpers may spot someone with potential before you do—maybe even someone you already know. However, please remember to set clear, appropriate boundaries with others to ensure they don't interfere with your choice of a partner or put pressure on either of you.

Consider the social circles below in the left-hand column to clarify your thinking and possibly generate some new ideas. For each category, write in the middle column the names of people you think might be able to support you. Then, write in the right-hand column how they might be able to help you expand your life experiences, prepare further for marriage, and potentially discover a possible marriage partner. If you struggle to identify people, begin in a small way by asking one person you know. Then, you can gradually expand your support team.

Social Circles	Names of Those I Want on My Encouragement and Support "Team"	Specific Help Each Person Could Provide
Family Members		
Friends		
Community Members		
Other Social Circle		
Other Social Circle		

Reflection:

1. How do I envision approaching these people and asking for their help?

   _____
   _____
   _____

2. What concerns might they have about assisting me in this way? How could I address these?

   _____
   _____
   _____

3. How will I express my appreciation to those who help me?

   _____
   _____
   _____

4. If my list of people who can encourage and support me is shorter than I prefer, how can I expand the pool of people I would feel comfortable asking to help me in this way? Which of my friendships, acquaintanceships, or other relationships could evolve to the stage in which we mutually support each other in our lives? How can I nurture these connections to reach this stage?

_____
_____
_____

Creating Friendships

As you know, friendship is central to a healthy marriage. This is evident in many ways. For example, people often say their marriage partner is their best friend. In this section, we'll explore several ways in which friendship can help with marriage preparation. As you read through it, you may wish to make note of any ideas or people that come to mind. "PrepSheet 9: Widening My Circle of Friends and Experiences" (later in this chapter) will also help you think of—and record—practical next steps.

We begin with quotations below that speak to the high value of fellowship and friendship, and the power of trustworthiness as a character quality to keep people connected.

1. "Trustworthiness is the greatest portal leading unto the tranquility and security of the people. In truth the stability of every affair hath depended and doth depend upon it. All the domains of power, of grandeur and of wealth are illumined by its light."[186] Bahá'u'lláh

2. "The Lord ... hath made woman and man to abide with each other in the closest companionship, and to be even as a single soul. They are two helpmates, two intimate friends, who should be concerned about the welfare of each other. If they live thus, they will pass through this world with perfect contentment, bliss, and peace of heart, and become the object of divine grace and favor in the Kingdom of heaven."[187] 'Abdu'l-Bahá

3. "If a small number of people gather lovingly together, with absolute purity and sanctity, with their hearts free of the world, experiencing the emotions of the Kingdom and the powerful magnetic forces of the Divine, and being at one in their happy fellowship, that gathering will exert its influence over all the earth. The nature of that band of people, the words they speak, the deeds they do, will unleash the bestowals of Heaven, and provide a foretaste of eternal bliss."[188] 'Abdu'l-Bahá

4. "Do not be content with showing friendship in words alone, let your heart burn with loving kindness for all who may cross your path."[189] 'Abdu'l-Bahá

5. "You must love your friend better than yourself; yes, be willing to sacrifice yourself."[190] 'Abdu'l-Bahá

6. "... [E]stablish ties of friendship, on the basis of shared understanding, with those previously regarded as strangers."[191] Universal House of Justice

An unmarried person can meet a prospective future marriage partner and begin to develop a close friendship anytime and anywhere. Getting to know someone can be the same process whether you simply wish to make a new friend or think of the person as a prospective partner. Either way, it helps to know if you enjoy each other's company and want to learn more about each other.

Early friendship can be relaxed—an interchange in which two people see if they enjoy chatting and getting to know each other. The distinction society has made between how we should get to know a potential marriage partner, versus someone we just want to be friends with, can be misleading. Some people believe that for a relationship to be possible, there has to be an almost instant attraction when people first meet. However, many people find that building a close and loving friendship can later spark an attraction. There is no formula or single method for friendships to unfold and relationships to develop. We do know that we want to build and sustain a friendship with someone we'll spend our life with. So why not get to know someone in a relaxed and easy friendship from the outset?

Friendships can help us prepare for marriage in several ways. They give us opportunities to expand our self-knowledge, strengthen our relationship skills, and develop our character qualities. We can also improve our ability to notice how a friend practices various virtues. Reflecting on how we carry out our friendships helps us determine which skills and qualities we would benefit from developing further.

Creating new friendships expands the pool of potential relationships, which enhances the possibility of finding a potential marriage partner. It's often necessary to broaden our perspective of who could be a good marriage partner for us. Sometimes, this requires removing or addressing a prejudice or factor that restricts our view—whether it relates to economic level, race, ethnicity, culture, nationality, religious affiliation, physical appearance, personality, lifestyle preferences, geographical location, or any other limiting factor.

As you see others' behaviors and learn about their characters, you'll discern which of their attributes, values, and personality traits complement yours. It's generally wise to withhold judgment until you have a broader view of who they are, since pre-conceptions are often misleading. For instance, when you first meet someone, you might observe several superficial aspects about them that you initially think would not make them a suitable partner to live with, based on your understanding of what you're looking for.

As you observe these aspects, you might automatically make judgments about other aspects of the person's life and choices. However, if you get to know the person better, you will probably discover several positive behaviors that could only be seen through a friendship, such as that they:

- Regularly listen to and spend quality time with friends
- Always tell the truth
- Pray continuously throughout their day
- Enjoy lively group activities
- Treat everyone with an open, friendly attitude

In other words, everyone is complex, and it's easy for our prejudices and assumptions to initially interfere with getting to know someone. In case you wondered, the five traits mentioned above belong to an actual individual who is an excellent marriage partner but was almost discounted because they also possess attributes sometimes considered unsuitable for marriage. The world contains countless multi-dimensional people who defy common assumptions and stereotypes. It takes time to get to know people, to study their characters, and to discover what interests, challenges, or delights us about them.

One way to expand your circle of friends is to live a coherent life that focuses your time and energy on community-building and service—as encouraged in Chapter 1 and throughout the book. This can naturally foster qualities needed for a strong relationship and lead to friendships that may result in marriage. While building friendships through service, you may also see the value you bring to your community and what you gain from participating. A wide range of social spaces might be considered your "community", including:

- Neighborhoods
- Parks
- Homes of friends and neighbors
- Volunteer centers and activities
- Community centers
- Religious or spiritual activities and events
- Non-profit organizations

- Coffee and tea shops
- Local clubs and organizations
- Educational facilities
- Libraries or media centers

Some of the activities listed below could also enhance your life and provide opportunities to meet new people. What appeals to you?

Interested?	Activity
	Facilitate a study session or ongoing group to explore a meaningful or interesting topic
	Host a prayer gathering
	Visit neighbors and friends in their homes
	Coordinate or participate in a community service project
	Volunteer your time to support a worthy cause
	Visit or volunteer at an elder care facility or with a children's group
	Offer classes for the moral and spiritual education of children
	Offer friendship, mentorship, and guidance to groups of youth
	Attend conferences or workshops
	Join a committee addressing a civic or social issue
	Enroll in a course at a college, university, community center, or other institution
	Take classes related to the arts
	Volunteer at a museum, concert hall, theater, or library
	Join a book group, hiking group, community theater, sport club or team, game-playing group, or any other group that interests you (meetup.com is one good resource for this)

To consider: What other types of places and spaces could help you expand your activities, perspectives, and friendships? What do you have access to? Where can you visit or travel to? What opportunity can you create where it doesn't yet exist?

Other activities I want to participate in:
1. _____
2. _____
3. _____

Community involvement provides opportunities to observe and appreciate others' character qualities. For example, interacting with people in our communities reminds us of the vital virtue of trust. We learn how to be trustworthy—how to earn others' trust—and how and when to trust others, which requires discernment about whether someone is trustworthy. We also engage in meaningful conversations, strengthen communication and consultation skills, learn to treat others with equality and respect, and more. By participating in a community, we can also learn skills suitable for marriage and family life—such as childcare, managing time and finances, decision-making, commitment, and follow-through.

If you are involved in Bahá'í community activities, you will have opportunities to familiarize yourself with the institutions and agencies that guide community life, some of which were introduced in the Welcome message at the beginning of the book. Involvement in a religious or spiritual community offers a valuable arena to determine how one's religion or spirituality can reinforce the principles and nurture the behaviors that lead to a sound, long-term commitment like marriage.

You can see how this community connection can be useful in this story below. A woman shares about meeting a potential marriage partner and getting to know his character through a long-term service project in her Bahá'í community.

> "I see myself and the person I am serving alongside as complements to each other—interdependent—like the cells in the human body, as Bahá'u'lláh said. We are equal, as two wings of a bird, but not the same. I appreciate it when someone has strengths and qualities I don't excel in. That makes our service as a team dynamic and symbiotic.
>
> "I've served together with a man for about a year now. It has been a learning experience, and it feels rich with the breezes of confirmation and the will of God. I'm not sure exactly why it feels right. Perhaps because of our unity? Our mutual respect? Our mutual desire and commitment to serve our Faith and our community? Our being inspired by the way the other teaches and shares spiritual truths, and treats others? The fact that we share a lot of the same interests and backgrounds? Or that we share similar sorrows and challenges that have shaped us? Whatever it is, I am grateful for the many blessings coming forth from it, including the magnetic spirit we share that seems to benefit those we serve—as well as benefiting us. I am noticing there are many ways to meet people and become acquainted with their character but, for me, working together in service to our community and our Faith is ideal.
>
> "I personally am not the dating type, nor am I one to go out looking for a partner. Becoming acquainted with another's character in those circumstances seems so formidable, complicated, and tricky. God has blessed me with this gift of connecting with this man, and I just need to trust the process and be grateful for what is now. I don't have an agenda for where this friendship is going. I am focused on being of service and praying for God's will. I am learning that to follow the will of God means to trust it working in my life, choices, and commitments—and in my becoming acquainted with another's character. I find it a delightful experience in itself, just being a friend to someone else—and loving that friend with no attachments or feeling that I need that person to complete my life.
>
> "I'm not going with my imagination into the future, wishing the friendship was more than it is now. I am staying true to myself, whole within my own core, and reflecting on my actions every day. I'm grateful to be getting better acquainted with myself through the process too. I find that through natural reflection following our service, and honest sharing, humble learning occurs. I feel an acceptance for who I am, as I am, which fosters the natural desire to be better and improve myself in specific areas. This is helping me realize that becoming acquainted with someone else's character includes how they are when they encounter my weaknesses and shortcomings. Are they going to be judgmental, critical, controlling, or arrogant? Are they going to have contempt for my faults, and 'magnify' them, as Bahá'u'lláh advised us not to do with others' faults? Or are they going to honestly and tactfully share their feelings and needs, in reflection, staying true to themselves, and staying focused on their own work, trusting I will do the same?"

Of course, not every friendship you develop will result in a marriage partner. While we strongly encourage you to begin with friendship, even then, your emotions might run high. Either person's feelings could be hurt if the friendship doesn't evolve into a long-term prospect of marriage. Therefore, if you sense there is an imbalance in attraction between the two of you, and it doesn't appear the friendship would result in a happy, healthy marriage, it will be especially important to communicate.

It will help if you exercise integrity, courage, and respect, using clear yet tactful words with each other, to convey your hesitations. If you are careful and gentle, and do not make assumptions about the other's feelings, a thoughtful, candid conversation can lessen hurt feelings and prevent either of you from getting the wrong impression. These conversations can be very difficult, so you may wish to allow prayer, meditation, and reflection—and perhaps consultation with trusted others—to guide you in how to open and have the conversation. This transparency, while difficult, may serve the continuation of the friendship at hand, and will likely help each of you grow in your emotional capability, character, and communication skills.

You have now explored some of the benefits of friendship and community service, as well as ideas for activities to meet and get to know new people. We now invite you to complete PrepSheet 9, to help you broaden the number of people you know and enhance the diversity of your experiences.

Starting with Me—Knowing Myself Before Finding a Partner

PrepSheet 9: Widening My Circle of Friends and Experiences

Date: _____

Purposes:
1. To expand the number of close friends I have, so I'm more likely to meet potential marriage partners and get to know them in a way that would prepare us for a possible marriage together.
2. To have more personal and meaningful experiences with other people that help me build skills, such as understanding others and learning about their character qualities.

Complete the following:

1. What sincere services can I offer my community that will also connect me with a wider circle of potential friends?
   a. _____
   b. _____

   I will initiate these services by this date: _____.

2. Here are two additional places where I could meet someone new (consider both online and in-person opportunities):
   a. _____
   b. _____

   I will initiate these connections by this date: _____.

3. What 1 or 2 new activities could help me meet a potential marriage partner?
   a. _____
   b. _____

   I will initiate these activities by this date: _____.

4. What can I do to overcome any fears I may have about participating in these activities, and to increase my courage to do so? Who on my encouragement and support team could help me?
   _____
   _____
   _____

5. **Note:** Please complete the items below after participating in the activities you listed above.
   a. How successful was I at trying out the new activities? Do I want to continue doing them? Why or why not?
   _____
   _____

   b. What did I learn about people that will help me in a relationship?
   _____
   _____
   _____

6. Are there other activities I want to try next? If so, by when?
   a. _____ By when: _____
   b. _____ By when: _____
   c. _____ By when: _____
   d. _____ By when: _____

Reflection

1. What attitudes and behaviors are present in excellent friendships? Do I practice these?
   _____
   _____
   _____

2. Do I choose friends who show these attitudes and behaviors? What else do I find valuable about my friendships?
   _____
   _____
   _____

3. What actions sustain a friendship over time? Do I demonstrate these actions in my relationships? How could I build on them?
   _____
   _____
   _____

4. What are my favorite conversation topics with friends?
   _____
   _____
   _____

5. What are my favorite activities with friends?
   _____
   _____
   _____

6. When have I jumped to a quick conclusion about someone and that caused problems I regretted? What helps me be more patient with the organic process of getting to know someone?
   _____
   _____
   _____

7. What might prompt me to stop developing a friendship with someone?
   _____
   _____
   _____

Activity

1. Create a collage or some other artistic expression that demonstrates true friendship. Alternatively, you could think of a particular close friend of yours and illustrate what you see in that person's attitudes, words, and actions. [Note: If you're new to collages, here's how to create one: Cut out photos and/or words relating to a particular topic or theme from magazines or other sources. Glue them onto a large piece of paper or cardboard. You can also use markers to add your own artwork or words to the collage.]

    After making the collage, ask yourself the questions below to uncover insights from the activity.

    a. What did I learn about the attributes of friendship? (Or the attributes of a particular friend.)
    _____
    _____
    _____

    Do I consistently demonstrate these attributes with my friends?
    _____
    _____
    _____

    b. How would I like to grow and improve as a friend to others?
    _____
    _____
    _____

    c. How well do I attract, as potential friends, people who show these attributes?
    _____
    _____
    _____

    d. If I want to increase my capacity to attract these types of friends, how can I do so?
    _____
    _____
    _____

Continuing My Marriage Preparation Process

We are approaching the end of this book, but this is also the beginning of the next stage of your journey toward marriage. You will meet people, participate in activities with them, refine what you are looking for, and continue to prepare for marriage. As you proceed, it will be good to assess where you could benefit from further knowledge and skill-building. You might read relationship, marriage, parenting, and stepfamily books; watch helpful videos; or read excellent articles. It can be beneficial to better understand men, women, and the equality of the sexes. If you are a Bahá'í, of course you'll want to assess where the advice you find aligns with the Faith's teachings, and where it doesn't.

You can also consider other areas where you might benefit from practical skill-building, such as money management, home maintenance, cooking, or other domestic skills. Of course, marriage organically strengthens many of these capacities. Still, it can be helpful to begin your marriage with skills that contribute to the smooth running of a household and family. Remember to avoid getting stuck in gender stereotypes as you think about these tasks.

We invite you to consider the perspectives below from several people. We hope they strengthen your optimism about your future marriage and help as you create your life and your future.

"I look at the older generation and all the divorce and dysfunction in marriage. I wonder if it might be a simpler, more organic process than most people realize, and so they unintentionally complicate it. Maybe it's more like everything else that grows. For me, I see that I will serve with someone as a team, and we will naturally become acquainted with one another, in many different situations. If it grows into attraction, friendship, and love, and it feels like the Will of God to become a couple and to court, then marriage is just the natural fruit of that process. I hope to find someone who shares those values, and to have them as the foundation of our marriage."

"While it may be one aspect of the process, reducing potential partners only to checklists inevitably misses some of our humanity. I feel that people need to take a more relaxed and natural approach to courtship, to integrate their good judgment with their instincts, to rise above the 'head vs. heart' dichotomy. In this way, they can meet their needs for romance and adventure within marriage, rather than outside of it, and without repressing these vital aspects of a healthy personality. Marriage has the potential to be the human institution through which the need for passion and romance can best be fulfilled."

"What I noticed after getting married the first time, with very little clue about what to look for in a partner, was that I chose someone who was emotionally needy and very troubled. I got pulled into years of taking care of him and trying to get help for all his issues. The marriage was very inwardly focused, always trying to survive, and very unstable and fear-based. Yes, there was growth for both of us, but a lot of destruction and almost no service to others. It ended in divorce.

"When I married a second time, and we were thorough in getting to know each other and figuring out together what we wanted to create in our marriage, our inner unity was secure. We both grew, separately and together, and we worked through some major tests together in love and unity. Because we were in harmony, we were free to do a tremendous amount of service to others, both as individuals and as a couple. We weren't focused all the time on marriage-repair work.

"My observation is that there are enough problems that happen normally in life and in adjusting to living with someone, so I don't need to deliberately set up a marriage to have built-in problems and weaknesses. If I meet someone who has problems that I know would be very difficult to live with, and he says he wants to change, then I would want to see some very solid evidence of it first. And, I would want to be certain that there was room for me to have input, for us to consult together on solutions and seek professional help, and for us to pray together for solutions. I wouldn't assume that 'I want to change' means everything necessary will fall into place."

"There are no guarantees. At a certain point, marriage is a leap of faith. Be careful in your process and be honest with yourself about you and them. Don't make excuses for behavior when you have doubts and questions. Does he or she go in the kitchen and help clean up unasked? How does he or she handle money? Does he or she interrupt others in a rush to get an opinion heard? Does he or she listen to others? Is the car messy beyond what you think is good? Does he or she speak kindly of others? What type of things have you noticed that 'impress' him or her? Do those things impress you?"

You will continue to expand your knowledge about what makes marriage successful, and there are many factors that help marriages not only survive but thrive. For example, relationship author Susan Page identified the vital practice of couples demonstrating "goodwill partnership"—a consistent way of positively influencing their relationship. She writes:

"I interviewed thirty-five couples who described themselves as 'thriving'. I thought I might find that they all came from happy, functional families, or that they had unusual degrees of compatibility,

or that their problems were relatively minor compared with other couples—none of that was true. Some of them had rotten childhoods and enormous challenges. But there was a quality I found in all of these thriving couples that I find is usually missing in more troubled relationships. I now believe that quality is a deeper key to happiness than even good communication or mutual respect.

"It's a quality I call a *spirit of goodwill*. Successful couples are on each other's side. They view themselves as allies, not adversaries. They *want* to be happy together, and together they make this happen. In a spirit of goodwill, they accept the traits in their partner that they wish were different. They have given up trying to change each other. When they argue, they understand that a different point of view may be valid. Because they want to experience their love all the time, they would rather work toward a solution than hang on stubbornly to their own "'right" point of view.

"The most widespread belief about marriage is that it is hard work—that true happiness in marriage is a myth, ... and that 50 percent of all marriages end in divorce and the other half are just barely escaping it. But what you *believe* has a great deal to do with what you *experience*, because you view all of life through your beliefs! This pervasive negativity about love in our culture is extremely damaging.

"Happy couples simply don't buy it! They *believe* they can be happy together, and their happiness is a priority for them. They keep a sense of adventure and excitement in their lives."[192]

Reflection

1. What gives me hope that I will find and create a healthy marriage?
   _____
   _____
   _____

2. What will help me learn more about sustaining a marriage?
   _____
   _____
   _____

3. What topics will be helpful for me to learn more about?
   _____
   _____
   _____

4. What skills will I build before I am in a relationship or marriage?
   _____
   _____
   _____

Note: The book *Marriage Can Be Forever—Preparation Counts!* (Susanne M. Alexander and Johanna Merritt Wu) is an excellent choice for courting couples who are becoming acquainted and want to prepare themselves for marriage. This book likewise draws from and applies wisdom from the Bahá'í writings—in addition to scientific and scholarly sources and life experience. A copy can be acquired from your favorite online bookstore or https://marriagetransformation.com/shop.

Reflecting on the Whole-Book Experience and Next Steps

Your focused attention on preparing yourself to be an excellent marriage partner will surely serve you well. The foundational steps you've taken give you a platform from which you can move into the next stages of building a future marriage: forming and nurturing friendships that may lead toward marriage, getting to know a chosen partner much better, and then seeing what comes next. To orient yourself to your next steps moving forward, we suggest you reflect below on what you've learned.

1. Thinking back to when I began *Starting with Me*, what are five new insights I've learned about preparing myself to be married?

    a. _____
    b. _____
    c. _____
    d. _____
    e. _____

2. What have I enjoyed about the preparation process offered in *Starting with Me*?

    _____
    _____
    _____

    What has been challenging about this process?

    _____
    _____
    _____

3. What parts of the process will be an ongoing part of my life?

    _____
    _____
    _____

4. What are three action steps I will begin right away to help move me to the next stage of finding a partner?

    a. _____
    b. _____
    c. _____

Encouraging Reminder: To assist you in tracking and completing all the reflections and growth steps in this book, we have provided suggestions and tools in "Appendix A: Tracking My Action Commitments".

Closing Inspiration

Congratulations on having come this far in preparing yourself for marriage. More growth and more choices are ahead in your life, and we sincerely say, "Well done! Well done!" You've created an excellent foundation for your ongoing process of marriage preparation.

We hope this quotation will inspire you to move toward marriage at your chosen pace:

"Persevere in your efforts, let not obstacles damp your zeal and determination and rest assured that the Power of God which is reinforcing your efforts will in the end triumph and enable you to fulfill your cherished desire."[193] Shoghi Effendi

We also hope that many friendship, relationship, marriage, and family blessings will come into your life. This fun family story from Rúhíyyih Rabbaní, Shoghi Effendi's wife, who is also known as Rúhíyyih Khánum, may lighten your heart and encourage you to be in motion:

"Shoghi Effendi, like his grandfather ['Abdu'l-Bahá] and great-grandfather [Bahá'u'lláh] before him, had a delightful sense of humor which was ready to manifest itself if he were given any chance to be happy or enjoy a little peace of mind. His eyes would fairly dance with amusement, he would chuckle delightedly and sometimes break out into open laughter. To a young pilgrim, who had expressed his interest in getting married, Shoghi Effendi remarked: 'Don't wait too long and don't wait for someone to fall from the sky!'"[194]

Here are also some wise, encouraging words written on behalf of the Universal House of Justice to inspire you:

**"Concerning your wish for a marriage partner to enhance your life and service,
you are encouraged to
trust in God,
pursue your purposes with a joyful heart, and
identify opportunities,
through your own prayerful consideration or
through consultation with others,
to meet [someone] to whom
you could consider being married."**[195]

Appendices

Appendix A: Tracking My Action Commitments

One of the biggest challenges for many of us in accomplishing our goals and making progress in our lives, is keeping track of and meeting our commitments. We have suggested, in numerous *Starting with Me* sections, PrepSheets, reflection questions, and activities that you form personal goals, take action, reflect on your actions, and monitor your progress. You may have already scheduled your next steps in your calendar, set up automated reminders, or put them in a notebook or journal.

Monitoring your action steps and progress toward your goals is one means of ensuring that you continue to learn, grow, and advance. If you would like to use a more systematic approach for tracking your goals, and you would appreciate some ideas for how to start, here are a few suggestions that may appeal to you:

1. In one location (paper or electronic), create a list with each goal you created while working through the book, with the dates by which you will reflect on your progress toward them. You might also leave room for notes that capture your reflections on how your process is going and how you think you're doing.

2. Using one of our PrepSheets as a guide, create your own worksheet with columns that represent the goal, timing, purpose, check-in dates, and so on; enter each of the goals you created over the course of the book. (We provide a version below, if it's useful.)

3. Draw a representation of the themes and principles that relate to two of your highest priority goals; use this drawing as a guide in your meditations or daily reflection.

4. Enter each of your goals separately into your paper or electronic calendar on the dates by which you want to accomplish them, and the dates on which you plan to check your progress toward them; if helpful, set a reminder to do this.

5. Create a "buddy system" with a friend who wants to strengthen their goal management capabilities; talk with them about a system that will help each of you; determine how you will check in with each other regularly on how the system is working and how your goals are progressing.

6. Highlight sections from *Starting with Me*—or fold down the corners of certain pages—where you wrote down goals you are committed to meeting; review the book regularly; for example, every Wednesday and Sunday morning, or using whatever rhythm and timing helps you—to see how you're doing on your goals.

7. Try to make all of your goals "S.M.A.R.T. goals": Specific, measurable, agreed-upon, realistic, and time-bound.
(Source: Peter Drucker, George Doran; http://en.wikipedia.org/wiki/SMART_criteria - cite_note-1)

8. *Starting with Me*, of course, does not need to be a "one and done" experience. Instead, you can benefit greatly from re-reading sections of it occasionally, as needed. As you reflect on your progress and plans, and possibly revise your goals and action steps, it may be helpful to return to relevant sections of the book to re-read about themes you may want to refresh your understanding of, and to continually inform your marriage preparation process as you move forward.

These strategies are, of course, only suggestions that are offered with the intent to empower you and not constrain you. You'll determine through your own process of action and reflection, what systems work best for you. The best systems will help you meet commitments and achieve your goals for relationships and marriage and also for other aspects of your life, such as work, education, family, friends, health and physical fitness, and service to others.

WHAT: Goal/Action Item	WHEN: Completion Date	*Additional Check-In Dates (If Needed)*	HOW: Resources, People, and Virtues That Will Help Me Complete This	NOTES

Appendix B: Forming a Book Study Group

After looking through this book, you may decide you'll be most successful at studying its content and carrying out its activities if you involve a few friends to complete parts of it—or all of it—with you. Informal study groups can help participants progress through the material and allow each to gain new insights from the group discussions.

Groups can also help friends keep each other accountable for actions they decide to take as a result of activities and reflection questions. Youth may wish to convene a group of their friends to study this content together. You will determine if a supportive older youth or adult is needed.

Note: Group participants will be at different stages of literacy, so naturally they can support and accompany each other in their collective learning process. If appropriate and welcome, they could gently encourage and lovingly assist each other to strengthen their capacity to read and write.

Consult About Ground Rules

At the beginning, before diving into the content, discuss and agree on a few ground rules. It may be useful to write these on a whiteboard or easel pad, so everyone can see them throughout the discussion. This practice allows each participant to feel a sense of ownership of the group and its guidelines. It also helps the group refer to them as needed, or to add or revise an agreement.

Here are some ground rules your group may wish to consider, if they don't come up naturally in your initial discussion:

1. Uphold confidentiality through a firm agreement that "what's said in the group stays in the group," and—most crucially—is not mentioned outside the group.
2. Scrupulously avoid the tendency in society to engage in gossip and backbiting—either within or outside of group sessions.
3. Don't use personal devices (mobile phones, tablets...) during group discussions and social time, to give full support and attention to the group, out of respect for its purpose and intentions. (Exceptions can be agreed upon, such as for taking notes or using a smartphone in a way that advances the efforts of the group, or arranging breaks where people can check their electronic devices before they put them away again.)
4. Allocate time for prayer, meditation, or other spiritual enrichment activities.
5. Allocate time for social connection and fellowship.
6. Integrate the arts into your group's activities. Expressing ideas artistically often brings vitality to the learning process and enables participants to understand a concept in a new, refreshing way.
7. Be respectful and considerate of others. Give everyone time to share, and guard against individuals dominating the conversation.
8. Avoid terminology, jargon, and acronyms—religious or otherwise—that some group members might not understand.
9. Agree on what everyone will read—and do—between sessions. At the same time, if life circumstances and events prevent a participant from fulfilling their commitment, they can still attend sessions, and strive to catch up with the reading and activities, perhaps with another group member accompanying and supporting them.
10. Participants can invite and bring friends to the group, and new people can join the group at any time. (Or, alternatively, once the group begins, no one new should join.)

Consider the Logistics

Groups are more successful and function more smoothly when they agree on some of the logistics and other basic considerations. These questions may serve as useful prompts for your group:

1. How often, when, and where will you meet? (Meeting at least every week or two usually helps participants stay motivated and purposeful.)
2. Who, if anyone, will be responsible for sending the meeting details to the group members? What method of communication will work for all members?
3. Will there be food? If so, who will provide it?
4. Will anyone facilitate the sessions? If so, will it be the same person each time, or will it rotate among the members?
5. Would it be beneficial, for any reason, to take notes of the discussion? If so, who will record the notes and what types of information will they capture from the conversation? Will it be the same person each time, or will it happen on a rotating basis?
6. Do you need or want a group name? How will you talk about the group with others?
7. Will the group share what they learn with others (without sharing confidential information, of course)? What opportunities exist for this? Perhaps you could share your learning with a youth group? At a community meeting? With family members? How and when will you carry this out?

Additional Resources

If you are leading or participating in a group and discover that additional resource materials or any assistance would be helpful, please contact Marriage Transformation. Remember that our conversation book for groups, *Relationship Talk: Exploring Meaningful Questions Inspired by the Bahá'í Faith* is a potential tool for you.

Providing Feedback

We, the authors, invite you to consider sharing what you have learned with us if your group is willing. We are constantly striving to grow as well. If you would be willing to share your reflections about how you used the book, what worked, and what didn't, we would be truly grateful. We want to continue to understand the book's impact, improve the process we propose, and share it with other groups. Your insights may inform those efforts. If you think anything might be helpful to share with us, please contact Marriage Transformation.

Contact Information:

Marriage Transformation
Susanne M. Alexander
susanne@marriagetransformation.com
cell/text/WhatsApp: +1.423-599-0153

Appendix C: Using Consultation in Marriage Preparation

The teachings of the Bahá'í Faith advise couples and groups to reach decisions using a process called "consultation". Effectively applying this Bahá'í principle can benefit all aspects of one's life, including a relationship and marriage. Making decisions as a couple requires you to engage in the consultation process as equals, with full collaboration and mutual respect. For most relationships and marriages, this healthy pattern of communication is not developed quickly and is instead the result of a longer skill-building process.

We've asked you throughout the book to draw on the power of consultation, especially in seeking input from others who could help you reflect and understand yourself better. Therefore, this appendix aims to ensure you understand some of the basics of Bahá'í consultation. The quotations below shed light on its importance.

1. "Consultation bestoweth greater awareness and transmuteth conjecture into certitude. It is a shining light which, in a dark world, leadeth the way and guideth. For everything there is and will continue to be a station of perfection and maturity. The maturity of the gift of understanding is made manifest through consultation." (Bahá'u'lláh, *Compilation of Compilations, Vol. I*, #168)

2. "Man must consult on all matters, whether major or minor, so that he may become cognizant of what is good. Consultation giveth him insight into things and enableth him to delve into questions which are unknown. The light of truth shineth from the faces of those who engage in consultation. Such consultation causeth the living waters to flow in the meadows of man's reality, the rays of ancient glory to shine upon him, and the tree of his being to be adorned with wondrous fruit. The members who are consulting, however, should behave in the utmost love, harmony and sincerity towards each other. The principle of consultation is one of the most fundamental elements of the divine edifice. Even in their ordinary affairs the individual members of society should consult." ('Abdu'l-Bahá, *Compilation of Compilations, Vol. I*, #180)

3. "Consultation has been ordained by Bahá'u'lláh as the means by which agreement is to be reached and a collective course of action defined. It is applicable to the marriage partners and within the family...." (Universal House of Justice, January 24, 1993)

4. "... Bahá'í consultation is to be undertaken with the utmost love, sincerity, and unity. Its participants must come together in a prayerful attitude, seeking assistance from the Realm of Glory, expressing their thoughts freely, surrendering all attachment to their individual opinions, and giving fair-minded and careful consideration to the views of others, in an effort to reach consensus. 'Abdu'l-Bahá advises us that should it be found, in the course of coming to a decision, that discussion has become prolonged or given rise to disputation, consultation should be deferred and taken up at a more propitious time. ... Of course, it must be remembered that the purpose of consultation need not always be to arrive at a particular or final decision. Often the aim may simply be to engage in an exchange of views so as to help clarify a certain matter and bring about unity of vision. Further, you should recognize that, given current circumstances, there may be issues that cannot be resolved at present and which should be left for future consideration." (Universal House of Justice, May 19, 2009)

5. "Consultation is no easy skill to learn, requiring as it does the subjugation of all egotism and unruly passions, the cultivation of frankness and freedom of thought as well as courtesy, openness of mind and wholehearted acquiescence in a majority decision. In this field Bahá'í youth may demonstrate the efficiency, the vigor, the access of unity which arise from true consultation and, by contrast,

demonstrate the futility of partisanship, lobbying, debate, secret diplomacy and unilateral action which characterize modern affairs." (Universal House of Justice, *Messages 1963 to 1986*, p. 95)

6. "The preservation of unity within the family, and the maintenance of a setting in which all members of the family may grow spiritually, requires moderation and restraint by all concerned. Family consultation is a vital element in the development of a sound relationship; the principles of consultation enumerated by the Master, including courtesy, respect for the views of others, and the full and frank expression of opinions, are applicable to relationships within the family as well as to the functioning of a Spiritual Assembly." (On behalf of the Universal House of Justice, January 2, 1990, Ruhi Book 10 "Building Vibrant Communities", Unit 2 "Consultation")

7. "It is important to note that truth emerges after the 'clash' of carefully articulated views (which may well be expressed with enthusiasm and vigor), not from the clash of feelings. A clash of feelings is likely to obscure the truth, while a difference of opinion facilitates the discovery of truth." (Research Department of the Universal House of Justice, "Issues Concerning Community Functioning", section 2, p. 6)

Unity is a central and vital aspect of marriage, and it relates directly to the quality of a couple's efforts to build understanding, their decision-making process, and the resulting decisions. In a serious relationship and in marriage, you'll likely reflect on how you can strengthen the unity in your relationship, so that you and your partner can consult smoothly and effectively. This will require seeing each other as being on the same "team" and sharing your differing opinions without personally attacking each other. As you get to know each other, you'll learn what helps you carry out a decision together—and what prevents you from doing so.

The fields of marriage education and marriage therapy tend to assume that all couples fight and have conflict. They often indicate that couples can manage it, "fight fair", and reduce the tension. However, in calling all of humanity to maturity and sustainable peace, the Bahá'í teachings forbid conflict, dissension, and contention. While we wouldn't expect that everyone can achieve that high standard all the time, it would greatly benefit all of us to strive to avoid conflict. One tool we can use in our efforts for peace is to become excellent at consultation and committed to creating loving unity. Learning how to do this is part of the adventure of being a couple.

While the Bahá'í teachings offer powerful guiding principles for consultation, there is no simple 1-2-3 method for consultation that will work for every couple in every situation—nor do the Bahá'í teachings define a specific technique or procedure for consultation. Every individual has a unique personality and character, which also makes every couple unique. Every family, likewise, has its own circumstances, culture, and needs. However, some essential principles, approaches, and skills can apply universally.

The quotation excerpts below highlight some of the components and gifts of consultation. They can guide your thinking about how you engage in consultation in your life generally as well as more specifically as a couple in a potential marriage relationship.

- Consultation "must have for its object the investigation of truth."
- "The light of truth shineth from the faces of those who engage in consultation."
- When we engage in consultation, "that which is agreeable will of course be investigated and unveiled" to our eyes and "the truth will be disclosed".
- Through consultation, we endeavor "to arrive at unity and truth".
- Consultation "is the lamp of guidance which leadeth the way, and is the bestower of understanding."
- Consultation gives us "insight into things" and enables us "to delve into questions which are unknown".

- Consultation "is and will always be a cause of awareness and of awakening and a source of good and well-being."
- "The right solution will certainly be revealed" through a consultative process.
- Consultation leads us "to the depths of each problem" and enables us "to find the right solution".
- "The process of Bahá'í consultation is designed to ensure that every believer's voice can be heard, and his or her views considered."
- Consultation is "indispensable for the ordering of human affairs."
- Without consultation, "no welfare and no well-being can be attained".
(Excerpts are from Ruhi Institute, "Building Vibrant Communities", Book 10, Unit 2 on "Consultation")

Some aspects of consultation include:

- Open and unified communication between two (or more) people that assists them to build understanding or before making decisions or taking action
- A mindful and/or prayer-centered approach that includes a desire to be guided by facts, others' perspectives, moral and spiritual principles, and religious quotations that inform the decision-making process, when relevant for those consulting
- Focusing on the truth and ideal outcomes—understanding each other and clarifying each person's thoughts, feelings, views, preferences, requests, goals, and beliefs
- Each person contributes equally to the process, sharing information, offering opinions for consideration, and seeking to understand and gain new insights from different perspectives—even those which appear to clash with other ideas
- Each person proceeding with a flexible and open mind, receiving new information, and shifting their thinking to incorporate new understanding
- The group harmonizing its purposes and directions to reach a mutually-agreeable decision about the best course of action (or no action), often resulting in a solution of higher caliber than any being considered at the outset; Even if a decision or plan doesn't produce the desired results or appears to have been misguided, when made and carried out in unity, it's usually quickly corrected through further consultation

Some Ways to Consult As a Couple

The guidelines below may help you implement and improve consultation in your relationship or marriage or in any premarital discussions you have. Creating an atmosphere of openness, desire for objectivity, and humility will empower you to resolve issues successfully.

Please note that while this process is presented below in a formal, sequential way, in real life it need not, and usually will not, follow this order. Couples often consult in casual and relaxed settings—during a walk, while driving, during a meal, or while working on a project together. Therefore, we encourage you to view these guidelines as hints or tips that may or may not be useful to you, depending on the situation. While they are outlined in a matter-of-fact manner, they can sometimes require considerable emotional and mental effort to yield the best outcomes.

Some Potential Elements of Consultation

At the Beginning

1. **Set the Goal:** Agree together on the purpose and/or goal of the consultation, and refrain from bringing up unrelated issues.

2. **Prepare in Advance:** Find or prepare any applicable background information, relevant facts, and spiritual guidance. If it may be a difficult conversation, try to make sure your well-being is in good shape. For example, it may help if you are sufficiently rested and fed (not tired and hungry), and you have a sufficient level of attention and concentration. Pray and prepare yourself to be open and detached, eager to come to a common understanding or a solution that you can commit to together.

3. **Assess Timeliness and Privacy:** Assess whether it's timely to address the matter—sometimes there is an immediate need, and sometimes it's better to set a time in the future. Protect your privacy when appropriate; for example, you may not want to have a difficult consultation with other people around. Consider whether working through an issue would be good for others to see, especially children—sometimes it is, sometimes it's not.

4. **Focus:** Stay aware of thoughts, views, preferences, requests, goals, beliefs, and feelings that you may wish to or are wise to share related to the agreed topic. Also, stay aware of how and when you express these, so you encourage rather than discourage someone else from sharing as well. Try to stay centered on coming to a solution by sharing in a unified manner and avoid manipulating each other or the outcome.

5. **Explore Openly:** Strive to understand the problem at a deep level. Detach from any particular outcome and be open to learning. Consider which values and beliefs you both hold and are relevant to the situation. Allow the creative process to generate solutions that neither of you planned ahead of time.

6. **Build Love and Unity:** Build a loving and unified connection before consulting. Begin with prayer or another unifying action; incorporate these practices as needed throughout the consultation. Remember that your individual interests are interwoven with your couple's and family's well-being.

Throughout the Consultation

1. **Include Others:** When needed and appropriate, include other people, particularly those affected by the situation and potential outcome or those who have expertise related to the issue. If there are children in the family or situation, involve them when appropriate for their age, maturity, and the topic. Be clear in your own mind—and with any children—about whether they are only sharing their views, thoughts, and feelings, or whether they will also participate in the decision-making part of the process. The same would be true of course if you involved professionals, other family members, close friends, or mentors who may have important perspectives that you each want to consider. Again, generally, these may be private consultations between just the two of you, but there will likely be several scenarios in any relationship or marriage where other informed and wise reflections are beneficial.

2. **Share and Listen:** Share opinions, feelings, perspectives, and ideas frankly, honestly, respectfully, and in a balanced manner. Invite each other to fully express what is on your minds and hearts. Search for truth and do not stubbornly insist upon your own views—recognizing that each of you has something to offer and that the solution will often arise from "the clash of differing opinions". Listen patiently, attentively, and compassionately, and check in with each other to ensure that you are understanding each other throughout the process. Take a break when you need it—to clear your head, reflect, say a prayer, meditate, eat, sleep, walk, or whatever is needed. You may find it helpful to practice this wisdom from the Research Department of the Universal House of Justice:

> "It is important to note that truth emerges after the 'clash' of carefully articulated views (which may well be expressed with enthusiasm and vigor), not from the clash of feelings. A clash of

feelings is likely to obscure the truth, while a difference of opinion facilitates the discovery of truth." (Research Department of the Universal House of Justice, "Issues Concerning Community Functioning", section 2, p. 6)

3. **After Sharing, Let Go:** At the heart of consultation is relinquishing your own agenda, ego, and investment in the outcome, in recognition that shared understanding or a shared solution to an issue is the desired result. To help with this, you might imagine that you release your ideas and contributions into an imaginary central area where neither of you "owns" them. They belong to both of you—not individually but collectively—and you can change them as needed. As you gain new perspectives, and you are open to inspiration, you create mutual solutions—often solutions that are unique, creative, and may be very different from your starting points.
   Hint: It can be a helpful reminder to put an empty bowl or another beautiful container or object between you to symbolically and metaphorically "receive" your words. If you are struggling to express yourselves, you can also write down your thoughts and exchange them by hand or by putting them in the container for each other to read.

4. **Practice Equality, Respect, and Fairness:** Participate equally, recognizing all contributions are worthy of respect. Avoid domination, blame, repeated complaints, negative non-verbal signals, abuse, or threats that would sabotage the process or force a specific decision or outcome to happen. Ensure that you consider each other's perspectives with fair-mindedness, recognizing that this is focused on a positive outcome of well-being for you as a couple, in addition to each of you as individuals. Resolve not to cause or take offense at each other's words. If either of you notices you're repeating things you've already said, it's likely that you don't feel heard. It may be helpful to write key points down and share them, or have the other person share a summary of what they think they have heard and see whether there is understanding. This understanding is not the same as agreement, but once your partner has said back to you what they think you are trying to convey, you can clarify your perspective as needed. It can also set your heart at rest that you have been heard—regardless of the outcome that follows. This is an important tool in any communication process, but particularly so with loved ones. The respect you show for each other can help you recognize ways in which you are strong as well as areas in which you need to grow in your ability to communicate with fairness and lovingkindness.

5. **Search for a Diversity of Solutions:** Share clear information, in an honest, calm, courteous, loving, and open-minded way. Search for new insights and facts and apply any pertinent information to the issue. Welcome both agreement and clashes of differing *opinions*, which can lead to a spark of truth and keep you focused on finding solutions. On the other hand, avoid other types of clashes. You will, of course, experience emotions, but stay aware of their impact, as they may hinder the effectiveness of the consultation as noted above, but ensure you communicate about them. For example, one of you might share that, while you feel frustrated or angry, you also feel deep respect for the other person and want the best outcome. Your awareness of your own emotions and conveying your feelings in a respectful way can help relieve tension. On the other hand, feeling anger or frustration and expressing it as an attack will likely derail the effectiveness of the consultation.

6. **Monitor the Quality:** Encourage and affirm each other's positive participation and progress. Pause if serious disunity begins to arise, especially if you experience a physiological response, and do what's needed to calm down and rebalance before consulting further. (See Chapter 6.) Be thorough. Avoid rushing understanding or decisions that need more time.

Making a Decision

1. **Make a Unified Decision:** Some of your consultations will be focused on gaining mutual understanding about a matter. In other cases, you will need to explore thoughts and feelings about a topic in harmony and love and conclude with a unified decision. Your aim is not perfection, but rather to achieve the best possible decision from among the options available. Ensure that you assess whether the decision will serve your relationship well and that it will be beneficial for any others affected by it.

2. **Defer As Needed:** At times you may struggle to find an agreed-upon solution. You may also note that one of you may have more expertise on the matter, or one of you does not have a strong opinion about the issue. When these situations arise, one of you may choose to defer to the other's opinion. This is still a unified decision that you will benefit from carrying out together as a couple. Remember that deferring is not intended to be used regularly in place of full consultation, but generally only when there is a genuine lack of need or energy about the particulars of a decision from one of you or when one of you has the expertise that the other lacks.

3. **Seek Additional Help:** If you find it impossible to reach a unified decision and this is causing disunity, seek out sincere, trustworthy people whose judgment and wisdom you respect. This may include family members, friends, or experts. Invite them into the consultation and ask for their input on the issue as a means of helping preserve the well-being of your relationship, your marriage, and your family. Only choose to expand the consultation to people you both agree should be included and continue the wider consultation always demonstrating respect for each other.

Carrying Out a Decision

1. **Share Responsibility:** Commit to carrying out a decision wholeheartedly and in unity. Agree on the best ways to carry out the decision, such as what will be done together and what will be left up to individual initiative and judgment. Execute the agreed-upon actions with a learning-in-action mindset, to discover the merits of the decision.

2. **Set up Support Systems:** Put in place a system of accountability that you both agree will assist the decision to be carried out smoothly. This system could include calendar notifications, cell phone reminders, text reminders, specific goals with dates assigned, checking in with each other periodically, or anything else that works for you.

3. **Pause for Reflection, Assessment, and Next Actions:** Consultation includes the capability to review and revisit decisions to assess any progress, successes, or difficulties. When solutions are identified through a unified approach, everyone involved is working to create that solution. With everyone investing their energy to see the understanding and resolution occur, the opportunity then exists for seeing the flaws in the solution, should there be any. As you reflect and consult, you can determine if you simply need more time and energy to see its effective implementation. Alternatively, a new, modified decision may be needed instead. Capture any learning that occurred and avoid criticism or blame for anything that happened. Focus on the next best and unified actions to take.

Remember that how you consult will be up to you to create as you apply the spiritual principles. As you practice and apply virtues like compassion and respect, your outcomes will improve.

Appendix D: Many Sources About Character

Inspiring Quotations on Character

Some people refer to character qualities as "virtues". The scriptures of the world's religions, the writings of philosophers, the work of relationship experts and psychologists, traditional wisdom, and others include the importance of developing character strengths and virtues so that relationships function well. For example:

1. "Love is patient, love is kind. It does not envy, it does not boast, it is not proud. It is not rude, it is not self-seeking, it is not easily angered, it keeps no record of wrongs. … Love never fails…." (*The Bible*, 1 Corinthians, 13:4, 5, 8)

2. "… [M]ake your ear attentive to wisdom and your mind open to discernment…. You will then understand what is right, just, and equitable—every good course." (*Tanakh*, Mishlei (Proverbs) 2:2, 9)

3. "The light of a good character surpasseth the light of the sun and the radiance thereof." (Bahá'u'lláh, *Tablets of Bahá'u'lláh*, p. 36)

4. "But indeed if any show patience and forgive, that would truly be an exercise of courageous will and resolution in the conduct of affairs." (*The Qur'án*, XLII-43)

5. "… [G]reater than all is loving-kindness. As the light of the moon is sixteen times stronger than the light of all the stars, so lovingkindness is sixteen times more efficacious in liberating the heart than all other religious accomplishments taken together." (*The Gospel of Buddha*, XX:22)

6. "A man should not hate any living creature. Let him be friendly and compassionate to all." (*The Song of God: Bhagavad-Gita* (Swami Prahavananda translation), XII)

7. "Make it your guiding principle to do your best for others and to be trustworthy in what you say." (Confucius, *The Analects*, Book IX, p. 99)

8. "Virtuous action depends not just on what we do but also on doing the right thing for the right reasons, and knowing that we are acting for the right reasons." (Blaine J. Fowers, *Beyond the Myth of Marital Happiness*, p. 116)

9. "When you relax into the virtues of moderation, peacefulness, and contentment, you will find that you no longer digress into scattered, anxious multitasking. Thus, the energy you spend working on whatever task is before you will be far more purposeful and focused." (Linda Kavelin Popov, *A Pace of Grace*, p. 139)

10. "Kind words do not wear out the tongue." (*More African Proverbs* (Liberia), p. 47)

11. "We need to realize the seeds we plant in the spring will be what show up in our summer season of growth and will be the fruits that we will harvest in our fall season. We really have a lot to do with what shows up in our lives." (Don Coyhis of the Mohican Nation, whitebison.org)

12. "Sensitivity to the feelings and needs of others and a willing disposition to help and serve are hallmarks of a person committed to the path of spiritual development." (Joan Barstow Hernández, *Love, Courtship, and Marriage*, p. 41)

13. "We ... believe that positive traits need to be placed in context; it is obvious that they do not operate in isolation from the settings ... in which people are to be found." (Christopher Peterson and Martin E. P. Seligman, *Character Strengths and Virtues: A Handbook and Classification*, p. 11)

14. "All too often we underestimate the importance of a smile, an embrace, a kind word, a sincere compliment, or the giving of one's attention. It is precisely the small things that can change difficult moments into special ones." (Mehri Sefidvash, *Coral and Pearls*, pp. 11-12)

Websites with Valuable Character Content

- https://marriagetransformation.com/
- bahaimarriage.net; bahairelationships.com
- viacharacter.org
- virtuesproject.com
- https://www.virtuesmatter.org/

Appendix E: Courses of the Ruhi Institute

To learn more about its courses, you may wish to visit the Ruhi Institute website at https://www.ruhi.org/en/, and peruse its pages, including that of "Programs and Materials," which provides links to its course descriptions. Its "Statement of Purposes of Methods" is also quite interesting and inspiring, as it explains the Institute's unique orientation and the refreshing approach it takes in building the capacity of individuals, families, institutions, and communities to take charge of their spiritual, social, intellectual, and cultural development—and transformation.

The Institute's courses follow a logical sequence and order, in which capabilities for service are progressively built, one on top of the other; therefore, it's recommended and beneficial to participate in prior courses in the sequence before taking Book 12, "Family and the Community: Unit 1, "The Institution of Marriage". Please also note that the study of these books is undertaken not individually, but collectively in a study circle: "In general, small groups of participants, working with the assistance of a tutor, meet together in an atmosphere of joy, calm and meditative serenity to engage in close study of the course materials." (https://www.ruhi.org/en/walking-a-path-of-service/)

Should you wish to participate in a Ruhi course, we recommend reaching out to Bahá'ís in your area. This can be done by searching for local Bahá'í institutions and agencies, or a Bahá'í website for your locality. In addition, many national Bahá'í websites contain a "contact us" form which can be used to express interest. (These websites can be accessed from the global Bahá'í website: https://www.bahai.org/national-communities).

ABOUT THE AUTHORS AND PUBLISHER

Susanne M. Alexander is a Relationship and Marriage Educator, author, coach, and character specialist, as well as President of Marriage Transformation® (https://marriagetransformation.com/; transformationlearningcenter.com; bahaimarriage.net). She is certified to conduct marriage readiness assessments with couples through Prepare-Enrich (prepare-enrich.com), and the Character Foundations Assessment with individuals through Peirce Group (peircegroup.com). She received a BA in Communications from Baldwin-Wallace College.

Susanne meets with clients globally to help them prepare for relationships and marriage or strengthen their existing marriages. As a journalist, Susanne has written hundreds of articles, including many pieces on relationships and marriage as a contributing writer for bahaiteachings.org, bahaiblog.net, *Simple Marriage, Strengthening Marriage, Marriage Partnership*, and *First Years and Forever*.

Susanne has been single, in dating relationships, engaged, married, divorced, and widowed. She is a daughter, stepdaughter, mother, stepmother, and grandparent. All of this has given Susanne a diversity of experiences to share! She is originally from Canada, where she embraced the Bahá'í Faith, which has guided her life ever since. She is married to Phil Donihe, and they live in Tennessee, in the United States.

To contact Susanne please email her at susanne@marriagetransformation.com.

Johanna Merritt Wu, Ph.D., is an organizational psychologist, who has focused her career and current consulting efforts on organizational development and human resources management. Her work includes executive coaching, teambuilding, leadership training, and career development for corporations, non-profits, and start-ups. Johanna served as a human resources and Six Sigma executive at General Electric and as the department chair of the Human Resources Management program at Franklin University in Columbus, Ohio. She served at the Bahá'í World Center in Haifa, Israel, in the 1990s, and she has lived and worked in several different places around the world. With Susanne M. Alexander (see above), she co-authored 3 editions of *Marriage Can Be Forever—Preparation Counts!* and other books underway.

In addition to her professional work, Johanna is involved in the community-building activities in her local area. Among other services, she has spent 15 years mentoring local youth and 20 years hosting gatherings for collective worship and reflection; she also serves on Bahá'í institutions. Johanna, her husband Steve Wu, and their daughter Haley Grace currently live in Indiana, in the United States. To contact Johanna, please email her at merrittwuassociates@gmail.com or through her website at johannawu.com.

Jeremy Lambshead is a writer, editor, and trainer who collaborates with youth and adults to release human potential and promote the advancement of society. He received a BA in the sociological study of religion, with a concentration in environmental studies, from Carleton College. He subsequently worked for the Midwest Energy Efficiency Alliance and as a writer at the U.S. Bahá'í National Center. He has since trained youth to serve their communities, worked as an instructor in high school, a music teacher and program manager, a freelance writer, editor and communications consultant, and the executive director of a diversity, equity, and inclusion nonprofit. Jeremy also loves to create and perform songs and poems, has dabbled in acting and voiceover work, and has written blog posts, essays, news articles, and this, his first book—*Starting with Me*. He has collaborated in a volunteer capacity with the Bahá'í International Community's United Nations Office in New York, Crossing Borders Music (as a founding board member), Interfaith America, Alternatives to Violence Project, and on local task forces and committees, and as a protagonist of the Ruhi Institute's community-building activities. He speaks Spanish, has lived in Ecuador for five months, and has traveled in India, Japan, Mexico, Canada, Turkey, England, and Israel. He can be reached at jeremy.lambshead@gmail.com.

About the Impact of Marriage Transformation®

In 1999, Susanne M. Alexander and her late husband, Craig Farnsworth, began to explore what they could do to help singles and couples create stronger relationships and marriages, particularly in the Bahá'í community. In 2004, they formed Marriage Transformation as a company to broaden their outreach, increase their services, and publish helpful materials. Many loving family members have subsidized their efforts throughout.

In the years since the company formed, thousands of people in approximately 50 countries have bought Marriage Transformation books, and hundreds of others have benefitted from coaching, mentoring, and educational assessments. Susanne has created and delivered over 85 online courses and webinars with hundreds of participants. She has presented over 200 workshops and keynotes at conferences and weekend retreats, with thousands of attendees. In addition to Susanne and Craig's work, many collaborators have also contributed to the company's reach and impact. Susanne has trained and inspired many people to become relationship and marriage educators and coaches. Many others involved in this process have gone on to facilitate study groups and workshops using Marriage Transformation materials.

Early collaborators were Linda Kavelin Popov and Dan Popov of The Virtues Project, and more recently Grant Peirce of Peirce Group. All have assisted with integrating character and virtues throughout materials.

Johanna Merritt Wu has been a valued collaborator since 2002 through several book projects and some workshops. Jeremy Lambshead has been involved since 2018, and his enthusiasm, skill, experience, and dedication are much appreciated.

We interpret all this excellent activity as indicating that more and more people are intentionally focused on creating and sustaining healthy relationships and marriages. We sincerely appreciate everyone's efforts in this learning-in-action endeavor—and more effort is still needed. The three of us sincerely hope that *Starting with Me—Knowing Myself Before Finding a Partner* will empower countless people to take charge of preparing themselves for healthy and happy relationships and marriages. We also hope many people will use this book to serve others, conscious of the transformative impact that lasting, unified marriages can have on the world.

ACKNOWLEDGMENTS

From Susanne:

In my ongoing learning and service that has informed this book, I especially appreciate the collaboration of many colleagues who contribute on projects, faculty teams, and author teams that benefit individuals, couples, and families. Johanna and Jeremy have been excellent partners as we have consulted, written, and edited our way through creating this book.

My husband, Phil Donihe, is a steadfast champion and encourager of my service in the relationship and marriage field, and he is my daily prayer partner. We are very conscious that God empowers and inspires all our efforts in this world. I also appreciate the love, support, and learning that comes from my extended family and loving friends. In addition, I know that my parents, Kay and Ed Muttart, are angels circling around all I do. I very much appreciate everything my mother taught me about writing, editing, and proofreading and my father's steadfast faith in Bahá'u'lláh.

From Johanna:

Over the years, so many people have shaped my thinking about this book and my approach to marriage preparation that it's impossible to list them all here, but I am so deeply grateful to each of you. My co-authors, Susanne and Jeremy, have been incredible co-travelers on this journey, and I am deeply grateful for our collaboration. I especially want to thank my sacrificing and loving family, especially my ever-encouraging and patient husband Steve and my precious companion and daughter Haley Grace. I also deeply appreciate my parents, Oscar and Winnie Merritt, for their extraordinary 60-year example of a healthy, united, joyous marriage. Their guiding hands helped shape my life—including giving me the gift of an opportunity to know the Bahá'í Faith and the teachings of Bahá'u'lláh, which guide my choices every day. Finally, I gratefully acknowledge the insights and feedback from my longtime weekly youth group, who make my life richer by sharing their input on current and future relationships.

From Jeremy:

First and foremost, I thank the Most High for the abundant, clear guidance on marriage and family life given to humanity at this time in history. I also wish to express my gratitude to my co-authors Susanne and Johanna for wonderful experience of collaborating on this book, and for their generosity, excellence, and consultative spirit.

In the past years, a good many friends and family members, and diverse writers and speakers—in the Baha'i community and beyond—have acquainted me with principles and truths that have progressively deepened my understanding of relationships and marriage. If you are one such person, I thank you for generously sharing your knowledge and for engaging in explorations that sparked new insights. My particular, heartfelt thanks goes out to my family members who each lovingly offered valuable suggestions and/or encouragement on the project: Jane Lardner Lambshead, Dot Lambshead Roche, Paul Lambshead, Deborah Fischer, Elizabeth Lambshead, Joan Paul, Terrence Roche, and Brett Mullin. I'm also grateful for the support of my spiritual brothers: Carlos Serrano, for our late-night chats, which yielded many insights that advanced my thinking; Micah Streiff, for the ideas and resources you shared; Jamar Wheeler, for your swift, thoughtful, and wise replies; and Ravi Starr, for his indefatigable encouragement, for our countless rich conversations on these themes, and for giving a copy of Susanne and Johanna's book *Marriage Can Be Forever—Preparation Counts!*—which launched me on this journey years ago.

From the Author Team:

Many people provided feedback on our approach and various aspects of the book as it unfolded—from subtleties in content to our choice of title to cover design. We deeply appreciate their input and the considerable loving encouragement they gave to us.

Our heartfelt THANK YOU goes out to: Tahereh Ahdieh, Linda Ahdieh Grant, Daniel Allen, Michelle Alexander, Carlo Amani, Bahiyyih Baker, Maya Baker, Stacey Barringer Burr, Candace Benn, Sohinee Bera, Carol Brophy, Jennifer Burke, Emily Carter, Anelli G.J. Castellanos Herrera, Nathan Cole McBurnett, Katie Compton, Lacey Davidson, Charlie Davis, Valerie del Cid, Dawn Dilley, Jessica Eise, Amanda Elam, Ada Emmett, Susan Engle, Melissa Evens, Catherine Field, Krista Forsgren, Melissa Fraterrigo, Angela Frezza, Craig Georgen, Takiyah Gross-Foote, Hope Gulker, Dean Hill, Gretchen Hill, Laura Hoffman, Nevin Jenkins, Zakiya Johnson, Ruebben Kalai Chelvan, Linda Kelleher, Linda Kelly, Sue Larson, Matt Lister, Suzy Lister, Corinne Logue, Melissa Love, AJ Lucky, Marabeth Lum, Rodney Lynch, Vahid Master, Susanne McConville, Marilyn Medlock, Genevieve Merritt, Matthew Merritt, Winnie Merritt, Alex Monik, Susan Morris Keller, Carol Mortazie, Kirsten Nordland, Dawn Oh, McKenzie Oh, Paul Oh, Rhonda Palmer, Paul Parsons, Maggie Paxson, Grant Peirce, Ann Marie Pigman, Karen Pollock, Asali Powers, Caity Quinn Parsons, Kim Radpour, Marzieh Radpour Wiley, Irina Rahimi, Hana Razzaq, Lev Rickards, Jennifer Riedinger, Liam Roche, Mina Sabet, Mojdeh Sahihi, Paul Schloemer, Soraya Shirazi, Hanna Sistek, Lisa Smits, JoAnn Maxine Stephens, Larkin Stephens, Anu Subramanian, Kris Taylor, Will Taylor, Anita Trent, Lexie Tyus, Ivy Vanderweilen, Donna Van Fleet, Tracey Wiley, Johann Wong, Marjan Yavari, Lisa Yazdani, Miranda Yeomans, Eric Zahrai, Maggie Zahrai, Susan Zamora, and Ying Zhang.

REFERENCES AND ENDNOTES

Note: Popular online sources to find the books referenced in *Starting with Me* are:
- bahai.org/library/ (authoritative Bahá'í texts)
- bahai-education.org/ocean.html (software download)
- bahaibookstore.com or bahaibooks.com.au/ (for purchases)

Introduction

[1] 'Abdu'l-Bahá, *Selections from the Writings of 'Abdu'l-Bahá*, #86
[2] Bahá'u'lláh, *Bahá'í Prayers* (2002 ed.), p. 117
[3] Bahá'u'lláh, *Gleanings from the Writings of Bahá'u'lláh*, CXVII

Chapter 1 - Living an Integrated, Joyful Life: Foundation for a Happy Marriage

[4] Bahá'u'lláh, *Gleanings from the Writings of Bahá'u'lláh*, CXVII
[5] Bahá'u'lláh, cited by Shoghi Effendi in *Advent of Divine Justice*, pp. 24-25
[6] On behalf of Shoghi Effendi, *Compilation of Compilations, Vol. I*, #3.3
[7] Universal House of Justice, July 1, 2013, to Bahá'í youth conferences
[8] Universal House of Justice, *Framework for Action*, #35
[9] Universal House of Justice, December 7, 1992, European Bahá'í Youth Council; Ocean software program
[10] Bahá'u'lláh, *Tablets of Bahá'u'lláh*, p. 26
[11] 'Abdu'l-Bahá, *Paris Talks*, pp. 176-177
[12] On behalf of Shoghi Effendi, *Lights of Guidance*, #391
[13] On behalf of Shoghi Effendi, *Compilation of Compilations, Vol. I*, #146
[14] Universal House of Justice, *Turning Point*, p. 165
[15] Universal House of Justice, *Framework for Action*, #35
[16] On behalf of the Universal House of Justice, "Choosing a Profession", #13
[17] Universal House of Justice, February 8, 2013
[18] Bahá'í Youth Conferences Participants' Handout, July-October 2013
[19] Bahá'u'lláh, *Tabernacle of Unity*, p. 74
[20] Bahá'u'lláh quoted in Shoghi Effendi, *Advent of Divine Justice*, p. 82
[21] 'Abdu'l-Bahá, *Secret of Divine Civilization*, p. 19
[22] 'Abdu'l-Bahá, *Promulgation of Universal Peace*, p. 236
[23] 'Abdu'l-Bahá, *Promulgation of Universal Peace*, p. 218
[24] 'Abdu'l-Bahá, *Paris Talks*, pp. 109-110
[25] 'Abdu'l-Bahá, *Paris Talks*, p. 108
[26] Shoghi Effendi; On behalf of the Universal House of Justice, *Compilations of Compilations, Vol. I*, #138
[27] 'Abdu'l-Bahá, *Tablets of 'Abdu'l-Bahá, Vol. 1*, p. 45 quoted on behalf of the Universal House of Justice, quoted in a Bahá'í World Centre Research Department Memorandum, "The Humorist", January 12, 1997
[28] Howard Colby Ives sharing the reported words of 'Abdu'l-Bahá, *Portals to Freedom*, p. 120

Chapter 2 - Learning from Family and Relationships

[29] Bahá'u'lláh, *Tabernacle of Unity*, #1.16
[30] Universal House of Justice, *Framework for Action*, #35
[31] Universal House of Justice, *Framework for Action*, #16
[32] "Social Action" document prepared by the Office of Social and Economic Development at the Bahá'í World Centre, November 26, 2012; *Framework for Action*, #59
[33] 'Abdu'l-Bahá, *Selections from the Writings of 'Abdu'l-Bahá*, #221

34 'Abdu'l-Bahá, *Promulgation of Universal Peace*, p. 168
35 'Abdu'l-Bahá, *Promulgation of Universal Peace*, p. 92
36 On behalf of Shoghi Effendi, *Lights of Guidance*, #2047
37 Universal House of Justice, *Lights of Guidance*, #954
38 Universal House of Justice, *Messages 1963 to 1986*, #289.2
39 On behalf of Shoghi Effendi; On behalf of the Universal House of Justice, *Lights of Guidance*, #955
40 'Abdu'l-Bahá, *Selections from the Writings of 'Abdu'l-Bahá*, #141
41 On behalf of Shoghi Effendi, *Lights of Guidance*, #927
42 Universal House of Justice, quoted in "Child Abuse, Psychology and Knowledge of Self", December 2, 1985
43 Universal House of Justice, "Issues Related to the Study of the Bahá'í Faith"
44 On behalf of the Universal House of Justice quoted in the "Understanding Tests" letter from the Research Department of the Bahá'í World Centre to the Universal House of Justice, July 17, 1989
45 On behalf of the Universal House of Justice, *Compilation of Compilations, Vol. II*, #2339
46 On behalf of the Universal House of Justice, *Lights of Guidance*, #311
47 Ruhi Institute, "Family and the Community Book 12, Unit 1, The Institution of Marriage"; pre-publication edition material in development: Version 1.1.1.PP, section 13, p. 21
48 Ruhi Institute, "Family and the Community: Book 12, Unit 1: The Institution of Marriage", pre-publication edition material in development: Version 1.1.1.PP, section 13, p. 22
49 'Abdu'l-Bahá, *Selections from the Writings of 'Abdu'l-Bahá*, #86

Chapter 3 - Observing and Knowing My Character

50 Bahá'u'lláh, *Tablets of Bahá'u'lláh*, p. 36
51 Bahá'u'lláh, *Tablets of Bahá'u'lláh*, p. 57
52 Bahá'u'lláh, *Gleanings*, CXXXVII
53 'Abdu'l-Bahá, *Some Answered Questions*, 2nd ed., #57
54 'Abdu'l-Bahá, cited in Shoghi Effendi, *The Advent of Divine Justice* p. 26
55 Shoghi Effendi, *Compilation of Compilations, Vol. I*, #162
56 Bahá'u'lláh, *Gleanings from the Writings of Bahá'u'lláh*, CXXII
57 Bahá'u'lláh, *Hidden Words*, Arabic, #22
58 Bahá'u'lláh, *Tablets of Bahá'u'lláh*, p. 35
59 'Abdu'l-Bahá, *Secret of Divine Civilization*, p. 19
60 'Abdu'l-Bahá, *Selections from the Writings of 'Abdu'l-Bahá*, #111
61 Universal House of Justice, *Framework for Action*, #3
62 Shoghi Effendi, *Light of Divine Guidance*, pp. 69-70
63 Summarized from Christopher Peterson and Martin E. P. Seligman, *Character Strengths and Virtues: A Handbook and Classification*, pp. 18-30
64 Bahá'u'lláh, *Gleanings from the Writings of Bahá'u'lláh*, p. 216
65 'Abdu'l-Bahá, *Secret of Divine Civilization*, p. 60

Chapter 4 - Strengthening My Character

66 'Abdu'l-Bahá, *Paris Talks*, p. 60
67 'Abdu'l-Bahá, *Paris Talks*, pp. 62-63
68 On behalf of the Universal House of Justice, May 9, 2014, to an individual
69 Bahá'u'lláh, *Gleanings*, LXXVII, quoted by Universal House of Justice, *Messages 1963 to 1986*, #425.6
70 'Abdu'l-Bahá, *Promulgation of Universal Peace*, p. 226
71 On behalf of Shoghi Effendi, *Lights of Guidance*, #704
72 Universal House of Justice, to the followers of Bahá'u'lláh in the Democratic Republic of the Congo, November 1, 2022
73 On behalf of the Universal House of Justice, *Compilation of Compilations, Vol. II*, #2347
74 On behalf of the Universal House of Justice, April 19, 2013, to an individual
75 Ana Morante, *All-in-One Marriage Prep*, p. 36
76 Ridván letter to the Bahá'ís of the World, April 2016

[77] 'Abdu'l-Bahá, quoted in "Understanding Tests" memorandum from the Bahá'í World Centre Research Department to the Universal House of Justice, July 17, 1989
[78] 'Abdu'l-Bahá, *Promulgation of Universal Peace*, p. 244
[79] On behalf of Shoghi Effendi, *Compilation of Compilations, Vol. I*, #159
[80] On behalf of the Universal House of Justice April 19, 2013, to three individuals
[81] Shoghi Effendi, *Compilation of Compilations, Vol. I*, #226
[82] Shoghi Effendi, *Bahíyyih Khánum*, pp. 42-43
[83] Bahá'u'lláh, *Hidden Words*, Persian #72
[84] Shoghi Effendi, *Lights of Guidance*, p. 83
[85] On behalf of Shoghi Effendi, quoted by the Universal House of Justice; cover letter to "Psychology and Knowledge of Self"; October 23, 1994
[86] Universal House of Justice, *Wellspring of Guidance*, p. 39
[87] The Gottman Institute eNewsletter, May 10, 2018; gottman.com
[88] Bahá'u'lláh, *Hidden Words*, Arabic #31
[89] Bahá'u'lláh, *Hidden Words*, Arabic #22
[90] 'Abdu'l-Bahá, *Lights of Guidance*, #1485

Chapter 5 - Aligning My Expectations with Reality

[91] 'Abdu'l-Bahá, *Lights of Guidance*, #733
[92] 'Abdu'l-Bahá, *Selections from the Writings of 'Abdu'l-Bahá*, #88
[93] 'Abdu'l-Bahá, *Foundations of World Unity*, pp. 73-74
[94] Bahá'u'lláh, *Hidden Words*, Arabic, #2
[95] 'Abdu'l-Bahá, *Foundations of World Unity*, pp. 73-74
[96] 'Abdu'l-Bahá, *Promulgation of Universal Peace*, p. 62
[97] On behalf of the Universal House of Justice, "Investigation of Character, Courtship Practices, and Selection of a Marriage Partner", #9
[98] On behalf of the Universal House of Justice, "Investigation of Character, Courtship Practices, and Selection of a Marriage Partner", #11
[99] Bahá'u'lláh, *Bahá'í Prayers* (2002 ed.), p. 117
[100] Bahá'u'lláh, *Gleanings from the Writings of Bahá'u'lláh*, CXXV

Chapter 6 - Avoiding Possible Pitfalls on My Journey

[101] 'Abdu'l-Bahá, *Compilation of Compilations, Vol II*, #2308
[102] 'Abdu'l-Bahá, *Selections from the Writings of 'Abdu'l-Bahá*, #86
[103] On behalf of Shoghi Effendi quoted in the "Understanding Tests" memorandum from the Bahá'í World Centre Research Department to the Universal House of Justice, July 17, 1989
[104] On behalf of Shoghi Effendi, Dec. 4, 1954
[105] On behalf of Shoghi Effendi, *Lights of Guidance*, #689
[106] On behalf of the Universal House of Justice, October 6, 1999
[107] Memorandum from the Research Department of the Bahá'í World Centre to the Universal House of Justice July 6, 1994; Bahá'í Library Online, bahai-library.com
[108] Bahá'u'lláh, *Bahá'í Prayers* (US 2002), p. 118
[109] Bahá'u'lláh, "To Set the World in Order: Building and Preserving Strong Marriages", compiled by the Research Department of the Universal House of Justice, August 2023, #1
[110] From a letter to Agnes Ghaznavi from the Research Department of the Bahá'í Faith's World Centre, March 10, 1991, published in Agnes Ghaznavi, *Sexuality, Relationships and Spiritual Growth*, p. 139
[111] Shoghi Effendi, *Lights of Guidance*, #1156
[112] On behalf of Shoghi Effendi, *Lights of Guidance*, #1211
[113] On behalf of the Universal House of Justice, March 16, 1992, quoted in a Memorandum from the Research Department to the Universal House of Justice, "Homosexuality", #17
[114] On behalf of Shoghi Effendi, *Compilation of Compilations, Vol. I*, #147
[115] On behalf of Shoghi Effendi, *Afire with the Vision*, #99

116 Dr. Mark Laaser, *All-in-One Marriage Prep*, p. 200)
117 On behalf of the Universal House of Justice, March 9, 2023, to an individual
118 Justin Baldoni, *Man Enough*, p. 226
119 On behalf of Shoghi Effendi, "Investigation of Character, Courtship Practices, and Selection of a Marriage Partner", #5
120 Dr. Emily Nagoski, *Come As You Are*, pp. 229-230
121 Dr. Emily Nagoski, *Come As You Are*, pp. 230-233
122 On behalf of the Universal House of Justice, October 27, 2010, to an individual
123 Emily Nagoski, PhD, *Come As You Are*, p. 140
124 Shoghi Effendi, *The Advent of Divine Justice*, pp. 25, 28
125 On behalf of Shoghi Effendi, *Lights of Guidance*, #1157
126 On behalf of the Universal House of Justice, *Compilation of Compilations, Vol. I*, #128
127 On behalf of the Universal House of Justice, *Lights of Guidance*, #1216
128 On behalf of the Universal House of Justice, February 5, 1992
129 Quoted in Agnes Ghaznavi, *Sexuality, Relationships and Spiritual Growth*, p. 139, from a letter to the author from the Research Department of the Bahá'í World Centre, March 10, 1991
130 On behalf of the Universal House of Justice, *Framework for Action*, 51.8
131 Bahá'u'lláh, *Hidden Words*, Arabic #29
132 Bahá'u'lláh, *Gleanings from the Writings of Bahá'u'lláh*, CXXV
133 Shoghi Effendi, *Compilation of Compilations, Vol. II*, #2075
134 On behalf of Shoghi Effendi, *Compilation of Compilations, Vol. II*, #2315
135 On behalf of Shoghi Effendi, *Compilation of Compilations, Vol. II*, #2327

Chapter 7 - Describing Myself and a Potential Partner

136 'Abdu'l-Bahá, *Foundations of World Unity*, p. 9
137 'Abdu'l-Bahá, *Paris Talks*, p. 178
138 Paul Coleman, PsyD, *All-in-One Marriage Prep*, pp. 76-77
139 Bahá'u'lláh, *Tablets of Bahá'u'lláh*, p. 35
140 Bahá'u'lláh, *Tabernacle of Unity*, 1.4
141 On behalf of the Universal House of Justice, *Messages 1963 to 1986*, #214
142 On behalf of the Universal House of Justice, "Investigation of Character, Courtship Practices, and Selection of a Marriage Partner", #20
143 Bahá'u'lláh, *Tablets of Bahá'u'lláh*, p. 66
144 'Abdu'l-Bahá, *Secret of Divine Civilization*, pp. 23-23
145 'Abdu'l-Bahá, *Selections from the Writings of 'Abdu'l-Bahá*, #34
146 On behalf of Shoghi Effendi, *Lights of Guidance*, #1268
147 On behalf of Shoghi Effendi, *Unfolding Destiny*, p. 440
148 On behalf of the Universal House of Justice, *Lights of Guidance*, #1269
149 On behalf of the Universal House of Justice, "Investigation of Character, Courtship Practices, and Selection of a Marriage Partner", #16
150 On behalf of the Universal House of Justice, "Investigation of Character, Courtship Practices, and Selection of a Marriage Partner", #13
151 Rúhíyyih Rabbaní, *Prescription for Living* (1978 edition), pp. 87-88

Chapter 8 - Creating My Future

152 'Abdul-Bahá, *Paris Talks*, pp. 174-175
153 On behalf of Shoghi Effendi quoted in "Understanding Tests" memorandum from the Bahá'í World Centre Research Department to the Universal House of Justice, July 17, 1989
154 On behalf of Shoghi Effendi, *Compilation of Compilations, Vol. II*, #2011; italics appear in the original text
155 Universal House of Justice, *Messages 1963 to 1986*, #375.5
156 Universal House of Justice, *Framework for Action*, #10
157 Universal House of Justice to Bahá'í youth conferences, July 1, 2013, *Framework for Action*, 27.5; 27.7
158 Shoghi Effendi, quoted on behalf of the Universal House of Justice, *Messages 1963 to 1986*, #214

[159] 'Abdu'l-Bahá, "To Set the World in Order: Building and Preserving Strong Marriages", compiled by the Research Department of the Universal House of Justice, August 2023, #7
[160] 'Abdu'l-Bahá, *Selections from the Writings of 'Abdu'l-Bahá*, #88
[161] 'Abdu'l-Bahá, *Selections from the Writings of 'Abdu'l-Bahá*, #86
[162] 'Abdu'l-Bahá, *Bahá'í Prayers* (US 2002), p. 119
[163] On behalf of Shoghi Effendi, *Lights of Guidance*, #1268
[164] Universal House of Justice, *Framework for Action*, #35
[165] On behalf of the Universal House of Justice, *Lights of Guidance*, #1303
[166] On behalf of the Universal House of Justice, "To Set the World in Order: Building and Preserving Strong Marriages", compiled by the Research Department of the Universal House of Justice, August 2023, #26
[167] Linda J. Waite and Maggie Gallagher, *The Case for Marriage*, p. 17
[168] Linda J. Waite and Maggie Gallagher, *The Case for Marriage*, pp. 31, 33
[169] Shoghi Effendi to an individual believer; cited by the Universal House of Justice, *Messages from the Universal House of Justice, 1968-1973*, pp. 109-110
[170] On behalf of Shoghi Effendi, *Compilation of Compilations, Vol. II*, #2316
[171] Universal House of Justice, *Lights of Guidance*, #1222
[172] On behalf of Shoghi Effendi, *Compilation of Compilations, Vol. II*, #2315
[173] Provisional translation from a talk by 'Abdu'l-Bahá, provided on behalf of the Universal House of Justice, June 2, 2023
[174] 'Abdu'l-Bahá, *Paris Talks*, p. 129
[175] On behalf of Shoghi Effendi, quoted in the "Understanding Tests" memorandum from the Bahá'í World Centre Research Department to the Universal House of Justice, July 17, 1989
[176] Universal House of Justice, *Framework for Action*, #34
[177] Universal House of Justice, *A Wider Horizon*, p. 27
[178] On behalf of the Universal House of Justice, quoted in the "Understanding Tests" memorandum from the Bahá'í World Centre Research Department to the Universal House of Justice, July 17, 1989

Chapter 9 - Completing This Stage of My Journey

[179] On behalf of the Universal House of Justice, *Lights of Guidance*, #1269
[180] 'Abdu'l-Bahá, *Compilations of Compilations, Vol I*, #179
[181] 'Abdu'l-Bahá, *Lights of Guidance*, #767
[182] Universal House of Justice, *Framework for Action*, #35
[183] On behalf of the Universal House of Justice, August 28, 1994, *Marriage Can Be Forever—Preparation Counts!* 3rd ed., p. 141
[184] On behalf of the Universal House of Justice, quoted in the "Understanding Tests" memorandum from the Bahá'í World Centre Research Department to the Universal House of Justice, July 17, 1989
[185] On behalf of the Universal House of Justice, *Compilation of Compilations, Vol. II*, #2161
[186] Bahá'u'lláh, *Tablets of Bahá'u'lláh*, p. 37
[187] 'Abdu'l-Bahá, *Selections from the Writings of 'Abdu'l-Bahá*, #92
[188] 'Abdu'l-Bahá, *Selections from the Writings of 'Abdu'l-Bahá*, #39
[189] 'Abdu'l-Bahá, *Paris Talks*, p. 16
[190] 'Abdu'l-Bahá, *Promulgation of Universal Peace*, p. 218
[191] Universal House of Justice, *Framework for Action*, #14
[192] Susan Page, essay in *All-in-One Marriage Prep*, pp. 284-285
[193] Shoghi Effendi, *Arohanui, Letters to New Zealand*, p. 25
[194] Rúhíyyih Rabbaní, *Priceless Pearl*, p. 129
[195] On behalf of the Universal House of Justice to an individual, August 25, 2010

Feedback and Resources

Please remember that this is the beginning of your learning journey about relationships and marriage. One of your many resources is Marriage Transformation. We welcome hearing from you about your experiences with our books, materials, courses, coaching, and more. Our books are available through online bookstores globally. Some are:

- Relationship Talk: Exploring Meaningful Questions Inspired by the Bahá'í Faith
- Be Brave and Arise: My Life Quest As a Bahá'í Man
- Marriage Can Be Forever—Preparation Counts!
- Creating Excellent Relationships: The Power of Character Choices
- All-in-One Marriage Prep
- Creating Well-Being for Couples and Families
- Couple Vitality
- Re-Vitalizing Our Marriage

Contact Information:

Susanne M. Alexander
Marriage Transformation®
susanne@marriagetransformation.com
cell/text/WhatsApp: +1.423-599-0153 (US Eastern)

https://marriagetransformation.com/

https://www.transformationlearningcenter.com/

https://bahaimarriage.net/

https://www.facebook.com/MarriageTransformation

https://www.instagram.com/marriagetransformation/

https://www.youtube.com/user/SusanneMAlexander

https://www.linkedin.com/in/susannemalexander/

www.ingramcontent.com/pod-product-compliance
Lightning Source LLC
Chambersburg PA
CBHW081446070526
44586CB00019B/2248